THE BIBLE
VERSUS
DISPENSATIONAL ESCHATOLOGY

REV. JOHN C. EGERDAHL

THE BIBLE

VERSUS

DISPENSATIONAL
ESCHATOLOGY

"Blow the trumpet in Zion, and sound an alarm in My holy
mountain" Joel 2:1

Pleasant Word
A Division of WINEPRESS PUBLISHING

FOREWORD

I sat across from a panel of men who represented a particular evangelical organization. They were evaluating me for approval to minister in their denomination. They had a list of 175 theological questions to ask me, the last thirty of which had to do with specific details relating to dispensationalism. When we got to a certain place in the interview, one kind-hearted gentleman said, "I just want you to know, I'm a pan-millennialist. I believe it will all pan out in the end."

Everyone laughed. I knew this man was trying to find some common ground for my acceptance into their organization. I agreed that day to be a pan-millennialist as well; after all, eschatology is not essential to salvation or fellowship. I convinced myself that I could push eschatology into the future or relegate it to some minor emphasis in my preaching, and all would be well. I reasoned this would be the best solution, as nearly 80 to 90 percent of evangelical churches in America are dispensational to some degree.

I think there are many ministers who are trying to do exactly the same thing. They are unwilling to even seriously look into or study this issue because of the economic and fellowship implications. Many of us say that we would be willing to die as martyrs for Christ, but we are often unwilling to search for truth if it goes against the status quo. I later reasoned to myself, *Wasn't this the very same position the Jewish leaders took when they rejected Christ? They feared losing their place at the royal table* (cf. Isa. 28; John 11:48).

During the next year or so, I found that I could not remain a pan-millennialist. As I studied for sermon preparations, I found that my view of eschatology gave understanding to the whole of Scripture, not just the scriptures that directly spoke of the end times. I knew I had to commit my life to the truth of God's Word no matter the consequences and regardless of whatever gain or loss I might incur. I also knew I must commit myself to knowing the truth and then freely proclaiming that truth to others. I had to simply leave the results in the Lord's hands.

I appreciate this book and commend it to you, because the author is simply uncompromising when it comes to truth. He does not present us with three or four possible views so that we may choose which one we like or which one is most convenient. He stands in firm conviction that the truth of God on this subject is clear and plainly revealed in God's Word and that it is our duty to believe it, teach it, and defend it. I believe this is a book that every pastor, seminary professor, board member, and president of an evangelical college or seminary around the world should read objectively. And not only read it, but also study it, looking up the Scripture references and reading their contexts. A person needs to read this book with the volume in one hand and a Bible in the other to fully understand it. As you read this book, you will see the author's arguments are powerful, for they are scriptural.

Over the years, I have met many people in the Church who have held the dispensational position simply because it is the most popular and widely held position. After all, how can so many people be wrong? If one person picks up a handful of dirt, it looks pretty insignificant. It is unworthy of notice. But if many people take their handfuls of dirt and together gather them into a great pile until it forms a mountain, then all eyes are drawn toward it. Because of the sheer quantity, the insignificant has become significant. I believe a similar thing has happened with dispensationalism. The sheer mass of people believing in it has become a greater persuasion for many than the arguments supporting the doctrine itself.

Beloved, our hearts tell us that spiritual truth can never be established on this basis. One of my favorite things about the author's writing and teaching in this book is that he has a way of laying out hard-to-understand truths very clearly and plainly. No one should feel that he must blindly follow others whom he considers better informed than himself. I do not want to mislead you; this book contains profound truths, and it may require reading several times before you are able to see the full implications.

I have met others who were afraid to read or study anything against dispensationalism because they believed such writing to be anti-Semitic. After all, they say, loving Judaism will bring blessing, and to say anything negative will likewise bring God's curse. Let me say, the author is not anti-Semitic, nor is the purpose of his writing in any way based on hatred. He is a very humble and loving man who loves all regardless of their origin or nationality. It will not take long for you to see that Christ is his all in all.

What the author has done in this book is to show how all of God's promises and curses are to be interpreted through Christ and the New Covenant. He puts the blessings and curses on the right biblical foundation. He has designed this book to point all men to Christ as the means of eternal blessing. This is an act of love, for if someone gives a false hope, telling a person he is blessed and loved of God when he is not, he has not loved but, in essence, hated that person.

I know there are others who will read this book who are dispensational by conviction. All of us should keep in mind that conviction itself does not determine whether a statement is true or false. Many are inclined to think, especially about spiritual things, that if a person is determined enough or zealous enough, he will win God's approval. After all, God sees the intent even if the belief may not be quite right. This is erroneous thinking. Stubbornness or obstinacy is never a virtue. It is our duty to be willing to change our views any time they do not align with God's Word.

The author is convinced that God has clearly stated His truth. We must study and compare scripture with scripture until our convictions stand squarely on His Word. The author has stated that he welcomes any critical reading and study of his book. If anyone, after reading his book, can show from Scripture where the author has misinterpreted God's Word, the author will freely change his position. He is a man who desires to stand for truth no matter the cost.

Another thing you will notice about Pastor John Egerdahl is that he is widely read in dispensational literature. I have often found that when many people of the dispensational persuasion are confronted with particular beliefs of the system, they will say, "Well, that's not what I believe" or "That's not what my pastor teaches." Just because we personally do not believe a particular point does not negate the fact that the system we espouse does. The author has defined dispensationalism from the statements of the leaders of the movement. He has not in any way darkened their position to make his own appear in a brighter light. The position is defined by their writings.

May God give you grace to read this book with an open mind and an open heart. It could change your life.

Rev. Dr. William E. Britt

PREFACE

In writing the manuscript for this book, I am aware of the material that exists both pro and con on the subject. This book is polemical and is based on the defense of the Christian faith that relates to biblical eschatology. Much prophecy has been interpreted on the basis of prognosticated newspaper headlines, which, in the long run, has amounted to false prophecies.

I became interested in eschatology and have studied it since I was discharged from the U.S. Navy in 1946, after which time I received five years of education under the G. I. Bill. Having worked with other churches and taught for four years at a Bible college, I became pastor of Bible Chapel in Auburn, Washington, where I served for forty-one years. I also started Auburn College of the Bible to train the local people in the Word of God. The school ran for over twenty-five years, until I retired.

During this time, much prophetic speculation regarding the end times has washed under the bridge and is still being promoted today. Many predictions of the rapture and the end of the world have been made, but we are still here. People are in a quandary as to what to believe. Therefore, a careful study of end time events is necessary today. This I have endeavored to do in this book. The great need is to subscribe to Scripture, not to newspaper headlines.

The scriptures cited in each chapter should not be glanced over but read and studied within the context from which they are taken. Each chapter is conclusive on the biblical evidence presented. Therefore, the passages cannot be interpreted to mean something else without making the Bible self-contradictory. This is an important factor. The Word of God cannot be juggled to mean two different things at the same time.

Because the theory of the "golden age" (one thousand years of peace on earth during the last days) is built on speculation and Jewish apocryphal writings, it does not carry biblical weight. We do well to remind ourselves that when our Savior came, He took away the first covenant and established the second under which we now live (Heb. 10:9), which is the eternal covenant (Heb.13:20). We learn from the New Covenant that there is no golden age to come, save for the new heavens and the new earth, at which time we will enter into eternity. The New Testament presents Christ and His Church to be the fullness of God (Eph. 1:22-23), outside of which there can be no other fullness. This leaves no room for any other fullness outside of the Church. Much that has been transferred to a so-called millennium really belongs to the Church Age or to eternity.

Peter is strikingly sure that at Christ's *parousia* (the bodily presence of Christ as His second coming), we will enter the new heavens and the new earth (2 Pet. 3:9-13). We should not play Ping Pong with God's Word. Because the Holy Spirit is the inspirer of the Word of God and is the Spirit of Truth, He cannot be the author of two views that are diametrically opposed to one another. Both views may be wrong, but both cannot be scriptural. So let us be like the people of Berea who were more fair-minded and searched the Scripture to see if these things were so.

Dispensationalism has used God's Word to speculate and then build a system based on Judaism's hopes of Israel being re-established by God for a golden age of one thousand years of peace on this earth. Dispensationalists even extend the word *parousia* to be a "pre-tribulation second coming of Christ." This we do not find in the New Testament, God's final revelation. When it comes to a future salvation for Israel as taught by dispensationalism (Rom. 11:26), Peter states that the salvation of which the Old Testament prophets prophesied was the salvation that Christ brought. Peter also states that this salvation applied to us of the New Testament Age and not to the salvation of Israel in a millennium (1 Pet. 1:9-12). Hopefully, I have made this evident in this book.

I have no reason for writing this manuscript other then to present the truth that the Bible alone represents. No personal esotericism is involved. Please hold in mind that it is against the doctrines of dispensationalism that I write, not against the people who express this view. Each chapter deals with a certain aspect of biblical eschatology that I feel dispensationalism has distorted by reverting to a Judaistic slant. It is my prayer that the reader will study each chapter and then reach his or her conclusions on what the Bible—and the Bible alone—has to say. I have no assumptions or conjectures to present but have based my conclusions solidly on Scripture. The Reformers based their conclusions on *sola scriptura*, the Scripture alone, and may I do the same. Not to be true to the scriptures is to falsify them. If the scriptures presented do not prove the point expressed, then I stand to be corrected by the scriptures that do!

I wish to express my appreciation to my wife, Muriel, who has allowed me the many days and years of solitary study and compilation of this manuscript. My deep gratitude goes to Jean Britt, who has untiringly spent time each week over several years to put this book in its proper order to be printed, and to her husband, Rev. William E. Britt, D. Min., who supported us in this writing. I am also grateful to Rev. Charles H. Robinson, D. Min., of Dayton, Tennessee, for the reading of the manuscript and editorial help given. I want to also pay due regard to Ronald and Barbara Lalime, who have painstakingly read and seen that all scriptural references were correct and in order, and to my son and his wife, Ryan and Peggy Egerdahl, and my granddaughter Michelle Anderson for their encouragement and support. I also want to express a sincere thanks to my many friends for their suggestions and critique.

My desire and prayer has been that of David in Psalm 19:14: "Let the words of my mouth and the meditation of my heart be acceptable in Your sight, O Lord, my strength and my Redeemer."

Chapter 1

AN INTRODUCTION TO ESCHATOLOGY

It is a historical fact (as reflected in newspaper headlines) that interest in *eschatology* has had and continues to have its greatest influence on people during times of world stress and its least influence during times of peace and prosperity.

Are we not living in a generation that is gambling with everything worthwhile in life? Are we not losing the spiritual battle because of it? One reason for this is because biblical truth is being compromised for modern-day headlines. Everybody wants to live in a better world, but sentiment and speculation have replaced scriptural truth.

Historically, eschatology took an entirely new stance in the Church during the nineteenth century.

- Paul had warned the Church of "winds of doctrine" (Eph. 4:14).
- Prior to this, our Lord had warned us of doctrines of men that were substituted for the doctrines of God (Matt. 15:9).
- Paul later warns that at the end of time, "doctrines of demons" would deceptively arise (1 Tim. 4:1).
- Jesus, when talking about catastrophes that would come on the world at the end of the age, warned mankind of a deception that would creep in (Matt. 24:4,11, 24).

It is not peculiar that it was during the times of world distress eschatologically that Jesus' warning applies. The Bible itself has forecast these things so that we might be on guard concerning them. However, when deception is as prevalent as it has become today, there are very few voices indeed that rise up against it.

The heartbeat of God for Israel in the Old Testament was for a better time to come in the person of a prophet similar to Moses (Deut. 18:15) who would lead them toward a new promised land. The New Testament reveals that this prophet has come and has brought God's revelation to the fullest. Truly, Jesus is that prophet greater than Moses (Acts 3:22-23):

- By Moses came the law, but by Christ came grace and truth (John 1:17).
- Christ is the high priest greater than Aaron and the king greater than David.
- He is the builder of the temple (John 2:18-19).
- He is greater than Solomon (Matt. 12:42).

This gives us a great hermeneutic in that the Old Covenant must be interpreted in the light of the New Covenant. Why not let the Bible interpret itself? Can man arrange his own hermeneutic? After all, did not our Lord say that Old Testament history came to its final conclusion in Himself (Luke 24:25-27)?

- What does the Bible mean when Christ says that He is the Alpha and the Omega (Rev. 22:13)?
- Does not Paul say that the fullness of God had arrived in Christ, that we are complete in Him, and that we are not to be otherwise philosophically deceived (Col. 2:8-10)?
- The Scripture has declared that all the promises of God find their fulfillment in Christ (2 Cor.1:20). How then can we be looking for something greater than what Christ has already done before the resurrection takes place, at which time all believers will have glorified bodies like that of Christ?

It is a fact that God's people have never been satisfied with what God has provided for them. Under the Old Covenant, people wanted what they only could have after Christ came to the world (John 1:17). Under the New Covenant, people want that which only can be theirs after the resurrection, when they will be together with Christ for eternity.

In Romans 2:28-29, Paul explains that a national Jew is not a Jew and an Israelite is not a true Israelite (Rom. 9:6), but that God has made every believer—whether Jew or Gentile—a true son of Abraham (Gal. 3:29), and that what God was doing in the Church He called the "Israel of God" (Gal. 6:15-16). Paul then bursts out with the phrase, "Oh, the depth of the riches both of the wisdom and knowledge of God! How unsearchable are His judgments and His ways past finding out!" (Rom. 11:33).

The wonder in eschatology today is that man has a greater vested interest in modern-day headlines than he does in the Word of God itself. How many prognostications have come and gone as to who the antichrist was or when the rapture and the end of the world would take place? But we are still here! Under the Old Covenant, those prophets would have been taken out and stoned to death for daring to presume upon God with their own predictions. God told Jeremiah that He did not send these types of prophets (Jer. 23:21).

If Scripture is given by the inspiration of God and "is profitable for doctrine, for reproof, for correction, for instruction in righteousness" (2 Tim. 3:16), it should then be evident that Scripture is plain enough to serve the purpose of interpreting itself. Does not this mean that contradictory views on the same subject should not be accepted? The Bible says that Christ who was preached to us "was not Yes and No, but in Him was Yes" (2 Cor. 1:19).

Because the Holy Spirit is the Spirit of Truth, how can it be possible that two views on a particular doctrine that are diametrically opposed to each other can both be true? Both may be wrong, but both cannot be right. Must we not look at all biblical truth in the light of Scripture only? The reformers called this idea *sola scriptura.*

Chapter 2

HERMENEUTICS: THE DOCTRINE OF BIBLICAL INTERPRETATION

Just how is the Bible to be interpreted? This is an ongoing problem within Christendom. The *Scofield Bible Correspondence Course* says, "A type must never be used to teach a doctrine" (*Scofield Bible Correspondence Course*, 1:45, rule 1). However, a note in the *Scofield Reference Bible* on Revelation 4:1 regarding John's call to *come up hither* states the following: "This call seems clearly to indicate the fulfillment of 1 Thess. 4:14-17" (Scofield 1945, 1334).

Those who believe that Christ postponed His kingdom are called "dispensationalists." This theory states that Christ postponed the kingdom until after His second coming. This means that the kingdom of God is not present now but will be in effect after Christ returns the second time, at which time He will set up the Messianic kingdom.

Under this dispensationalist theory, the Messianic kingdom (also called the Davidic kingdom or the millennium) is to last for only a thousand years. It is to be literally set up on the earth, with Jerusalem as its capital. Jesus will literally sit on David's throne, Satan will literally be bound, and there will come a literal one thousand years of peace.

Dispensationalists, including Scofield, say that the call of John to *come up hither* in Revelation 4:1 is the rapture of the Church and thus the fulfillment of 1 Thessalonians 4:14-17. This is a violation of his own rule, as it makes John a *type* of the Church, and is therefore a human invention. It is clear that dispensationalists, in order to establish their own doctrines, violate their own rules whenever they deem it necessary.

Arthur Pink quotes John Owen as saying, "Our inventions, though ever so splendid in our own eyes, are unto him an abomination, a striving to pull Him down from His eternal Excellency, to make him altogether like unto us" (Pink 1973, 243). Pink also quotes Jerome as saying, "God is dishonored by that honor which is ascribed to Him beyond His own prescription" (Ibid.)

Therefore, just how is the Bible to be interpreted? A true biblical hermeneutic is found in Acts 8:35, where Philip interprets Isaiah 53 to the Ethiopian eunuch. Through this passage, we see that the Bible lends itself to the fact that it must be interpreted to be fully understood.

In this story told in Acts, the Holy Spirit sent Philip on a preaching mission. On his way, Philip met up with an Ethiopian eunuch who was reading a passage in Isaiah 53:7-8. Philip asked the eunuch if he understood what he was reading. He answered, "How can I, unless someone guides me?" The Bible then states that Philip "opened his mouth, and beginning at this Scripture, preached Jesus to him" (Acts 8:35).

To this day, Jews do not believe that the Isaiah passage relates to Christ. However, the New Testament, written with the inspiration of the Holy Spirit, affirms that Philip gave the true interpretation of the text. Thus it is with many truths of the Old Testament: they need to be interpreted in the light of how the New Testament apostles and prophets interpreted them.

FAULTY SYSTEMS OF HERMENEUTICS

The "literal hermeneutic" system of interpretation violates sound biblical exegesis. Literalism separates the unity of the two Testaments. The Old Testament was never to be complete without the New Testament. H. F. Rall, in his book *Modern Pre-millennialism and the Christian Hope*, quotes Dr. Torrey as saying, "All prophecy is to be 'exactly and literally fulfilled'" (Rall 1920, 122). If the fulfillment of all prophecy has to be literally true, then in the story of Satan tempting Eve in Genesis 3:15, we would have a literal snake in combat with a human being. And then, for God's curse, there only would be a bruised head and a bruised heel. Would that be the true fulfillment?

Dr. J. Oliver Buswell says, "It is a sound rule of scripture interpretation that the didactic and historical ought to be used to interpret the figurative and apocalyptic" (Buswell 1937, 63). This grammatical-historical method of interpreting Scripture implies that the meaning of words must be the same as that of the author who penned them. While the original occasion may be seen this way, it does not follow that the words cannot have a spiritual fulfillment in the New Testament. The examples of Isaiah 53 and Genesis 3:15 mentioned previously are the very proof of this. To rigidly follow this method would put the New Testament in a straightjacket of interpreting the Old Testament.

From a human perspective, the Old Testament has been made to fit into a prearranged philosophical and historical framework, though the scriptures themselves argue against an artificial reconstruction. After his conversion to Christ, Paul, a strict Jew who was trained in the Old Testament, showed the unity of the two Testaments and demonstrated how the dependency of the Old Testament on the New brought the Old Testament to light through the gospel. He wrote:

> Share with me in the sufferings for the gospel according to the power of God, who has saved us and called us with a holy calling, not according to our works, but according to His own purpose and grace which was given to us in Christ Jesus before time began, but has now been revealed by the appearing of our Savior Jesus Christ, who has abolished death and brought life and immortality to light through the gospel.
>
> (2 Tim. 1:9-10)

This proves that it does take the New Testament to bring to light the writings of the Old Testament. It also becomes a hermeneutic for the interpretation of the Old Testament.

An example of this is found in the interpretation of Isaiah 7:14, "Behold the virgin shall conceive and bear a Son, and shall call His name Immanuel." The Holy Spirit, through Matthew, found the fulfillment of this verse in the birth of Jesus (Matt. 1:23). This gives us a key to the interpretation of other Old Testament prophecies as fulfilled in the New Testament. To avoid this method of interpretation is to void the divine inspiration of Scripture.

Paul lays down another hermeneutic in 1 Corinthians 4:6 when he says, "These things, brethren, I have figuratively transferred to myself and Apollos for your sakes, that you may learn in us not to think beyond what is written." To go beyond what is written is to add something to the text that is not there and convolute the Word of God. It is man himself taking the place of God and endeavoring to write Scripture.

Martin Kuske quotes H. F. Kohlbrugge as saying:

> For the purpose of scriptural interpretation one must put himself in the place of the apostles and the first Christian community. "Here there is no middle-of-the-road position. Either the Lord, His apostles, and the first Christians interpreted the writings of Moses and the prophets in completely the wrong way, that is granted that they themselves did not understand them and that they deceived others, or we have to understand and interpret these writings very simply as they are, without taking away from or adding to them. If one rejects the later option, he must realize what one does with the Lord and His apostles and that is destroying the basis of the Christian faith and the Christian hope as its foundation"
>
> (Kuske 1976, 71)

Paul writes in Romans 15:4, "For whatever things were written before were written for our learning, that we through the patience and comfort of the Scriptures might have hope." This, together with 1 Corinthians 10:1-11, affirms that these Old Testament events bear a spiritual significance in the New Testament.

A hermeneutic called "double fulfillment" has been used by some to save their particular interpretation of Scripture. However, if this were a true hermeneutic, we would then have to say that Isaiah 7:14 must also have a second fulfillment. Would that be likely? What theologian would agree with that? (Milton S. Terry has written on this subject in his book *Biblical Hermeneutics*, pp. 493-499).

E. W. Bullinger, a dispensationalist, says, "There is one great foundation principle in the science of logic which will meet all the difficulties, if we are careful to observe it; it is this: *We cannot reason from the particular to the general.* On the contrary, we must reason from the *general* to the *particular*, if we would reason accurately" (Bullinger 1930, p. vii).

There is a controversy over the literal and figurative (or spiritual) method of interpretation. The Jews of Jesus' day were literalists, as is evident from John 3. When Jesus talked with Nicodemus about being born again, Nicodemus only could think literally of entering his mother's womb. When Jesus talked to the woman at the well about living water, she looked for a vessel to draw water from the well. When Jesus said, "Destroy this temple and I will build it in three days" (John 2:19), the Jews responded by talking about a literal temple.

J. Dwight Pentecost, in his book *Things to Come*, states, "Literalism among the Jews. The prevailing method of interpretation among the Jews at the time of Christ was certainly the literal method of interpretation" (Pentecost 1964, 17). Pentecost could not have put it more clearly. But were the Jews right? It does not seem so, according to Jesus. Christ never agreed with the doctrine of the Pharisees or the Sadducees. On the contrary, He denounced their teachings and practices.

Matthew 16:1-12 provides the proof. In verse 6, Jesus warned His disciples of the teachings of these religious leaders: "Take heed and beware of the leaven of the Pharisees and the Sadducees." In verse 12, it states, "Then they understood that He did not tell them to beware of the leaven of bread, but of the doctrine of the Pharisees and Sadducees."

As if this is not enough, all we have to do is read Matthew 23, where Jesus uses the entire chapter of thirty-nine verses to denounce the Pharisees and Sadducees and their teachings. Jesus pronounces seven woes on their teaching, which culminates in His rejecting the temple as His house and pronouncing desolation on it. Prior to this, in Matthew 22:23-33, Jesus said to the Sadducees, "You are mistaken, not knowing the scriptures nor the power of God" (v. 29). If they did not know the Scriptures or the power of God, how can we then depend on the literalism of the Jews on which the dispensationalists have subscribed?

It was the hatred of the Pharisees and Sadducees regarding Christ's interpretation of Scripture as opposed to their literal method that put Christ on the cross. Ever since Christ's first sermon in Nazareth, the Jews had plotted to kill Him (Luke 4:16-30). The events in Matthew 23 took place during the last seven days of Christ's life.

Dispensationalists claim to be literal in their interpretation of Scripture. They say that this is rightly dividing the Word of Truth. The claim is that every Old Testament prophecy was literally fulfilled. Dr. William Pettingill wrote, "Likewise, the promises brought to the virgin Mary by the angel Gabriel have been fulfilled in part, and literally fulfilled; therefore we have a right to expect the literal fulfillment of the remainder" (Pettingill 1948, 69-70). Is this biblically true?

A. C. Gaebelien, a literalist, makes the following comment on Daniel 12:2: "This is a spiritual resurrection of literal Israel" (Gaebelien 1911, 200). The verse in Daniel states, "And many of those who sleep in the dust of the earth shall awake, some to everlasting life, some to shame and everlasting contempt." Most theologians take this to mean a literal physical resurrection in the last day. The question is: How can a literalist make a spiritual resurrection out of this passage and still be literal? How literal *are* the literalists? It seems that they can jump in and out of their own hermeneutics at will to produce their own ends. Gregory of Nysan said of literal interpreters: "They have enveloped their ears with the Jewish veil."

Leonard Woods said of biblical writers, "If in setting forth they employed language more or less figurative, they did it, not to detract from the reality or the importance of truth which they declared, but to illustrate it more clearly, and to impress it on our minds more strongly and permanently" (Woods 1829, 2:182).

In 1 Corinthians 2:13, Paul states that the Bible is a spiritual book and should be spiritually discerned: "These things we also speak, not in words which man's wisdom teaches but which the Holy Spirit teaches, comparing spiritual things with spiritual." Literalism would reduce many Scriptures to absurdity. In John 6:53, Jesus said, "Unless you eat the flesh of the Son of Man and drink His blood, you have no life in you." The content of the communion table cannot be interpreted as being literal! In John 10:9, Jesus said, "I am the door." There is nothing literal about either of these verses. To make them literal would be cannibalism and to say that Jesus swung on hinges. Literalism here would reduce the scriptures to absurdity.

Isaiah 40:3-4 states, "Make straight in the desert a highway for our God. Every valley shall be exalted and every mountain and hill brought low." Is this literal or spiritual? If we interpret this passage literally, it would mean bulldozers would have to level Palestine. One person actually said this. Is this what God meant in these verses?

We are saved from literalism here by the Holy Spirit's interpretation of the same passage in Luke 3:3-4. In these verses, Luke implies that the ministry of John the Baptist was to take away the spiritually crooked places and the stumbling blocks that the Jews had put in the way of people coming to God so that "all flesh shall see the salvation of God." This is why Jesus could say, "Tax collectors and harlots enter the kingdom of God before you" (Matt. 21:31).

Isaiah 2:2 states, "Now it shall come to pass in the latter days that the mountain of the Lord's house shall be established on the top of the mountains." Is this verse literal or spiritual? Consider the following:

- If this were interpreted literally, we would have a mountain on top of a mountain.
- In Acts 2:16-21, when Peter interpreted the events of Pentecost, he said that the *last days* mentioned in Joel 2:28-32 were now being fulfilled. Therefore, the *last days* had to begin with the beginning of the New Testament. Hebrews 1:1-2 verifies this fact. After the last days, there can be no other days, or words are meaningless.
- Joel 2:32 is interpreted in the New Testament as being the time when all who call on the name of the Lord shall be saved, Israel included. The prophetic fulfillment is seen in Romans 10:13 and not after the second coming of Christ.

In Isaiah 11:6-9, the kingdom of the Messiah is spoken of as a kingdom of peace, yet in Isaiah 9 and 11:14-15, the prophet speaks of the wars and victories of the Messiah's reign. A reference to the New Testament of the same prophet will show that Isaiah 9:5 is spiritually applied as it is related to verses 6 and 7, which speak of the Messiah on the throne of David.

In Acts 2:30, Peter spiritualized the throne of David to be the throne to which Christ ascended in heaven. There is no literalism here. Who then can truthfully say that all Old Testament prophecies must be literally fulfilled in a literal kingdom for the Jews here on earth? To do so would violate the New Testament application of these verses and destroy the divine inspiration of the Scriptures.

In Matthew 10:34, Jesus says, "Do not think that I came to bring peace on the earth. I did not come to bring peace but a sword." What kind of a literal sword did Jesus bring? Or was Jesus spiritualizing the word *sword* to mean the sword of the Spirit, which is the Word of God (see Eph. 6:17; Heb. 4:12)?

In the same way, to interpret Isaiah 66:20 literally requires that verses 21 and 23 also be interpreted literally. This involved the Jewish priesthood and its worship. Does not Hebrews 10 contradict a literal interpretation of the same? Many eschatological doctrines of dispensationalism include such methods of literal interpretation. This, however, voids much of the New Testament's interpretation, application, and fulfillment of the Old Testament.

Furthermore, the persons of Ishmael and Isaac, Hagar and Sarah are interpreted spiritually by the New Testament in Galatians 4:21-31.

Similarly, Hebrews 12:18-24 parallels the Old Testament relationship of the people of God with that of the New Testament people of God. The Old Testament people came to Mount Sinai; the New Testament people come to Mount Zion, which is the city of the living God, the heavenly Jerusalem. Was this not the city that Abraham was looking for in Hebrews 11:10? There is no literal Jerusalem found here. Certainly, neither Jesus, who gave to John the Revelation (Rev. 1:8), nor His apostles always followed the literal method in their interpretation of the Old Testament.

Joseph Angus, D.D., states the following on the interpretation of prophecy:

> It is the golden rule, that as prophecy is not self-interpretative (of private interpretation, 2 Pet. 1:20-21), each of the predictions of Scripture must be compared with others, on the same topic, and with history, both profane and inspired. Parallel predictions will often throw light upon one another, and recorded fulfillments will explain predictions or parts of predictions still unfulfilled. History and the New Testament will thus often fix the meaning of individual passages, and these will illuminate and explain their respective connections.
>
> (Angus 1857, 294)

In the following section, it will be shown that the "principles of God are eternal," but that the application of those principles are spiritually interpreted when transferred to the New Covenant.

ETERNAL PRINCIPLES OF BIBLICAL INTERPRETATION

Paul, speaking to the Ephesian church, states that what was accomplished by Christ was God's eternal purpose (Eph. 3:11). Nothing ever takes God by surprise. All of God's works from eternity are known to Him (Acts 15:18). In the Bible, the principles of God are eternal; they never change. However, the function of those principles changes from the Old Covenant to the New Covenant.

Religion has made God's Word antique in the light of today's high-tech knowledge. But God's Word is always up to date. It never becomes antiquated. Paul, writing to the church in Corinth, lays down an eternal biblical principle of interpretation in 1 Corinthians 15:46: "However, the spiritual is not first, but the natural, and afterward the spiritual." Ira

Landis puts it this way as he amplifies this rule of interpretation by seven analogies found in 1 Corinthians 15:43-49:

First The Natural, Then The Spiritual

THE NATURAL	THE SPIRITUAL
Sown in dishonor	Raised in glory
Sown in corruption	Raised in incorruption
Sown in weakness	Raised in power
Sown a natural body	Raised a spiritual body
First Adam, a living soul	Last Adam, a quickening Spirit
First man of earth, earthly	Second Man, Lord from heaven
Borne the earthly image	Bear the image of the heavenly

With a sweep of the past and a comprehension of the future, Paul saw that here was the principle of God's dealings with man throughout the ages: "First the natural, afterward the spiritual" (Landis 1946, 81). Is not Paul saying that the rule of first the natural and then the spiritual applies from the "first Adam" on through to the "last Adam," and then on to that of bearing the heavenly image at the time of the resurrection?

The creation narrative (Gen. 1) is a type of redemption as seen in the New Testament (2 Cor. 4:6; Eph. 5:8; John 1:4-5; 3:19; 8:12; 1 John 1:5). In these references, we find no literalism in the fulfillment of God's dealings with man from the Old Testament to the New Testament. Comparing parallel passages of the Old Testament with the New Testament function and fulfillment of the same forms the proper interpretation of Old Testament texts.

This is enough to prove that the principles of God are eternal and that their functions change under the New Covenant. In addition, it shows that the physical or literal of the Old Covenant becomes a spiritual principle under the New Covenant.

Does God Walk Backward?

To say that God is going to reverse these principles would be to say that God changed His mind. Of course, we know that this is not true, as He said, "For I am the Lord, I do not change" (Mal. 3:6). To suggest that the

GOD IS KING ETERNAL Ps.10:16; 103:19; Acts 15:18 The Bible Has One Theme—Redemption This Redemption God Expresses in Two Covenants		
◄——————— From Eternity		To Eternity ———————►
The Old Covenant—the natural	**Cross Rev. 13:8**	**The New Covenant—the spiritual**
The first creation—heaven and earth, Gen.1		The second creation—a new heaven and earth, 2 Pet. 3; Rev. 21
The Edenic paradise lost, Gen. 3		Paradise restored, Rev. 21: 22
A bride for Adam, Gen. 2:20–23		A bride for Christ John, 3:29; Rev. 21:2
Animal blood sacrifice, Gen. 3:21		Blood of Christ, Matt. 26:26–29
Seed of the woman, Gen. 3:15		Christ is the Seed of the woman, Gal. 3:16; 4:4
The Mosaic covenant, Ex. 20		Christ's new covenant, Luke 22:20; Heb. 10:9
The Tabernacle, Ex. 30–40		Christ is the new tabernacle, John 1:14
The Temple, 2 Chron. 2–8		Christ is the new temple, John 2:19–21
Israel—God's people		The Church—God's people, 1 Pet. 2:10
Natural Israel, 1 Cor. 10:18		Spiritual Israel, Rom. 9:6; Gal. 3:1–29
Physical circumcision		Spiritual circumcision, Col. 2:11
Passover lamb, Ex.12		Christ is our Passover, 1 Cor. 5:7
Old Covenant of the letter, 2 Cor. 3:3, 6, 7, 9, 11		New Covenant of the Spirit, 2 Cor. 3:3, 6, 8, 9, 11
Ministry of death, 2 Cor. 3:7		Ministry of righteousness, 2 Cor. 3:8
Covenant of works (thou shalt)		Covenant of faith, Eph. 2:8–9

restoration of Judaism is the fulfillment of the Old Covenant after the New Covenant has been put in place is to have God walking backward instead of forward to a restored paradise and a new heaven and new earth.

Did Jesus not say that new wine should not be put into old wineskins? Nor should we put a new cloth on an old garment. With Christ as the new Melchizedek, there is no way that He can be replaced by priests of Judaism offering animal sacrifices. God never intended to patch up Judaism with the new cloth of the gospel or put His new wine into the wineskins of Judaism. May God deliver us from a Christless interpretation of the Old Testament.

Chapter 3

THE KINGDOM OF GOD IN THIS PRESENT AGE

No civilization or earthly kingdom lasts forever. Kingdoms of men come and go. They rise and fall under the mighty hand of a sovereign God (Jer. 18:1-9). In just my generation, we have seen this exhibited in the Nazi regime under Hitler, in the fascist regime under Mussolini, in the communist regimes in Russia, and in many other smaller regimes in Third World countries. However, there is a kingdom among men that is eternal and enduring. It is the kingdom of God. Nebuchadnezzar found this out back in 600 B.C. (Dan. 4). Needless to say, 2,600 years later, the governments of this world still have not learned this lesson.

It was in the fullness of time (Eph. 1:10; Gal. 4:4) that Jesus came from heaven and preached this eternal kingdom (Matt. 25:34). It is at this point that our biblical study of the kingdom of God that was brought to us by our Lord and Savior, Jesus Christ, begins. What is this kingdom? F. F. Bruce makes clear in his comments on Exodus 15:18, "The Lord will reign forever and ever":

> This is the first explicit mention of the kingdom of God in the Bible, and from it we learn that His kingdom is not to be understood territorially (as when we speak of the kingdom of England), but in the sense of His royal dominion, exercised over nature and man alike—over nature as we have seen in His curbing of the Red Sea, and over men, both in His vindication of those who put their trust in Him and in His judgment on their enemies.
>
> (Bruce 1978, 5)

Both Jesus and John the Baptist drew their message about the arrival of the kingdom of God from the Old Testament. As to John the Baptist's message in Matt. 3:9, Bruce continues:

> It was useless for John's hearers to assert that they were Abraham's descendants, as though God were concerned about pedigrees. God if he so wished could have created children of Abraham out of the stones on the ground. What God wanted was a heart-devotion and righteous living. These were the qualities that marked His kingdom, and they would be acceptable to Him apart from any question of natural parentage.
>
> (Ibid., 27)

JESUS SETS UP THE STONE KINGDOM OF DANIEL

When Jesus said in Mark 1:15, "The time is fulfilled, and the kingdom of God is at hand," time-wise He had to be referring to a prophecy in the Old Testament relating to a kingdom that God would establish on the earth. This prophecy we find in Daniel 2:44-45:

> And in the days of these kings the God of heaven will set up a kingdom which shall never be destroyed; and the kingdom shall not be left to other people; it shall break in pieces and consume all these kingdoms, and it shall stand forever. Inasmuch as you saw that the stone was cut out of the mountain without hands, and that it broke in pieces the iron, the bronze, the clay, the silver, and the gold—the great God has made known to the king what will come to pass after this. The dream is certain, and its interpretation is sure.

This "stone kingdom" never would be destroyed; it would stand *forever*, not just for a thousand years. Daniel foretold, and history has revealed, that there were four successive nations that ruled the then-known world up to the time when this stone kingdom would be set up. Those nations were Babylon, Medo-Persia, Greece, and Rome.

Rome, the fourth kingdom, was the ruling power of the world when Christ came. It was then that Jesus announced that the kingdom of God had come. Mankind was to repent and believe the gospel, and through the acceptance of the gospel enter the kingdom of God (John 3:3-5). This was the message that John the forerunner had already proclaimed (Matt. 3:1-12).

In Matthew 21:42-44, Jesus declared that He was the stone that Israel had rejected: "Jesus said to them, 'Have you never read in the Scriptures: The stone which the builders rejected has become the chief cornerstone. This was the Lord's doing, and it is marvelous in our eyes? Therefore I say to you, the kingdom of God will be taken from you and given to a nation bearing the fruits of it. And whoever falls on this stone will be broken; but on whomever it falls, it will grind him to powder.'"

This stone is the same stone spoken of in Daniel 2:34-35, 44-45, which hit the image on its feet and ground it to powder. The stone broke the other kingdoms into pieces and consumed them, and then the wind like that of a summer threshing floor blew them away, never to return again. The stone became a great mountain and filled the whole earth.

Dispensationalism teaches that the ten toes of the image did not come under the falling stone, which are to be the future revival of the Roman Empire. How could anyone scripturally come up with such reasoning? We are assured in the prophecy that the toes were crushed with the image and blown away by the wind of the threshing floor so that no trace of them was to be found. The Roman Empire is *never* to be revived again. Furthermore, the Bible never says that "toes" are kings or kingdoms; it uses horns instead. We must keep our symbols straight:

- This Messianic Stone was prophesied in Genesis 49:24. In this prophecy, Christ is called "the Shepherd, the Stone of Israel."
- The Psalmist declared the stone would be rejected by Israel (Ps. 118:22).
- Jesus used this Psalm to state that this was being fulfilled in Himself (Matt. 21:42-43). Although rejected, the stone would become the chief cornerstone.
- Peter declared in Acts 4:11-12 that this prophecy was fulfilled in Christ. "This is the 'stone which was rejected by you builders, which has become the chief cornerstone.' Nor is there salvation in any other, for there is no other name under heaven given among men by which we must be saved."
- Likewise, in Romans 9:32-33, Paul declares that Christ was the stone the Jews stumbled over. You cannot stumble over something that has not yet come.

Peter declared that the stone had been laid in Zion as the foundation of the New Testament Church: "Therefore it is also contained in the scripture, 'Behold, I lay in Zion a chief cornerstone, elect, precious, and he who believes on Him will by no means be put to shame.' Therefore, to you who believe, He is precious; but to those who are disobedient, 'The stone which the builders rejected has become the chief cornerstone,' and 'a stone of stumbling and a rock of offense'" (1 Pet. 2:6-8). Prophecy thus fulfilled cannot be irrelevant!

CHRIST'S KINGDOM IS ESSENTIALLY A KINGDOM OF SALVATION

History has revealed that since Calvary, no one nation has ruled the world as did the four kingdoms prior to the cross. Rome eventually fell through the preaching of the kingdom of God by the Early Church. The kingdom that Jesus preached became the reign of God through salvation in experiencing the new birth (John 3:3-5). Isaiah prophesied that the Messiah's reign would be by proclaiming the saving power of God: "How beautiful upon the mountains are the feet of him who brings good news, who proclaims peace, who brings glad tidings of good things, who proclaims salvation, who says to Zion, 'Your God reigns!'" (Isa. 52:7).

In Romans 10:15, Paul quotes this passage of Isaiah as being fulfilled in the saving message: "And how shall they preach unless they are sent? As it is written: 'How beautiful are the feet of those who preach the gospel of peace, who bring glad tidings of good things!'" Paul further states in Romans 15:12, "There shall be a root of Jesse; and He who shall rise to reign over the Gentiles, in Him the Gentiles shall hope."

This constitutes one aspect of the Messiah's reign. "For if by the one man's offense death reigned through the one, much more those who receive abundance of grace and of the gift of righteousness will reign in life through the One, Jesus Christ…so that as sin reigned in death, even so grace might reign through righteousness to eternal life through Jesus Christ our Lord" (Rom. 5:17, 21).

After the believer experienced the new birth in Christ, God's law would be written on his or her heart (Ezek. 36:26; Heb. 10:11-17; 2 Cor. 3:2-3). This, in essence, is the reign of the kingdom of God that Christ inaugurated. Jesus never promised a materialistic kingdom. The reason the Jews rejected Jesus as their Messiah was because they were looking for a king that would deliver them from Rome and set up an earthly materialistic kingdom with Israel as the head nation and the Messiah as their literal king. When Christ did not comply, they refused to see Him as their Messianic king (Luke 4:28-32), and therefore had the right to reject Him. The truth of this is seen in Acts 13:27, "For those who dwell in Jerusalem, and their rulers, because they did not know Him, nor even the voices, of the prophets which are read every Sabbath, have fulfilled them in condemning Him."

Charles C. Ryrie in *The Final Countdown* says the following about the kingdom: "Obviously, at His first coming Christ did not even establish a kingdom in Palestine…Therefore we are forced to conclude that the kingdom will be set up at His second coming" (Ryrie 1989, 23). Where is this implicitly stated in the Bible? It would nullify the entire New Testament account of the kingdom that Jesus set in motion!

However, the Scripture does verify the fact that Christ did set up His kingdom at the time when Rome, the fourth kingdom of Daniel, was in power. At His trial, Jesus said that He was the king and that He had a kingdom (John 18:36-37). This kingdom was not to be left to another people. It was to stand forever, and nowhere in the Bible is it said that this kingdom would be postponed once it was started. After all, Jesus came into this world to battle sin and the kingdom of Satan, not to battle Rome (Matt. 1:21; 4:8-10).

WHAT IS THE KINGDOM OF GOD?

The theological idea concerning the kingdom of God is a puzzle to many. In the scriptures, there sometimes seems to be immediacy about the kingdom of God; at other times, it appears in its ultimate as being far off. Scripturally, there is a reason for this discrepancy, as will be seen below.

Jesus undoubtedly uses the idea of the kingdom as the all-encompassing category for the full sovereignty of God over all created things and for all time. The New Testament depicts the kingdom fully present as expressed in Christ. The fact that Christ is presently reigning is seen in 1 Corinthians 15:25-27. Spiritually, all things are now under Christ's feet (1 Cor. 15:27; Eph. 1:20-22), but we do not see them that way as yet. But we do see Jesus (Heb. 2:5-10). Furthermore, the New Testament writers seem to extend the kingdom to include the final perfection of creation itself at the resurrection and redemption of the body (Rom. 8:18-23). This, no doubt, will be expressed in the eternal kingdom: the new heavens and new earth.

Some people think God has been idle and is not involved in the affairs that take place on earth. To the contrary, as the chart on the next page indicates, God has been and is an eternal king over the entire universe. He guides the stars of the heavens in their courses (Pss. 8:3; 104:19). He provides for man—the just and the unjust—by sending rain and supplying crops. All nations are under His watchful eye. He pulls one down and builds another up according to His circumscribed sovereign will (Jer. 18:1-9).

God had an eternal plan for man long before the ages began (Eph. 3:11; 2 Tim. 1:9; 2 Thess. 2:13-14). This plan is revealed in His redemptive relationship to the Church through His Son, Jesus Christ our Lord. God gave kingship to Adam when He placed Him in the garden. He was given dominion (kingship) over all living creatures. Adam forfeited this kingship by disobeying God. However, the promised seed of the woman, the Messianic Christ, came to restore the dominion that Adam lost (Ps. 8:4-8; Heb. 2:6-9).

From eternity to eternity, God's kingdom is expressed in three phases: the Old Covenant as seen in Israel, the New Covenant as expressed in Jesus Christ, and the eternal or eschatological kingdom. Time-wise, every reference in the Bible relating to the kingdom of God can be seen as coming under one of these three categories.

ON THREE PHASES

First, God's kingdom on earth began with the nation of Israel. Exodus 19:6 states, "And you shall be to Me a kingdom of priests and a holy nation. These are the words which you shall speak to the children of Israel."

The New Testament aspect of the kingdom of God began with Christ. Mark 1:14-15 states, "Now after John was put in prison, Jesus came to Galilee, preaching the gospel of the kingdom of God, and saying, 'The time is fulfilled, and the kingdom of God is at hand. Repent, and believe in the gospel.'" In Luke 16:16, Jesus says, "The law and the prophets were until John. Since that time the kingdom of God has been preached, and everyone is pressing into it." Matthew 11:12-13 states, "And from the days of John the Baptist until now the kingdom of heaven suffers violence, and the violent take it by force. For all the prophets and the law prophesied

THE KINGDOM OF GOD IN THREE PHASES

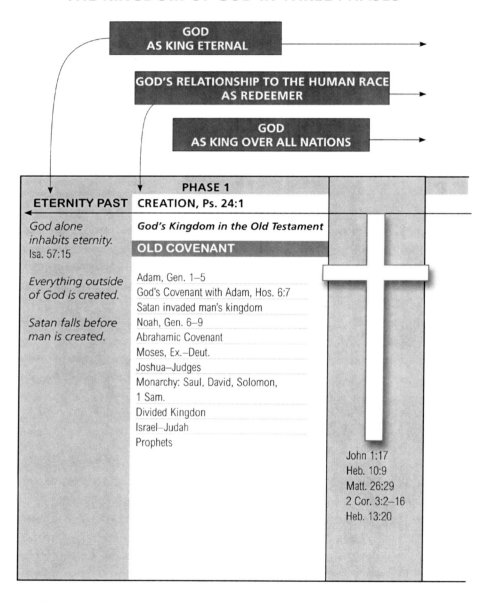

	GOD AS KING ETERNAL	
	GOD'S RELATIONSHIP TO THE HUMAN RACE AS REDEEMER	
	GOD AS KING OVER ALL NATIONS	

	PHASE 1	
◄ **ETERNITY PAST**	**CREATION, Ps. 24:1**	
God alone inhabits eternity. Isa. 57:15	***God's Kingdom in the Old Testament***	
	OLD COVENANT	
Everything outside of God is created.	Adam, Gen. 1–5	
	God's Covenant with Adam, Hos. 6:7	
	Satan invaded man's kingdom	
Satan falls before man is created.	Noah, Gen. 6–9	
	Abrahamic Covenant	
	Moses, Ex.–Deut.	
	Joshua–Judges	
	Monarchy: Saul, David, Solomon, 1 Sam.	
	Divided Kingdon	
	Israel–Judah	
	Prophets	John 1:17 Heb. 10:9 Matt. 26:29 2 Cor. 3:2–16 Heb. 13:20

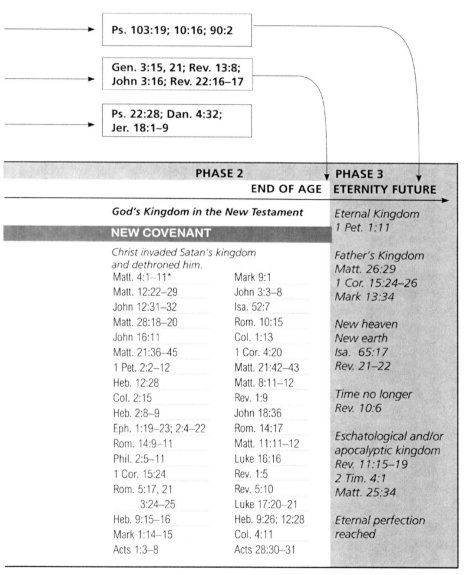

Ps. 103:19; 10:16; 90:2

Gen. 3:15, 21; Rev. 13:8;
John 3:16; Rev. 22:16–17

Ps. 22:28; Dan. 4:32;
Jer. 18:1–9

PHASE 2	PHASE 3
END OF AGE	ETERNITY FUTURE
God's Kingdom in the New Testament	*Eternal Kingdom*
	1 Pet. 1:11
NEW COVENANT	
Christ invaded Satan's kingdom	*Father's Kingdom*
and dethroned him.	*Matt. 26:29*
Matt. 4:1–11* Mark 9:1	*1 Cor. 15:24–26*
Matt. 12:22–29 John 3:3–8	*Mark 13:34*
John 12:31–32 Isa. 52:7	
Matt. 28:18–20 Rom. 10:15	*New heaven*
John 16:11 Col. 1:13	*New earth*
Matt. 21:36–45 1 Cor. 4:20	*Isa. 65:17*
1 Pet. 2:2–12 Matt. 21:42–43	*Rev. 21–22*
Heb. 12:28 Matt. 8:11–12	
Col. 2:15 Rev. 1:9	*Time no longer*
Heb. 2:8–9 John 18:36	*Rev. 10:6*
Eph. 1:19–23; 2:4–22 Rom. 14:17	
Rom. 14:9–11 Matt. 11:11–12	*Eschatological and/or*
Phil. 2:5–11 Luke 16:16	*apocalyptic kingdom*
1 Cor. 15:24 Rev. 1:5	*Rev. 11:15–19*
Rom. 5:17, 21 Rev. 5:10	*2 Tim. 4:1*
3:24–25 Luke 17:20–21	*Matt. 25:34*
Heb. 9:15–16 Heb. 9:26; 12:28	
Mark 1:14–15 Col. 4:11	*Eternal perfection*
Acts 1:3–8 Acts 28:30–31	*reached*

*Note: study the verses in column 1 first, and then column 2

until John." This phase of the kingdom will end when Christ delivers His redemptive kingdom to God the Father (1 Cor. 15:24-26).

The third aspect will be the eternal or eschatological kingdom that begins after Jesus returns the second time. Jesus called it the kingdom of the Father (Matt. 26:26-29; 13:43; 25:34; 1 Cor.15:24).

I first came to understand these aspects of the kingdom of God after I was discharged from the United States Navy in 1946. I had read about the kingdom of God in the Bible, but I had never heard anyone preach on it. At about the same time, I started witnessing to a Jehovah's Witness and began to hear about the kingdom as they know it. They even call all their meeting places "kingdom hall." However, I found that they had no new birth experience in their kingdom model, as Jesus stated in John 3:3-5 we would have. Neither was their kingdom related to Jesus Christ, who announced and preached the kingdom as being present in His day (Mark 1:14-15).

I concluded that these Jehovah's Witnesses twisted the biblical truths to their own destruction (2 Pet. 3:16). Their claim is that they are the ones who were in the kingdom and were actually setting it up in the earth—and I quote: "That God's kingdom by his promised Seed was born in A.D. 1914 remains an established fact" (*New Heavens and New Earth* 1953, 213).

HAS THE KINGDOM BEEN POSTPONED?

At a later time in my life, some literature came into my possession that declared Jesus had postponed His kingdom until after the Church Age. Now I really was confused. A cult was claiming to be the kingdom and a Christian group was saying the kingdom was postponed. This drove me to study Scripture to see what God actually had to say about the kingdom in His Word.

Remember, dispensational hermeneutics are supposed to be literal. That would mean that Christ's kingdom must be a literal kingdom set up on the earth. Because there is nothing in the world today that depicts a kingdom in such form, the dispensationalists invented the theory that the kingdom was postponed and that God put the Church Age in its place. There is *nothing* in the Bible about a postponement of the kingdom, but this postponement theory is at the heart of dispensational premillennialism. They cannot teach their doctrines without it. Take away their unscriptural postponement and their system falls apart.

Listen to some of the authors that propose this theory and their state-ments. (Note that my purpose here is not to write against people but against the doctrines that they so tenaciously espouse.) First, in *There's a New World Coming*, Hal Lindsey writes, "Had the people received Him, He would have fulfilled the kingly promises in their day…But when the Jewish nation as a whole rejected Christ, the fulfillment of His kingship was postponed until the final culmination of world history" (Lindsey 1974, 30).

In this passage, Lindsey concedes that the cross would not have been necessary if Jesus had fulfilled the kingdom promises at that time. If Jesus had fulfilled these kingdom promises, He would not have had to die. But what does that do to the inspired Word of God? What would that mean in Revelation 13:8 when John refers to "the Lamb slain from the founda-tion of the world"? Furthermore, where in the Bible is the postponement directly stated?

Lindsey assures us, "The apostles didn't realize that the Kingdom promised to Israel had been temporarily postponed until God could call out from among the Gentiles a people who would accept His Messiah" (Ibid., 167). How does he know that the kingdom was postponed? Is he not saying that he knows more than the Holy Spirit-inspired apostles? What does this do to a closed canon and to biblical inspiration?

Dwight Pentecost, another dispensationalist, states the following on the theocratic kingdom offer:

> It has been shown in tracing the theme of the Gospel of Matthew that the pivotal point in the Lord's ministry to Israel was reached in *the twelfth chapter, where the rejection of Israel by Christ,* because of their announced rejection of Him, and the withdrawal of the offer of the kingdom is re-corded. Gaebelein, speaking of the events in chapters eleven and twelve, says: "It is the great turning point in this Gospel and with it the offer of our Lord to Israel as their *King,* as well as the offer of the Kingdom ceases…Because the nation has rejected Him, the Lord announces *the severance of every natural tie* by which He was bound to the nation. (Mt. 12:46-50)" (Pentecost 1978, 463, emphasis mine.)

Let it be noted that in Matthew 12:46-50, there is no statement of Jesus withdrawing an offer of the kingdom. If in the twelfth chapter of Matthew Jesus postponed the kingdom, why does He in Chapter 16 give the keys of that kingdom to Peter? And why as late as Matthew 24:14 does Jesus commission them to preach the gospel of the kingdom until the end of this age?

Scofield says that it was in Luke 19:11-27, the parable of the pounds, where Jesus "postponed" the kingdom (Scofield 1945, 1102). This parable is the equivalent of the parable told in Matthew 25:14-30, the parable of the talents. So, if it is truly in Luke 19:11-27 that Jesus postponed the kingdom, how is it that He already took the kingdom away from Israel in Matthew 21:43? After Jesus took the kingdom away from Israel, there is no promise in Scripture that the kingdom will be given back to the nation of Israel.

In Matthew 21:19, Jesus stated that He was through with national Israel by cursing the fig tree, which was representative of Israel. He said, "Let no fruit grow on you forever." This truth is further confirmed in Luke 13:6-9, where the fig tree was to be cut down because it bore no fruit. Who has the authority to reverse what Jesus said? The fig tree is gone forever, and He never promised that the vineyard would be returned to the nation of Israel. As Gaebelein said about the reference above, "The Lord announces the severance of every natural tie by which He was bound to the nation." How true—and where is it stated that He will reverse this severance?

J. E. Jeter, in an article in the *Voice,* says, "The Kingdom of God is at our very door! This great fact should thrill the soul of every child of God. What a glorious thought to know that we soon will be in a righteous kingdom…the kingdom is not here now" (*Voice,* January 1962, vol. 9, no. 12). W. S. Hottel, in *The Earthly Kingdom and Kingship of the Lord Jesus Christ,* wrote, "The earthly kingdom of Christ was offered to the nation of Israel at Christ's first advent, and was not accepted by them, but was rather deliberately rejected" (Hottel undated, 11). Yet where in Jesus' teaching did He offer an earthly kingdom to Israel? If true, it should be stated in the Bible, but it is nowhere to be found.

Hottel goes on to say, "Upon rejection of Christ as King the kingdom entered a mystery form and was transferred to human hands to be administered" (Ibid., 13). Where in the Bible does it state that the kingdom went into a "mystery form"? In his notes on Matthew 13:11, Scofield also states that the kingdom is in mystery form (Scofield, 1945, 1014-1016). However, while Jesus spoke about mysteries *of* the kingdom, He never once said that the kingdom *itself* was a mystery. In fact, "of" is in the genitive case and speaks of things that belong to the kingdom or are an aspect of the kingdom, not the kingdom itself. Nicodemus surely thought it a mystery as to how he could be born again and thereby enter the kingdom of God (John 3:1-8).

Perhaps Frederick Grant best sums up what has happened to prophecy and the kingdom today: "Modern ideas have been read into prophecy. Or ancient Jewish apocalyptic has been made the key to unlock the whole 'Mystery of the Kingdom of God.'" Grant says that the modern game is to "take an idea and see what you can make of it…Shuffle the cards once more and deal yourself a solitaire hand" (Grant, 1940, viii-ix).

DID MAN'S SIN PREVENT CHRIST FROM SETTING UP HIS KINGDOM?

Hottel goes on to say, "The rejection of Christ the King by His own people and nation, His crucifixion, death, resurrection, and ascension *prevented* Him from taking possession of His earthly Kingdom and from reigning as King" (Hottel undated, 14, emphasis mine).

In dispensationalism, because all dispensations in the Old Testament failed and Christ failed to bring in the kingdom when He came the first time, He must therefore have a one-thousand-year millennial kingdom to fulfill what He failed to accomplish. Ultimately, this kingdom also fails in bringing man under God's subjection because of the great rebellion of Satan at the end of the thousand years.

Since when can man's doings prevent God's omnipotence? "All the inhabitants of the earth are reputed as nothing; He does according to His will in the army of heaven and among the inhabitants of the earth. No one can restrain His hand or say to Him, 'What have You done?'" (Dan. 4:35). The gospel of the kingdom that Christ brought in is the same one that Paul preached by declaring, "Now thanks be to God who always leads us in triumph in Christ, and through us diffuse the fragrance of His knowledge in every place" (2 Cor. 2:14). There is no failure here!

Another classical dispensationalism theory says that Christ postponed the kingdom because of the rejection of the Jews, which prevented Him from setting up the kingdom. However, Psalm 2:1-3,6 speaks to the opposite position:

> Why do the nations rage, and the people plot a vain thing? The kings of the earth set themselves, and the rulers take counsel together, against the Lord and against His Anointed, saying, "Let us break their bonds in pieces and cast away their chords from us"...*Yet I have set My King on My holy hill of Zion.* (emphasis mine)

Peter used this same Psalm in Acts 4:25-26 and affirmed that in spite of Christ's rejection by national Israel, God had set up Christ as king. He was now on David's throne (Acts 2:29-35).

Hottel continues, "When the Lord Jesus returns to earth in power and great glory the prophecy of Zechariah 9:9 will be literally fulfilled" (Hottel undated, 19). However, Scripture states that Zechariah 9:9 was fulfilled by Jesus in Matthew 21:4-5 as He rode into Jerusalem on Palm Sunday. Therefore, dispensationalists cannot use this prophecy for a second fulfillment in the future.

> Dwight Hervey Small says concerning the kingdom, "We recall how God summoned Israel to be the people of His rule; He entered into irrevocable covenants with them. Their disobedience and consequent judgment could not cancel out God's purpose or reverse His covenants. But it did allow men's failings to bring about a delay in the final enactment of God, the establishment of the Messianic kingdom. It brought about a postponement. But with the postponement came an interim pre-form of the kingdom in the birth of the church."
> (Small 1989, 177)

If the Old Testament spoke of the glorious kingdom to come with the Messiah, where is it written that it would be rejected by Israel, and God would have to institute the church in its place? The silence of this in scripture does not allow man to fill in the blanks with human speculation as if it were God's Word! John 3:3-5 describes the new birth that Jesus said would place a person into the kingdom of God. Jesus put no difference between this kingdom and the one that He introduced in Mark 1:14-15. Ezekiel 37:24-26 prophesied that it would be David's greater Son who would bring in this everlasting covenant. The new and everlasting covenant was brought in by Jesus (Luke 22:20; Hebrews 13:20). After this there can be no other covenant because Jesus' covenant is the everlasting one. Small tells us that the covenant with Old Testament Israel was irrevocable. But

Jeremiah says that Israel broke the covenant and that God was going to make a new one that could not be broken (Jer. 31:31-34). Hebrews 8:8-12 and 10:16-17 affirms that Jesus' covenant was the one that Jeremiah described. Furthermore, Hebrews 10:9 states that Jesus took away the first covenant to establish the second (and final) covenant. Nowhere in Scripture is a temporary or interim covenant mentioned.

Related to the time of Christ's return, in 1974, Dr. Charles Taylor wrote in his book *Get All Excited! Jesus Is Coming Soon*, "Jesus will return within this decade! The Jews will build their Temple in the tribulation" (Taylor 1974, 1). The decade was up in 1984. What is Dr. Taylor saying now?

Stanley Horton, one of my Bible college professors, states, "Jesus will come and set up a literal kingdom, just as real as the empires of the past but without their imperfections" (Horton, *Bible Prophecy Student Manual #10*). Dwight Pentecost says, "This kingdom was proclaimed as being 'at hand' at Christ's first advent (Matt. 3:2; 4:17; 10:5-7); but was rejected by Israel and therefore postponed (Matt. 23:37-39). It will again be announced to Israel in the tribulation period (Matt. 24:14)" (Pentecost 1978, 142). Matthew 24:14 is a commission of the Church to preach the gospel of the kingdom until the end of the age.

THE ATONEMENT AND THE CROSS IN DISPENSATIONALISM'S KINGDOM

Scofield writes the following concerning the postponement: "When Christ appeared to the Jewish people, the next thing, in the order of revelation as it then stood, should have been the setting up of the Davidic kingdom. In the knowledge of God, not yet disclosed lay the rejection of the kingdom (and King), the long period of the mystery-form of the kingdom, the world-wide preaching of the cross, and the out-calling of the Church. But this was as yet locked up in the secret counsels of God (Matt. 13:11, 17; Eph. 3:3-10)" (Scofield Reference Bible 1945, 998).

According to Scofield's statement, what does this do to the cross? Is it not saying that the cross would have been unnecessary if Christ would have set up His earthly kingdom when He came the first time? Does this not affect the atonement of Christ? What do other authors say on the same subject?

To fulfill their doctrinal presuppositions that the nation of Israel must yet have a kingdom on earth ruled by Jesus Christ in person, dispensationalists circumvent the cross of Christ. This view is therefore unbiblical and presents a false and heretical view of the atonement and of the kingdom of God. It is preposterous to think that Jesus, who knew all things, would teach, preach, and demonstrate His kingdom with miracles and then turn around and postpone it, only to have it reappear after more than two thousand years had passed. The kingdom miracles are the outcome of who Jesus was as king. Therefore, the character of the kingdom of God takes on the nature of the king. A. T. Robinson says on Mark 1:14, "The kingdom of God had arrived with the presence of the King" (Robinson 1930, 257). Dispensationalism bypasses these truths by stuffing them in a glove box to be used only in the millennium.

Note the following on the subject: John F. Walvoord wrote, "The Old Testament saints anticipated that if the second advent was fulfilled in their lifetime they would see Christ establish His millennial kingdom on earth" (Walvoord 1978, 360). Where in the Old Testament is such an anticipation stated? The theory of a millennial kingdom only arose after John wrote the book of Revelation around A.D. 96-98 (see Rev. 20). Before that time, there was no mention of a thousand-year millennial kingdom. Therefore, there could not have been such a thing as a millennial kingdom in the mind of Old Testament writers. Would not this also say that the cross would not have been necessary if Christ had set up His millennial kingdom at that time?

G. H. Pember wrote, "For both the Fore-runner and the Lord Himself begin their ministry with the cry, 'Repent for the Kingdom of the Heavens has come nigh.' The Four Hundred and Eighty-three Years were drawing to a close; but the *dreary interval* would not be necessary if Israel could at that time repent and receive the Anointed Prince" (Pember 1984, 1: 210-211, emphasis mine).

So, the Church Age is a "dreary interval!" What does this do to Christ's victory of the cross (2 Cor. 2:14)? The dispensational position then is that the cross of Christ was not victorious and would have been unnecessary if the Jews had repented! This is further affirmed by the following authors.

S. D. Gordon states in *Quiet Talks About Jesus*, "It can be said at once that His dying was not God's own plan. It was a plan conceived somewhere else, and yielded to by God. God had a plan of atonement by which men who were willing could be saved from sin and its effects. That plan is given in the Hebrew code" (Gordon 1906, 114). He continues:

> Clearly Jesus' dying does not in any way fit into the old Hebrew form of sacrifice…nor into the spirit of the man who caused the death of the sacrifice…The Old Testament scheme is Jewish. The manner of Jesus' death is not Jewish, but Roman. As a priest He was not of the Jewish order, but of an order non-Jewish and antedating the other by hundreds of years. In no feature does he fit into the old custom…the kingdom plan has been broken by the murder of the King."
>
> (Ibid., 115,117)

Gordon concludes, "It must be kept clearly in mind that there is a difference between God's plan and that which He knows ahead will occur. Sovereignty does not mean that everything God plans comes to pass" (Ibid., 60). No plainer statements could be made by a dispensationalist. Note that some deny these words as being true. Charles C. Ryrie, in his book *Dispensationalism,* calls this charge untrue because some did not document it (Ryrie 1965, 149-150). But it is documented in S. D. Gordon's book as just quoted.

Leslie D. Weatherhead writes:

> Was it God's intention from the beginning that Jesus should go to the Cross? I think that answer to that question must be no. I don't think Jesus thought that at the beginning of his ministry. He came with the *intention* that men should follow him, not kill him. The discipleship of men, not the death of Christ, was the intentional will of God, or if you like, God's ideal purpose—and I sometimes wish that in common language we could keep the phrase "the will of God" for the intentional will of God…But when circumstances wrought by man's evil, set up such a dilemma that Christ was compelled either to die or to run away, then in those circumstances the Cross was the will of God, but only in those circumstances which were themselves the fruit of evil.
>
> (Weatherhead 1944, 12)

This is a direct violation of what the Word of God says. The Bible declares that Jesus was "the Lamb slain from the foundation of the world" (Rev. 13:8). Jesus Himself declared that He came into the world "to give His life a ransom for many" (Matt. 20:28).

Each one of these authors is saying that the cross would not have been necessary if Christ had set up His millennial kingdom when He came to earth the first time. This is heresy, and the system must be rejected on that basis. How easy it has become to accept what is said without searching the Scriptures.

Because of these statements, dispensationalism must be held suspect—not only in this area that affects the atonement, but in other areas as well. Dispensationalists do all this to preserve a national kingdom for Israel in the millennium, which is unqualified by Scripture. It was never intended by Christ that the "rent veil" of Judaism would be patched up by the new cloth of the gospel. Neither under the New Covenant can we put new wine into old wineskins.

In the *Scofield Reference Bible,* Scofield writes that the kingdom will be given back to Israel (Scofield 1945, 1147). In his comments on Acts 1:6, Scofield states that Jesus left out one point: "One point was left untouched viz., the time when He would restore the kingdom to Israel;…the time was God's secret (Matt. 24:36, 42; 25:13, cf. 1 Thess. 5:1)." In other words, Christ left out a point to which Scofield had the answer.

THE CHURCH IS GOD'S KINGDOM

As to whether or not the Jews will yet inherit a kingdom for themselves apart from the Church must be answered on the basis of how the Scriptures themselves relate to that subject. A true hermeneutic is that the Old Testament should be interpreted in the light of the New Testament and that all indirect scriptures should be interpreted in the light of direct passages of Scripture.

Regarding the Jews inheriting their former status and having a millennial kingdom, there is nothing in the writings of Christ or His apostles relative to that subject. The New Testament is silent on that theme, and it is not in accord with Scripture to build a doctrine on the basis of silence. To construct a kingdom for the Jews after Jesus comes back would be to reconstruct and perpetuate the Old Covenant for a thousand years. Hebrews 10:9 states that Jesus already took away the first covenant to establish the second; thus, to say the opposite would be a direct violation of Scripture. It is also stated that Jesus is now the mediator of the new and better covenant (Heb.8:6-13; 12:24). Let us not forget that Jesus took the kingdom away from Israel (Matt.21:42-43) and gave it to a nation to bring forth the fruits. Peter says that this was the Church (1 Pet. 2:4-12).

Therefore, when the disciples asked Christ, "Lord will You at this time restore the kingdom to Israel?" (Acts 1:6), the answer cannot be based on the silence of Scripture. But did not Jesus answer the question by telling His disciples that they would live to see the kingdom come with power (Mark 9:1)? In Acts 1:3-8, Jesus spoke of the kingdom and told His disciples that they would receive power when the Holy Spirit had come upon them. Then they were to be the witness of Christ to the whole world. Was not this Christ's answer to the kingdom question? Does not the continuation of the kingdom find its fulfillment in its continued preaching and as the hope of Israel (Acts 26:6-7; 28:23-31)?

THE MILLENNIAL KINGDOM TO DISPENSATIONALISM IS DAVID'S KINGDOM

Scofield states the following regarding the Davidic kingdom in his comments on Ephesians 1:10: "The Dispensation of the Fullness of Times. This seventh and last of the ordered ages which condition human life on earth is identical with the kingdom covenanted David (2 Sam. 7:8-17; Zech. 12:8; summary Luke 1:31-35; 1 Cor. 15:24) and gathers into itself under Christ all past 'times.' The time of oppression and misrule ends by Christ taking His kingdom (Isa. 11:3,6). The times of the Gentiles end in the smiting of the image and the setting up of the kingdom of the heavens (Dan. 2:34-35; Rev. 19:15-21)" (Ibid., 1250).

To the contrary, the Scriptures reveal that the kingdom was set up by Christ, as He was the Stone of Daniel (Dan. 2:34-35). In Romans 9:32, Paul states that the Jews stumbled over that stone. How can you stumble over a stone that has not yet come? Peter says that Christ was the stone that the builders rejected and that He is the chief cornerstone (Acts 4:11-12; 1 Pet. 2:4-10). How is it possible to miss this point? (For more on this topic, see appendix B, "Daniel's Stone and Prophetic Biblical History.")

How do the dispensationalists deal with this problem? They have to invent a scheme. They postpone the kingdom that Jesus set up in Mark 1:14-15. This postponement theory makes the Church a substitute for the kingdom that Christ failed to establish during His time on earth. The Church became an afterthought of God, whose ability in setting up the kingdom was waylaid by sinful man. In his comment on Luke 19:10, Scofield calls this "the postponed kingdom" (Ibid., 1102).

So Jesus died a king without a kingdom. But what do the Scriptures say? To the very last, Jesus confessed that He was king and that He had a kingdom (John 18:33-37). The inspired Word declares that Jesus was hailed as king on Palm Sunday when He marched into Jerusalem (Matt. 21:5), which was the prophetic fulfillment of Zechariah 9:9.

Rather than postponing the kingdom, Jesus took the kingdom away from Israel: "Therefore I say to you, the kingdom of God will be taken from you and given to a nation bearing the fruits of it" (Matt. 21:43; see vv. 33-46). Isaiah wrote, "Therefore thus says the Lord God; 'Behold, I lay in Zion a stone for a foundation, a tried stone, a precious cornerstone, a sure foundation; whoever believes will not act hastily'" (Isa. 28:16). The New Testament takes this stone of Jewish prophecy and applies it to the Church (1 Pet. 2:6-8; Eph. 2:20; Matt. 21:42-45). Do not these scriptures tell us that the Church has inherited the kingdom aspects and the promises that were given to Old Testament Israel?

Scofield states what Christ's return to Israel would mean: "To Israel, the return of the Lord is predicted to accomplish the yet unfulfilled prophesies of her national re-gathering, conversion, and establishment in peace and power under the Davidic Covenant (Acts 15:14-17 with Zech. 14:1-9)" (Ibid., 1148). Does this mean that God is going to favor a handful of Jews with the Davidic Covenant at His second coming while bypassing the millions of Jews in this present age?

The scripture concerning the return of Israel to their land was fulfilled at their return from Babylon under the decree of Cyrus. After the Babylonian captivity, where are scriptures to back up this claim? There are none!

In his commentary on Acts 15:14-17, Scofield has James reprophesying the prophecy of Amos 9:11-12 as being yet future instead of saying that prophecy was fulfilled when the Gentiles came into the Church. On Matthew 11:20, Scofield continues, "The kingdom of heaven announced as 'at hand' by John the Baptist, by the King Himself, and by the twelve, and attested by mighty works, has been *morally* rejected. The final official rejection is later (Matt. 27:31-37)" (Ibid., 1011).

If Scofield is correct in his comments on Matthew 11:20, would this mean that Jesus forgot He had postponed the kingdom when later He gave the keys of that kingdom to Peter (Matt. 16:19)? Why did Peter on the Day of Pentecost quote so profusely from the Jewish Old Testament (Joel 2; Pss. 16; 110) and apply it to the Church if the kingdom was supposed to be postponed? Dispensationalists say these prophecies are all about Jesus and the Messianic or millennial kingdom, whereas Peter applies them to the Church. Is biblical inspiration fallible? (See appendix C, "Jesus Is King of His Kingdom, As Prophesied by the Prophets.")

If the promises of the Old Testament were written to literal Israel and not to the Church, why did Peter call the New Testament Church a kingdom of priests (1 Pet. 2:5, 9), as taken from Exodus 19:6 in which Israel became God's kingdom people? Why did Jesus call the Church a kingdom of priests in Revelation 1:6 and 5:10 if He was not applying Exodus 19:6 to the Church?

Since Abraham is the father of the Jewish nation, why is his covenant of redemption then applied as being fulfilled in the New Testament Church (Acts. 3:22-26; Rom. 4; Gal. 3:15-19,29) if the Church does not inherit the promises of Israel? Paul said that he received his truths by revelation from Jesus Christ (Gal. 1:12). Why then was he still preaching the kingdom and Christ as king as late as A.D. 63 (Acts 17:7; 28:31) if Jesus had already postponed the kingdom? Was Jesus wrong in His revelation to Paul?

Gabriel's annunciation to Mary in Luke 1:30-33 was the fulfillment of Psalm 2:6. Why was the throne of His father David promised to Mary's son at the time of his birth (Isa. 9:6-7), stating it would be from "this time forth," if it was to be postponed for several thousand years? Did not God who sent the angel know about the postponement? Or is God not omniscient?

Furthermore, why did Peter, who was supposed to know about the postponement, later proclaim in Acts 2:29-35 that it was thus prophesied of Christ that on His resurrection and ascension He would take the throne of David? In Romans, Paul also affirms this prophecy as being fulfilled by Christ's resurrection when he quotes the prophet Isaiah, "There shall be a root of Jesse; and He who shall rise to reign over the Gentiles, in Him the Gentiles shall hope" (Rom. 15:12).

Do not these references bespeak the fact that Christ took His reigning position on the throne at His resurrection and ascension into heaven? How could both Peter and Paul, inspired by the Holy Spirit, be wrong and the dispensationalists be right?

In 2 Corinthians 4:2, Paul states, "But we have renounced the hidden things of shame, not walking in craftiness nor handling the word of God deceitfully, but by manifestation of the truth commending ourselves to every man's conscience in the sight of God." With this warning that Paul uses in Corinthians, do you suppose that Paul or the dispensationalists are mishandling the Word of God when they deny that Christ set up His kingdom when He came?

Was John, the apostle of love, wrong in Revelation 1:9 when he said he was "in the tribulation and kingdom and patience of Jesus Christ"? How long after Calvary was this? How come John, an apostle of Christ who suffered in the kingdom of Christ, did not know that Jesus had postponed the kingdom? Was John not there at the time it was supposed to have been postponed?

In Revelation 12:10, John says the following regarding Christ's arrival into heaven: "Then I heard a loud voice saying in heaven, 'Now salvation, and strength, and the kingdom of our God, and the power of His Christ have come, for the accuser of our brethren, who accused them before our God day and night, has been cast down.'" In his comments on this verse, Scofield says, "The Dispensation of the Kingdom (2 Sam. 7:16 refs.) begins with the return of Christ to the earth, runs through the 'thousand years' of His earth-rule, and ends when He has delivered up the kingdom to The Father (1 Cor. 15:24, note)" (Ibid., 1341).

Scofield also notes, "Zechariah 12-14, form one prophecy the general theme of which is the return of the Lord and the establishment of the kingdom...Point (5) the cleansing fountain (Zech. 13:1) then to be *effectually* 'opened' to Israel" (Ibid., 976). Is this not saying that there is no cleansing fountain for Israel until the millennium?

In a TV broadcast on November 1981, Jerry Falwell said, "Jesus will literally sit on David's literal throne in Jerusalem. The Sermon on the Mount is the constitution of the millennium and is a word picture by Jesus; is dispensational and therefore useless to be lived out through us by the indwelling Holy Spirit." Falwell went on to say, "It is a comfort to know that it will be a 1,007 years after the rapture before the world blows up."

W.S. Hottel, in *The Earthly Kingdom and Kingship of the Lord Jesus Christ,* wrote, "If the reader will carefully follow this brief but comprehensive outline sketch, he will clearly see how the plan for a glorious Kingdom of Christ, to be set up in the earth, and to be centered in Israel, dates from the very beginning of world history; and he will see how the Church is not that kingdom, but is altogether differentiated from the earthly kingdom, and has another hope, calling, destiny and glory altogether, far more spiritual and more glorious than is realized in an earthly kingdom of Christ" (Hottel undated, 4).

Rutgers, in his book *Premillennialism in America*, wrote, "The kingdom postponed will then 'be restored to its rightful place *as soon as the church gets out of the way*'" (Rutgers 1930, 202-204, emphasis mine). Harry Ironside, a dispensationalist, wrote an entire book on the Church called *The Great Parenthesis* (Ryrie 1978, 136). On this basis, the dispensationalists postpone Christ's kingdom for a Jewish millennium and thus make the Church a substitute for a failure on Christ's part to establish the kingdom when He came the first time. So the Church that Jesus started is in the way of His establishing His earthly kingdom! Nonsense!

A brief note: If the *Scofield Reference Bible* has been edited to mean something different than what Scofield originally intended (as some have claimed), then we have to take his notes to be faulty to begin with. And if some were faulty, who knows how many more were also faulty? In addition, if Scofield's notes were edited to mean something other then what he originally intended, how come modern writers are drawing the same conclusion as Scofield? If progressive dispensationalism has changed anything, why do they still believe that the kingdom Christ started is yet to be that of an earthly millennium?

To dispensationalists, the millennium and the Messianic kingdom of David are one and the same. They have merely changed the wording on some of the topics, because they still come up with some of the same conclusions. If there is such a thing as "progressive dispensationalism," does that mean the same theologically as the doctrine of "open theism"? Is God progressively learning? Or do we believe that God is omniscient and that the canon of Scripture is closed?

THE BIBLE AND THE KINGDOM OF GOD

A biblical view of the kingdom is important because it will determine one's outlook on the entire New Testament. It will also determine one's outlook on the second coming of Christ and the consummation of the world.

Micah prophesied a king was to be born. "But you, Bethlehem Ephrathah, though you are little among the thousands of Judah, yet out of you shall come forth to Me the One to be Ruler in Israel, Whose goings forth are from of old, from everlasting" (Mic. 5:2). Matthew declared Micah's prophecy to be fulfilled in Christ (Matt. 2:1-12). So the king was born.

Early in the Gospel of John, Jesus was hailed as king: "Nathanael answered and said to Him, 'Rabbi, You are the Son of God! You are the King of Israel'" (John 1:49)! A.T. Robinson says, "The kingdom of God had arrived in the presence of the King" (Robinson 1930, Mark 1:14-15).

John the Baptist, Christ's forerunner, began his message by saying, "Repent, for the kingdom of heaven is at hand" (Matt. 3:2)! How could John the Baptist preach the kingdom of God if it was not a present reality to him by the results of his preaching? Who sent John with his message (John 1:33)? Is the inspiration of Scripture faulty? Jesus said that John the Baptist was "more than a prophet" (Matt. 11:9). Have we today more spiritually intelligent people on this subject than John the Baptist?

In Mark 1:14-15, Jesus said three things about the kingdom. First, He said that *the time was fulfilled.* To what time being fulfilled was Jesus referring? It had to be something prophetically recorded by the prophets concerning the kingdom that He was now preaching and setting up. Second, Jesus said that *the kingdom was at hand.* What kingdom? Daniel 2 foretold the kingdom that would be set up by the arrival of the Messianic king: "In the days of these kings the God of heaven will set up a kingdom, which shall never be destroyed; and the kingdom shall not be left to other people; it shall break in pieces and consume all these kingdoms and it shall stand forever" (Dan. 2:44).

God's kingdom was to be set up *in the days of these kings,* and Rome was the last of those kingdoms. It was then that Christ the "stone" was born; therefore, this kingdom could not be yet future. This stone kingdom would last forever and could not be postponed. In it, Jesus would stand in the forefront as the person of the kingdom with salvation and eternal life as its motif. Innate in this motif lies the reign of Christ and His kingdom (Isa. 52:7; Rom. 10:15). Rome, the fourth kingdom in the prophecy of Daniel 2:31-45, was in power when Jesus the Messiah came. Note the following:

- It was then that Jesus was born as king (Matt. 2).

- It was then Jesus set up His kingdom (Mark 1:14-15).
- Jesus was hailed as king as He marched into Jerusalem (Matt. 21:4-5).
- Jesus died as king (John 18:36-37; 19:19-22).
- Jesus rose from the dead and gave instruction to His disciples regarding His kingdom, which was still in existence after the resurrection (Acts 1:3). How could the kingdom have been postponed prior to this?
- Jesus declared that the power of the kingdom would be in the coming of the Holy Spirit (Acts 1:1-8; Mark 9:1; Matt. 16:28; Luke 9:27). Either the kingdom came with power at Pentecost as Jesus said, or the people to whom He was talking are still alive today. Which is it?

Repent and believe the gospel was the third thing Jesus said in Mark 1:14-15 concerning the kingdom. In the proclamation of the kingdom of God, sinners enter that kingdom (John 3:3-5). Dispensationalists say the kingdom was postponed, but not the gospel of that kingdom, which is the basis for entering the kingdom. This gospel Christ ordered to be preached until He returned (Matt. 24:14). Could it be possible that Jesus did not know what He was saying about the kingdom at the time?

THE BIBLICAL USE OF THE PHRASE, "AT HAND"

"The kingdom of God is at hand" (Mark 1:15). What is meant by the term "at hand," and how is it used in the Bible? In his comments on Matthew 4:17, Scofield states, "'At hand' is never a positive affirmation that the person or thing said to be 'at hand' will immediately appear, but only no known or predicted event must intervene" (Scofield 1945, 998).

Scofield's statement that "at hand" does not mean present or going on at the time is a ploy to take one's eyes off the reality of the kingdom that Jesus brought. It makes it easier for him to take the kingdom references and apply them to a millennial kingdom in which Jesus sits on a literal throne of David, literally ruling on earth for a thousand years under restored Israel and its animal sacrifices. All of this is said without a New Testament scriptural basis.

In addition, where in the Bible is it stated that "only no known or predicted event must intervene" before the kingdom is set up? Where is the scriptural proof for such reasoning? The Bible is silent on this aspect; therefore, it must be but human reasoning to avoid the truth of the kingdom's presence. Scofield talks as if what he says is gospel truth on the subject of "at hand"! But what does the Bible teach on this subject?

"At hand" comes from the Greek word (εγγυσ)(*engus*). Jesus used this word in Mark 1:14-15 when He preached that the kingdom of God was at hand. "Now after John was put in prison, Jesus came to Galilee, preaching the gospel of the kingdom of God, and saying, 'The time is fulfilled, and the kingdom of God is at hand. Repent, and believe in the gospel.'" In this verse, the word *is* is used in the present tense. That would mean that it was present right then! Consider the following other instances of this word *engus* in the Gospel of John:

- John 2:13: "Now the Passover of the Jews was at hand [*engus*], and Jesus went up to Jerusalem." In this passage, "at hand" meant going on right then.
- John 6:4: "Now the Passover, a feast of the Jews, was near [*engus*]." This is the same relationship as was found in John 2:13.
- John 6:19: "They saw Jesus walking on the sea, and drawing near [*engus*] the boat." In other words, Jesus was in their immediate presence.
- John 7:2: "Now the Jews' Feast of Tabernacles was at hand [*engus*]." Jesus goes up to the feast as beseeched by his brothers, which indicates that the feast was immediately taking place.

All of these verses prove that the word for "at hand" (*engus*) meant that something was taking place right then without any intervening period between. Other references in the Bible also prove that the kingdom was present at the time Christ was on earth.

Matthew 4:23 states, "And Jesus went about all Galilee, teaching in their synagogues, preaching the gospel of the kingdom, and healing all kinds of sickness and all kinds of disease among the people." Healing was a manifestation of the presence of the kingdom. How could the kingdom, the reign of God, not be present?

Matthew 12:28 states, "But if I cast out demons by the Spirit of God, surely the kingdom of God has come upon you." Jesus was casting out devils and said that thereby the kingdom of God had come upon them. Christ's kingdom has power over the kingdom of Satan.

Matthew 11:12-13 states, "And from the days of John the Baptist until now the kingdom of heaven suffers violence and the violent take it by force. For all the prophets and law prophesied until John." Since the kingdom was suffering violence, it had to be presently in manifestation. Question: When in these verses did Jesus say the kingdom had come?

Luke 17:20-21 states, "Now when He was asked by the Pharisees when the kingdom of God would come, He answered them and said, 'The kingdom of God does not come with observation; nor will they say, "See here!" or "See there!" For indeed, the kingdom of God is within you.'" Jesus' kingdom was not political but spiritual. Jesus' kingdom was not to come by outward visible means; it was to be the reality of His reign in the lives of those who believed.

The kingdom that dispensationalists talk about was one that would come with observation, a literal throne of David, with Jesus sitting on it, in the city of Jerusalem. Would this not put Jesus' statement of Luke 17:20-21 in the trash?

Acts 28:30-31 states, "Then Paul dwelt two whole years in his own rented house, and received all who came to him; preaching the kingdom of God and teaching the things which concern the Lord Jesus Christ with all confidence, no one forbidding him." Paul preached the kingdom of God for two whole years as a prisoner in Rome. This was at least thirty years after Calvary. Can it be said that the revelation of truth that Jesus gave to Paul was faulty? Or did Jesus forget to tell Paul that He had postponed the kingdom (Gal. 1:12)? Can it be said that Paul did not know what he was saying? Would it not be better to trust the biblical record over that of dispensationalism?

In conclusion, what does "at hand" mean scripturally? Would it be feasible to say that after having been commissioned by God (John 1:33), John the Baptist came preaching, "Repent, for the kingdom of heaven is at hand" (Matt. 3:2) if no kingdom were in existence? Likewise, would Jesus, the very Son of God who was sent by God, have preached the same message, saying, "The time is fulfilled [past tense], and the kingdom of God is at hand [present tense]; Repent and believe the gospel [present tense]" (Mark 1:15) if there were no kingdom to enter? Is it possible that both John the Baptist and Jesus had the wrong message and were preaching about a kingdom that could not be entered for now over two thousand years? What a demeaning thought! No! The kingdom was present and Christ was the king.

THE KINGDOM WAS NOT POSTPONED BUT
TRANSFERRED TO THE NEW TESTAMENT CHURCH

Where in the teachings of Jesus is there a direct statement that He actually postponed the kingdom? It simply is not found in Scripture. Rather, Jesus took the kingdom away from Israel and gave it to the Church (Matt. 21:33-43,46; 1 Pet. 2:4-12). "Therefore I say to you, the kingdom of God will be taken from you and given to a nation bearing the fruits of it" (Matt. 21:43). Peter affirmed this to be the Church: "But you are a chosen generation, a royal priesthood, a holy nation, His own special people, that you may proclaim the praises of Him who called you out of darkness into His marvelous light" (1 Pet. 2:9).

Prior to Jesus taking the kingdom away from Israel, he cursed the fig tree and said, "Let no fruit grow on you ever again" (Matt. 21:19). He concluded His thought by using a parable about Israel taken from Isaiah 5:1-7, in which Isaiah declared that Israel was God's vineyard. The chief priests and the Pharisees realized that Jesus was talking about them (Matt. 21:45). Therefore, there can be no mistake as to the timeframe in which the parable was meant to take place and to whom it applied. It was on the basis of not receiving the fruits of the land that the landowner's Son (Jesus) took the kingdom away from Israel (Matt. 21:43) and gave it to a nation bringing forth the fruits. In so doing, Jesus took away all the vineyard rights that Israel had in their position under God. (See Chapter 6 regarding the Land Question.)

Where in the Bible after this event does Jesus promise the kingdom will be given back to Israel? There is no such statement. Jesus' statement to Israel that "the kingdom of God would be taken from her [you]" is an admission that the kingdom of God existed in Israel when He came the first time. This kingdom was established in Israel when they came out of Egypt (Ex. 19:6). If there were no such kingdom on earth at the time, how could Jesus take something away from Israel that did not exist? Peter continued to apply Isaiah 8:14 and 28:16 and Psalm 118:22 to the Church:

> Therefore it is also contained in the Scripture, "Behold, I lay in Zion a chief cornerstone, elect, precious, and he who believes on Him will by no means be put to shame." Therefore, to you who believe, He is precious; but to those who are disobedient, "the stone which the builders

rejected has become the chief cornerstone." And "a stone of stumbling and a rock of offense." They stumble, being disobedient to the word, to which they also were appointed.

(1 Pet. 2:6-8)

In this passage, Peter calls the church: (1) a chosen generation, (2) a royal priesthood, (3) a holy nation, and (4) His own special people. This is what Israel was called when they came out of Egypt (Ex. 19:6). Does this not tell us that the Church has received the kingdom status, has inherited Israel's promises, and is God's new Israel (Gal. 6:15-16)? Can we not accept what the Bible says that the church is "a holy nation"?

Dispensationalists claim these promises of the Old Testament belong to Israel and not to the Church. But here we have Peter writing by divine inspiration and applying them to the Church. Because Christ was the foundation that was laid in Zion, Old Testament Zion had to be typical of the New Testament Church, as there was no other foundation that could be laid. "For no other foundation can anyone lay than that which is laid, which is Jesus Christ" (1 Cor. 3:11). Paul further avers this in Ephesians 2:20.

In Romans, Paul confirms the fact that the stone from the Old Testament is Christ, which the Jews stumbled over. "For they stumbled at the stumbling stone, As it is written: 'Behold, I lay in Zion a stumbling stone and rock of offense, and whoever believes on Him will not be put to shame'" (Rom. 9:32-33). How can you stumble over a stone that has not yet come?

After His resurrection, Jesus spoke to His apostles and sent them out to establish the New Testament Church. He connected the kingdom with the Church that they were commissioned to establish, "speaking of the things pertaining to the kingdom of God" (Acts 1:3-8). If Jesus had postponed the kingdom, why did He continue to teach them about the kingdom for forty days? Is not this indicative of the fact that Jesus never did postpone the kingdom? How could Jesus preach and teach the same message as John the Baptist on the kingdom of God if it were not present at that time? Jesus was the king of the kingdom. You cannot have a king without a kingdom, or vice versa.

THE BIBLICAL REALITY THAT THE KINGDOM OF GOD WAS IN EXISTENCE AT THE TIME OF CHRIST

In Luke 16:16, Jesus said, "The law and the prophets were until John. Since that time the Kingdom of God has been preached, and everyone is pressing into it." Again, Jesus stated the same truth in Matthew 11:12-13, "And from the days of John the Baptist until now the kingdom of heaven suffers violence, and the violent take it by force. For all the prophets and the law prophesied until John." Was Jesus wrong about the kingdom in these statements?

From these verses, it is plain that Jesus was teaching that a new transition was taking place through John the Baptist and His own coming. It is clear that the law and the prophets were to be until John and then the kingdom came.

What did Jesus mean in Matthew 12:28 when He inquired, "But if I cast out demons by the Spirit of God, surely the kingdom of God has come upon you"? Is Jesus not saying that by the casting out of demons, the kingdom of God was in manifestation?

Jesus told Nicodemus that by being born again, he would both see and enter the kingdom of God (John 3:3-5). Does this not tell us that the kingdom was a present reality at that time?

If Jesus had already postponed His kingdom, why in Matthew 21:31 does He say that "tax collectors and harlots enter the kingdom of God before you"?

In Luke 22:29, Jesus said to His apostles, "And I bestow upon you a kingdom, just as My Father bestowed one upon Me." If Jesus had already postponed the kingdom, why at this time would He bestow the same kingdom upon His apostles that the Father had bestowed on Him? To say that this kingdom would come into existence some two thousand or more years later is ludicrous.

Around A.D. 64, Paul still did not know about a postponed kingdom. Writing to the Colossians, he said, "He delivered us from the power of darkness and conveyed us into the kingdom of the Son of His love" (Col. 1:13). To the dispensationalist, the kingdom of the Son is the millennial kingdom that comes only after Jesus' second coming.

When the apostle John wrote the book of Revelation, he said at that time that he was in the kingdom of Jesus Christ. "I, John, both your brother and companion in the tribulation and kingdom and patience of Jesus Christ, was on the island that is called Patmos for the word of God and for the testimony of Jesus Christ" (Rev. 1:9). This does not concur with the prediction that the kingdom was postponed.

THE PROPHETIC REALITY OF THE THRONE OF THE KINGDOM

Isaiah 9:6-7 states, "For unto us a Child is born, unto us a Son is given; and the government will be upon His shoulder, And His name will be called Wonderful, Counselor, Mighty God, Everlasting Father, Prince of Peace. Of the increase of His government and peace there will be no end, upon the throne of David and over His kingdom, to order it and establish it with judgment and justice from that time forward, even forever. The zeal of the Lord of hosts will perform this."

Isaiah prophesied that when the Messiah was born, He would take the throne of David and set up His kingdom. The time of this prophecy began with the birth of Jesus: "Unto us a Child is born, unto us a Son is given…upon the throne of David and over His kingdom…from that time forward, even forever." From what time forward? It was to be from the time that the child was born and the son given. This prophecy does not indicate any postponement, but a continuous reign.

In Luke 1:31-33, this prophecy was reiterated to Mary by the angel Gabriel and applied to Jesus. This was not a prophecy about the future; it was prophecy that was coming into fulfillment.

In Luke 1:67-79, Zachariah's prophecy further accentuated the fact that Jesus was the fulfillment of the Davidic Covenant: "And has raised up a horn of salvation for us in the house of His servant David, as He spoke by the mouth of His holy prophets, who have been since the world began." The Abrahamic Covenant also accentuates the same truth: "To perform the mercy promised to our fathers and to remember His holy covenant, the oath which He swore to our father Abraham" (Luke 1:72-73).

Matthew, Mark, Luke and John in their Gospels introduce Christ as the king of the house of David and as heir to the fulfillment of the Covenant of Abraham (cf. Matt. 1; John 8:56; Luke 1:54-55; 2:25-32). In Mark 1:14-15 Jesus announced that the kingdom had come. Was Christ not omniscient? Why would He start something that later He would have to postpone because of the wrath of man? The wrath of man in rejecting Christ was prophetically revealed in the Old Testament. It did not take God or Jesus by surprise!

THE FULFILLMENT OF THESE PROPHECIES IN CHRIST BY HIS ASCENSION TO THE THRONE OF DAVID

Acts 2:30-31 states, "Therefore, being a prophet, and knowing that God had sworn with an oath to him that of the fruit of his body, according to the flesh, He would raise up the Christ to sit on His throne, He, foreseeing this, spoke concerning the resurrection of the Christ, that His soul was not left in Hades, nor did His flesh see corruption." This is a direct quote from Psalm 132:11 and is its fulfillment.

On the Day of Pentecost, Peter, inspired by the Holy Spirit, said that Jesus on His resurrection ascended to heaven and took the throne of David. For proof, Peter quoted Psalm 110:1: "The Lord said to my Lord, 'Sit at My right hand, till I make Your enemies Your footstool'" (Acts 2:34-35). Peter spoke of this as having taken place by the resurrection and ascension of Christ (Acts 2:30-31). Proof that Jesus was on the throne of David was that He had poured out the promised Holy Spirit. To deny the reality of this is to deny biblical truth and biblical inspiration.

The crowd, on seeing and hearing that Jesus was the fulfillment of the Davidic promise, recognized it as the fulfillment of prophecy. Jesus was the Davidic king they had been looking for but had now crucified. So they cried out, "What shall we do?" and three thousand entered the kingdom that day. Jesus is on the throne of David!

WHOSE THRONE WAS DAVID'S THRONE?

Dispensationalism states that Christ is to sit on David's literal throne when He comes back the second time to set up His Messianic kingdom. Is this what the Bible teaches? Whose throne was the throne of David? Consider the following:

- 1 Kings 2:12: "Then Solomon sat on the throne of his father David; and his kingdom was firmly established." Note that at David's death, Scripture says, "Then Solomon sat on the throne of his father David." David's throne!

- 1 Kings 8:20: "So the Lord has fulfilled His word which He spoke, and I have filled the position of my father David, and sit on the throne of Israel, as the Lord promised; and I have built a temple for the name of the Lord God of Israel." Solomon says he had filled the position of his father David and sat on the throne of Israel. Therefore, the throne of David and the throne of Israel are one and the same.
- 1 Chronicles 28:5: "And of all my sons (for the Lord has given me many sons), He has chosen my son Solomon to sit on the throne of the kingdom of the Lord over Israel." David was saying that the Lord had chosen his son Solomon to sit on the throne of the kingdom of the Lord over Israel.
- 1 Chronicles 29:23: "Then Solomon sat on the throne of the Lord as king instead of David, his father." Here David's throne is called the throne of the Lord [Jehovah]. Was it literally God's throne? What happens to literalism?

Are the four thrones in these scriptures the same throne? Why does God call David's throne the throne of the Lord? Which throne is the throne of David? Since David's throne was promised to the Messiah, which of these thrones, according to Acts 2:30-31, was Jesus resurrected to sit upon while being at the right hand of God in heaven?

Psalm 132:11 states, "The Lord has sworn in truth to David; He will not turn from it; I will set upon your throne the fruit of your body." Peter through the inspiration of the Holy Spirit on the Day of Pentecost takes Psalm 132:11 and applies it to the resurrected Christ: "Therefore being a prophet, and knowing that God had sworn with an oath to him that of the fruit of his body, according to the flesh, He would raise up the Christ to sit on his throne, he, foreseeing this, spoke concerning the resurrection of the Christ" (Acts 2:30-31).

This is a direct fulfillment of Psalm 132:11 in that Christ was the one who was the fruit of David's body. Therefore, after Christ's resurrection and ascension, He was seated on the throne of David in heaven. Would this throne be a literal or spiritual throne? Scofield makes the following comments on Isaiah 9:6-7: "The 'throne of David' is a phrase as definite, historically as 'throne of the Caesars' and as little admits of 'spiritualizing' (Luke 1:32-33)" (Scofield 1945, 721). John F. Walvoord says regarding

Luke 1:31-33, "If interpreted literally, the promises of the Old Testament assure a future restoration of Israel and a future kingdom of David in the millennial period" (Walvoord 1982, 16).

Stanley Horton, a professor of mine in Bible college, says, "Jesus will come and set up a literal kingdom, just as real as the empires of the past but without their imperfections" (Horton, *Bible Prophecy Student Manual #10*). This certainly leaves no room for Jesus to have a spiritual throne from which to reign.

However, according to 1 Chronicles 29:23, David's throne was "Jehovah's" or the "Father's" throne. In Revelation 3:21, Jesus says that He is sitting on the Father's throne. What kind of a throne would that be? Surely it is not the literal throne that David sat on.

To the truthfulness and respect of progressive dispensationalists, they have departed from both classical and revised dispensationalism in that they have seen and admitted that Christ is seated on the throne of David in heaven right now. However, dispensationalists do not believe that Jesus is *reigning* from heaven now—only that He has poured out the Holy Spirit. They stop short of conceding total fulfillment by saying that "the New Testament does indicate that the political aspects of Jesus' Davidic kingship will be fulfilled in the future" (Blaising and Bock 1993, 180).

In 2 Samuel 7:13, it states that the throne of David was to be established forever. However, because the last reigning king of David's line ended when Judah was taken over by Nebuchadnezzar, and because no human king from the line of David sat on the throne of David for over five hundred years prior to Christ, how could this prophecy be literal with such a vacancy? In giving the prophecy, God must have had something else in mind.

In 2 Samuel 7:19, David himself said that the prophecy of the ultimate fulfillment of the promise of his throne was "for a great while to come." Therefore, do not the following scriptures prove that it was meant for David's Seed (Christ) to be the fulfillment of the promise?

- Isaiah 9:6-7 states that from the time of birth of the Messiah, the throne of David would be given to the Son and it would be "from that time forward even forever."
- In Luke 1:31-33, the angel told Mary that she was to be the mother of the Messiah and that "the Lord God will give Him the throne

of His father David. And He will reign over the house of Jacob forever, and of His kingdom there will be no end."

- In Acts 2:25-36, Peter, quoting Psalm 132:11 and 16:10, affirmed that Christ was resurrected from the dead, ascended into heaven, and was seated on the right hand of God on David's throne in heaven (vv. 30-31).
- In Romans 15:12, Paul, quoting from Isaiah 11:1,10, states that Christ was resurrected to reign over the Gentiles. Christ cannot reign if He is not on the throne. Based on this New Testament affirmation, how can dispensationalists say that Isaiah 11 has not yet been fulfilled and that it belongs to a future age?
- In Revelation 3:21, Jesus Himself affirmed from heaven that He was on the Father's throne. This throne was the same throne attributed as being David's throne in 1 Chronicles 29:23, on which David's son Solomon sat when he took David's place. In Revelation 5:5, Jesus declared Himself to be the Lion of the tribe of Judah and the Root of David. There is no way we can forfeit these scriptures for literalism.

Both Peter and Paul were writing about the kingdom after the crucifixion of Christ—after the time when dispensationalism says that Christ had already postponed His kingdom. Why didn't Peter, who had direct communication with Christ while on earth, know that the kingdom was postponed? Peter was there when the kingdom was supposed to have been postponed!

Furthermore, Paul was converted several years after Calvary and received his teaching by direct revelation from Christ: "But I make known to you, brethren, that the gospel which was preached by me is not according to men. For I neither received it from man, nor was I taught it, but it came through the revelation of Jesus Christ" (Gal. 1:11-12). Paul did not seem to know a thing about a postponement of the kingdom when he quoted Isaiah in Romans 15:12 as prophesying that the Root of Jesse was to be resurrected to reign over the Gentiles. Was there a miscommunication between Jesus and Paul in the revelation given? Why did Paul write Romans 1:1-4; 4:1-25; 15:8-27; 15:8-27; and 16:25-27 if he knew that the kingdom was postponed? (See also Acts 26:22-23; 28:20-31.) It should not take much for a Bible believer to figure out who is giving us misinformation.

If dispensationalism is right, Jesus died a king without a kingdom. This would be an absolute absurdity! However, when absurdity reigns, confusion makes it look good. The postponement theory is confusing. It is a dispensationalist's main key for Israel to have a literal hold on the land and have a Jewish kingdom called the millennium. Without this man-made theory of postponement, they would find no place for a Jewish kingdom yet to come.

John 18:33-36, Matthew 21:1-9, and Zechariah 9:9 prove that Christ was king and that He had a kingdom. Matthew 21:1-11 interprets Zechariah 9:9 to state that Jesus was the king of the kingdom when He entered Jerusalem. Therefore, this prophecy was fulfilled on Palm Sunday and cannot belong to the millennium (see appendices B and C, which include scriptural testimonies to the fact that Jesus fulfilled these prophecies when He came the first time and thus could not have a second fulfillment thousands of years later).

Never once did Jesus ever cause us to believe that His kingdom would be racial (Jewish), national, or geographically located in Palestine. In the kingdom that Jesus instituted, the Bible says "For God so loved the world," not just one race in the world (John 3:16).

After Jesus was resurrected from the dead, He claimed universal authority over everything: "And Jesus came and spoke to them, saying, 'All authority has been given to Me, in heaven and on earth'" (Matt. 28:18). Paul says this includes even those "under the earth" (Phil.2:10). This sounds like a king in supreme authority, not someone who failed and had to postpone His kingdom!

THE DANGER OF THE POSTPONEMENT THEORY

The postponement theory makes the Church a substitute for the failure of Christ to establish His kingdom. The Church then becomes an afterthought in the mind of God, whose plan was waylaid in setting up the kingdom. If Jesus postponed the kingdom, then the Jewish rabbis were right in rejecting and crucifying Christ for claiming to be their king.

The postponement theory is unscriptural. In no place in the teachings of Christ did He state that He had postponed His kingdom. It is an assumption, and a biblical doctrine cannot be built based on an assumption. Christ is silent on this subject, and doctrine cannot be built on the silence of Scripture. I believe it was Martin Luther who said when the Scripture is silent, we must be silent.

The claim of dispensationalism is that when Christ came the first time, He was to set up the messianic kingdom. When Israel rejected Him, He postponed the kingdom. However, to have postponed the kingdom, Jesus would have had to leave the world without divine guidance and in the charge of Satan. But Scripture states the kingdom was given to the Church, the new nation (1 Peter 2:6-10). Christ was fully in charge, as all authority in heaven and earth had been given to Him. He then sent His disciples to declare that message to the whole world (Matt. 28:18-20).

WHAT WOULD IT MEAN BIBLICALLY IF THE KINGDOM WERE POSTPONED?

In conclusion, if the kingdom were postponed, it would mean that God is subject to man and that when Christ was rejected as an earthly king, He had to suspend His kingdom. Yet the Bible states, "No one can restrain His hand or say to Him, 'What have You done'" (Dan. 4:35). God has *never* been subject to man—nor will He ever be!

Postponement would also mean, as dispensationalism teaches, that Christ came to set up the millennial kingdom on earth with Israel as the head nation, but when they rejected Him, He had to postpone the kingdom.

It would mean that in the setting up of the kingdom, there would have been no need for the cross. The cross would have been unnecessary. This is most dangerous! The Bible teaches that Christ's death was planned from the foundation of the world. Revelation 13:8 states, "All who dwell on the earth will worship him, whose names have not been written in the Book of Life of the Lamb slain from the foundation of the world." Revelation 17:8 echoes the same truth. In Matthew 20:28 Jesus in His own words said that He came "to give His life a ransom for many." Peter tells us that "the precious blood of Christ…was indeed foreordained from the foundation of the world" (1 Pet. 1:19-20).

The postponement of the kingdom is unscriptural because it would mean that if the kingdom had been set up, it would have lasted for only a thousand years. Where would that leave us today? Where do dispensationalists get their thousand years from for a millennial kingdom, as Revelation 20 had not yet been written? To the contrary, Daniel prophesied that when the Messiah came, His kingdom would stand forever (Dan. 2:44; 4:3; 7:14, 18, 22, 27).

The postponement of the kingdom would mean there would be a literal thousand years to come after the second coming, whereas Revelation 11:15 states that when Christ returns the second time, "He shall reign forever and ever," not just for a thousand years. Since the Bible does not contradict itself, the thousand years of Revelation 20 must be interpreted in the light of Revelation 11:15.

Why did the New Testament believers continue to talk about the kingdom and Jesus as king until the last book of the Bible was written? (cf. Acts 8:12; 14:22; 19:8; 20:25; 28:23; Rom. 14:17; 1 Cor. 4:20; Col. 1:13; 4:11; 2 Thess. 1:5; 1 Tim. 1:17; 6:15; Rev.1:9; 15:3, 17:14; 19:16)

Finally, if there is no kingdom now, why does the book of Hebrews positively affirm that we have received a kingdom that cannot be moved? "Therefore, since we are receiving a kingdom which cannot be shaken, let us have grace, by which we may serve God acceptably with reverence and godly fear" (Heb.12:28).

Chapter 4

JESUS AS KING IN THE BOOK OF REVELATION

—✦◎

Most scholars agree that the book of Revelation has been in prophetic fulfillment from the inception of the New Covenant and will continue until Christ returns and introduces Paradise Restored. This is based on the following data:

- Jesus is ruler of the kings of the earth (Rev. 1:5). This is the fulfillment of an aspect of the Davidic covenant as seen in Psalm 89:27, "Also I will make him my firstborn, the highest of the kings of the earth."
- Jesus rules the nations and grants the same to the overcomers (Rev. 2:26-27).
- Jesus the Davidic king has the key of David (Rev. 3:7; cf. Isa. 22:22).
- Jesus as the Davidic king sits on His throne, which is also called the Father's throne (Rev. 3:21). Peter declares that on Jesus' ascension, He sat upon David's throne (Acts 2:30-31). Therefore, the thrones in these passages have to be one and the same.
- King Jesus is the Lion of the tribe of Judah and the Root of David. He is the slain Lamb seen in the midst of the throne (Rev. 5:5-6).
- The King in the end will summon all nations to the bar of judgment (Rev. 11:15; 19:11-21).

- When the King comes, His reward will be with Him to give to every man according to his works (Rev. 11:18; 20:12-13).
- Jesus is the king of the saints (Rev. 15:3).
- The King is the Alpha and the Omega, the Beginning and the End, the First and the Last (Rev. 21:6). Therefore, there is nothing out of His jurisdiction.
- Jesus is the root and offspring of David (Rev. 22:16) and fulfills Isaiah 11:1,10. The book of Revelation refers to Isaiah 59 times.
- The King will usher in eternity and the restored paradise (Rev. 21; 22).

As king, Jesus is on the throne of David ruling over His kingdom, the Church, to which He had the seven letters of admonition and encouragement written. All this took place while they were under the power of Rome and her deities. As king, He has fulfilled all the functions of the Davidic covenant. There is nothing in that covenant left for Christ to fulfill.

Craig A. Blaising, in his book *Progressive Dispensationalism,* says, "We have traced in some detail the fact that the New Testament presents Jesus' present position and activity *as a fulfillment of the Davidic covenant*" (Blaising 1993, 179-180, emphasis mine). However, a sentence later he reverses himself by saying, "We need to note that the New Testament does indicate that the political aspects of Jesus' Davidic kingship will be fulfilled in the future."

How can Blaising state that Jesus was the fulfillment of the Davidic covenant and then in the next statement say that there is yet to be a future fulfillment of His kingship? Is this an endeavor to make room for a future millennial kingdom in which Jesus will sit as a political king on David's throne? The question remains: Where in the New Testament are the political aspects of David's kingship spoken that were not fulfilled in Jesus, the Root and Offspring of David, who is now on David's throne? There are none!

The promises of the Davidic covenant such as mercy, righteousness, and peace never saw their fulfillment under David (2 Sam. 23:1-5). However, they have now come to their fulfillment in the Lord Jesus Christ (Acts 13:34). Mercy was and is Christ ruling on the throne (Heb. 4:16; Luke 18:13). This Christ will continue until He returns the second time.

Only the king of righteousness could bring in perfect righteousness. Jeremiah calls the Messiah "the Lord our Righteousness" (Jer. 23:5-6). Isaiah 62:1-2 states, "For Zion's sake I will not hold My peace, and for Jerusalem's sake I will not rest until her righteousness goes forth as brightness, and her salvation as a lamp that burns. The Gentiles shall see your righteousness." This Jesus Christ has done: "But of Him you are in Christ Jesus, who became for us wisdom from God—and righteousness and sanctification and redemption" (1 Cor. 1:30). Likewise, 2 Corinthians 5:21 states, "That we might become the righteousness of God in Him." Is there yet a righteousness that will go beyond the righteousness of God that has been given to us in our Lord Jesus Christ?

Jesus Christ, the Prince of Peace, has brought in peace. "For He Himself is our peace…and He came and preached peace to you who were afar off and to those who were near" (Eph. 2:14,17, from Isa. 57:19). Jesus said, "These things I have spoken to you, that in Me you may have peace" (John 16:33).

Truly, Jesus is the total fulfillment of the Davidic covenant in all its aspects.

Chapter 5

JESUS IS THE FULFILLMENT OF THE BRANCH PROPHECIES

Isaiah 4:2 states, "In that day *the Branch of the Lord* shall be beautiful and glorious" (emphasis mine). Isaiah 11:1,10 states, "There shall come forth a *Rod from the stem of Jesse,* and *a Branch shall grow out of his roots...*and in that day there shall be *a Root of Jesse* Who shall stand as a banner to the people; for the Gentiles shall seek Him, and His resting place shall be glorious" (emphasis mine).

Who is this Branch of the Lord and the Root of Jesse? Through New Testament fulfillment, the Branch and Root of Jesse is the Lord Jesus. Consider the following:

- Matthew 1:1 states, "The book of the genealogy of Jesus Christ, the Son of David."
- Revelation 5:5-6 applies the "Root of David" to Christ the slain Lamb.
- In Revelation 22:16, Jesus Himself acclaims that He is "the Root and the Offspring of David."
- In Revelation 3:7, Jesus says that He has "the key of David," which is the fulfillment of Isaiah 22:22.
- In Romans 1:1-4, Paul introduces himself as, "Paul, a bondservant of Jesus Christ, called to be an apostle, separated to the gospel of God which he promised before through His prophets in the Holy Scriptures, concerning His Son Jesus Christ our Lord, who was born of the seed of David according to the flesh, and declared to

be the Son of God with power according to the Spirit of holiness, by the resurrection from the dead."
- Romans 15:12 states, "And again, Isaiah says, 'There shall be a root of Jesse and He who shall rise to reign over the Gentiles; in Him the Gentiles shall hope.'"

In this last verse, Paul considered the prophecy in Isaiah 11:1,10 to be fulfilled and applied it to Christ's kingship, resurrection, and reign over the Gentiles when He came the first time. Jeremiah prophesied that the Babylonian captivity of Judah would be their "time of Jacob's trouble." Jeremiah 30:7,9 states, "Alas! For the day is great, so that none is like it; and it is the time of Jacob's trouble, but he shall be saved out of it...but they shall serve the Lord their God, and David their king [the Branch] whom I will raise up for them."

According to Jeremiah 30:9, Israel's trouble would last until God raised up for them "David their king," that is, Christ the Messiah. According to Psalm 132:11 (and its fulfillment in Acts 2:30-36), Christ at His resurrection and ascension was placed on David's throne in heaven.

Isaiah prophesied as to the functions of the throne: "That in mercy the throne will be established; and One will sit on it in truth in the tabernacle of David, judging and seeking justice and hastening righteousness" (Isa. 16:5). Luke 18:9-14 and Hebrews 2:17 and 4:16 declare that Jesus Christ was merciful and is on the throne of mercy now in heaven. Isaiah 16:5 further accentuates the fulfillment of Amos 9:11-12 and Acts 15:15-17, because Christ is sitting in truth in the tabernacle of David, seeking justice and hastening righteousness. All of these prophecies are already fulfilled in Christ.

JEREMIAH'S PROPHECY ABOUT THE BRANCH

In Jeremiah 23:5-6, the prophet wrote, "'Behold the days are coming,' says the Lord, 'That I will raise to *David a Branch of righteousness, a King shall reign and prosper*...In His day Judah will be saved, and Israel will dwell safely; now this is His name by which He will be called: "The LORD Our Righteousness"'" (emphasis mine). In Jeremiah 33:15-16, the prophet states that God promised Israel a Branch of David: "In those days and at that time I will cause to grow up to David a Branch of righteousness. He shall execute judgment and righteousness in the earth. In those days

Judah will be saved, and Jerusalem will dwell safely, and this is the name by which she will be called, 'The Lord Our Righteousness.'"

First Corinthians 1:30 states that Jesus Christ is our righteousness, and in 2 Corinthians 5:21, we read that we are made the "righteousness of God in Christ." Christ alone made satisfaction to the justice of God for man's sins, and He alone is the author of the righteousness that God will accept. Therefore, Jeremiah's prophecy is fulfilled in Christ. This leaves us with no doubt as to the fact that Jesus the Messiah is the king of righteousness and the root of Jesse, David's greater Son. Isaiah prophesied, "Behold, a king will reign in righteousness" (Isa. 32:1). That king is Jesus!

Jeremiah 22:1-10 speaks to the fact that Israel had broken God's Covenant and therefore would be carried into captivity, some never to return. In Jeremiah 31:31-34, God promised He would bring in a New Covenant that Israel could not break. This covenant the writer to the Hebrews repeats twice as being the covenant that Christ brought (Heb. 8:8-13; 10:15-17). Hebrews 13:20 calls it an "everlasting covenant." This means that there cannot be another covenant. Through this covenant, Christ fulfilled Daniel 9:24-27 and Hebrews 9:26 and 10:18, 26. It is not something *yet* to be fulfilled.

EZEKIEL'S PROPHECY OF GOD'S SERVANT DAVID

Ezekiel prophesied, "I will establish one shepherd over them, and he shall feed them—*My servant David*. He shall feed them and be their shepherd and I, the Lord, will be their God, and *My servant David a prince* among them; I the Lord have spoken. I will make a covenant of peace with them" (Ezek. 34:23-25, emphasis mine). Who would inaugurate this covenant, since David had been dead for some 350 years?

Ezekiel gave a prophecy in Ezekiel 37:24-28 of what would take place upon the return of Israel from Babylonian captivity:

- Israel was constituted as "the valley of dry bones" and was called "the whole house of Israel" (v. 11).
- God would put His Spirit in them (v. 14; cf. Acts 2:1-4).
- God would make Judah and Israel one nation again.
- Judah and Israel would have one king over them (v. 22).
- Who would that king be? "David My servant shall be king over them, and they shall all have one shepherd, and My servant David shall be their prince forever" (vv. 24-25).

These references never could apply literally to David. They had to apply to David's greater Son. In Ezekiel 37:26, God states that He would make "a covenant of peace" with them, which would be an everlasting covenant. Likewise, Christ's covenant was called a covenant of peace (John 14:27; 20:19, 21, 26; Rom. 5:1; Eph. 2:17) and also an everlasting covenant (Heb. 13:20).

There can be no doubt that this applied to and was fulfilled in the Lord Jesus when He came into this world the first time.

In Matthew 22:41-46, Jesus affirmed that He was the Son of David as well as David's Lord (Ps. 110:1). Peter declared in Acts 2:29-36 that Jesus was the Son of David and that upon His ascension was seated on the throne of David. Therefore, there can be no question but that these prophetic references of the Old Testament applied to Christ and were fulfilled in Him when He came the first time. On this basis, they are fulfilled and cannot be applied to a millennium, after Christ comes the second time.

Because both Jeremiah and Ezekiel spoke about the same David and the same covenant, which would be an everlasting covenant, the covenant referenced in Jeremiah 31:31-34 that is spoken of in Hebrews 8:7-13 and 10:9-18 is the eternal one that Christ made (Heb. 13:20).

ZECHARIAH'S PROPHECY ABOUT THE BRANCH

In Zechariah 3:8-9, the prophet writes, "Hear, O Joshua, the high priest, you and your companions who sit before you, for they are a wondrous sign; for behold, I am bringing forth *My Servant the Branch*. For behold, *the stone* that I have laid before Joshua: *Upon the stone are seven eyes*" (emphasis mine). Zechariah 4:10 states, "They are *the eyes of the Lord* which scan to and fro throughout the whole earth" (emphasis mine). Whose eyes are these?

Revelation 5:5-6 states, "But one of the elders said to me, 'Do not weep. *Behold, the Lion of the tribe of Judah, the Root of David,* has prevailed to open the scroll and to loose its seven seals.' And I looked and behold in the midst of the throne and of the four living creatures, and in the midst of the elders, stood *a Lamb* as though it had been slain, having seven horns and *seven eyes, which are the seven Spirits of God* sent out into all the earth" (emphasis mine). Christ has fulfilled this prophecy of Zechariah.

Zechariah 6:12-13, *"Behold the Man whose name is the Branch!* From His place he shall branch out, and he shall build the temple of the Lord;

Yes, He shall build the temple of the Lord. He shall bear the glory, and shall sit and rule on His throne; so He shall be a priest on His throne, and the counsel of peace shall be between them both" (emphasis mine). When Christ came and Israel rejected Him, He said concerning the temple: "Your house is left to you desolate" (Matt. 23:38). Jesus then proceeded to declare and build a new temple (John 2:19-21).

Zechariah 6:13 states, "He shall bear the glory," that is, the regal honors. John 1:14; 2:11; 17:5; Luke 9:32; 24:26; Acts 3:13; Hebrews 2:9; 2 Peter 1:17; and Revelation 5:12 all speak of Christ's present glory.

The Messiah would be a priest after the order of Melchizedek, wherein the priesthood and the throne were combined (Ps. 110:4; Heb. 5:6, 10; 7:14-15). The Branch was the Lord Jesus Christ. There is no literalism here. If there were, David himself would have to be resurrected to sit on the throne. Peter disproved that theory when he said David was still in the tomb (Acts 2:29-36) and Christ at His resurrection and ascension was seated on the throne of David (Acts 2:30-31).

DID CHRIST HAVE A RIGHT TO THE THRONE OF DAVID?

Hosea prophesied that Israel would be without a king: "For the children of Israel shall abide many days without king or prince, without sacrifice or sacred pillar, without ephod or teraphim. Afterward the children of Israel shall return and seek the Lord their God and David their king. They shall fear the Lord and His goodness in the latter days" (Hos. 3:4-5). According to the context, the "latter days" mentioned here certainly refer to the latter days of the Old Covenant, as is seen by the phrase "David their king," who was the Lord Jesus Christ. Jacob had prophesied, "The scepter shall not depart from Judah, nor a lawgiver from between his feet, until Shiloh comes, and to Him shall be the obedience of the people" (Gen. 49:10). Hebrews 1:8-13 declares that the throne, the scepter, and the kingdom belong to Christ and that He is to sit at God's right hand until God makes His enemies His footstool.

Christ had the legal right to the throne of David as conveyed to Him by His foster father Joseph, who was of the lineal descendant of king Jehoiachin, also called Jeconiah and Coniah (see 2 Kings 24:8-12; Jer. 22:24-30; Matt. 1:11-12). Jeremiah 22:30 says of Coniah (Jeconiah), the last ruling king from the line of David: "Write this man down as childless, a man who shall not prosper in his days; for none of his descendants shall prosper sitting on the throne of David, and ruling any more in Judah."

This prophecy was not waylaid. God raised unto David a righteous Branch, Jesus. Mary, the mother of Jesus, descended from David, and therefore she carried on the bloodline of David (Luke 3:23). Because of this, the continuity of the house of David is in Christ Jesus the Branch, and not in the natural line.

After Jeremiah prophesied that a righteous branch would come from the line of David (Jer. 33:15-16), he continued, "For thus says the Lord: David shall never lack a man to sit on the throne of the house of Israel" (v. 17). How could this be, as Coniah was the legal end of the Davidic line? The prophecy was that the line would continue in David's greater Son (see 2 Sam. 7:16-19) and in all the prophecies about the Branch.

In Ezekiel 21:25-27, God said that He would thrice overturn the throne and "give it to Him whose right it is." Looking at Genesis 49:10, we learn that the scepter belonged to Judah and that it would stay there "until Shiloh comes; and to Him shall be the obedience of the people." The dominion and rulership belonged to Judah, from whom both David and Christ the Messiah would come. Isaiah 11:10 says that the *Root of Jesse* would be as a *banner* or ensign of the gathering of the people. Jesus is the ensign, the flag under which Christianity flies.

Israel was to abide many days without a king. The kingly line could not have gone to Zedekiah, for he was put in power by Nebuchadnezzar and therefore did not have the legal right to the throne. Zedekiah was the uncle of Jehoiachin (2 Kings 24:17-18), and it was Jehoiachin's sons who were the heirs to the throne (1 Chron. 3:17-18; Matt. 1:11-12). Nebuchadnezzar killed Zedekiah's sons (2 Kings 25:7; Jer. 39:6) so the throne and the kingly line were empty until the Messiah, David's greater Son, came. Truly, Israel did abide many days without a king! Nevertheless, the real king has come, the Branch, David's greater Son, Jesus Christ our Lord.

It was through the branch prophecies that the *forever* of David's throne and kingdom (2 Sam. 7:13) was perpetuated and fulfilled by the Messiah, David's greater Son. Therefore, Jesus did have the right to the throne of David.

Chapter 6

DISPENSATIONALISM AND THE CHURCH

Is the Church God's new Israel? The rise of dispensationalism introduced into Christianity a new doctrine with distinctions that were unknown both in the Bible and in the Church for more than 1,800 years. Those distinctions included: (1) a separation between the Church and the elect of Israel of the Old Testament, and (2) a separation of the kingdom into two kingdoms—the kingdom of heaven for the Church and the kingdom of God for Israel. This would also make for two gospels, one for each kingdom, as each one is to be held separate and distinct from each other.

Dispensationalism states that God has two distinct peoples in the New Testament Age: Israel and the Church. Israel is said to be God's earthly people, while the Church (the Body of Christ) is said to be God's heavenly people. Thus, dispensationalism has an earthly theology for Israel. This theory aligns with the doctrines of a cult that has two separate people groups under God: the 144,000 who go to heaven and the remaining faithful who get to live on the renewed earth forever. This theology not only makes two destinies for God's people, but also calls for two separate methods of salvation. The theory is that Israel as a nation will get saved after the rapture. However, the Bible states that at that time, the door of salvation will have been closed (Matt. 25:10).

Keith A. Mathison quotes Lewis S. Chafer as saying, "The distinction between the purposes for Israel and the purposes for the Church is about as important as that which exists between the two testaments" (Mathison 1995, 18).

In *Dispensationalism Today*, Charles C. Ryrie states, "This is why the dispensationalist recognizes two purposes of God and insists in maintaining the distinction between Israel and the church" (Ryrie 1965, 96). J. Dwight Pentecost quotes the following from G. H. Pember's *The Great Prophecies*:

> The times of the Church are not properly a part of the fifth dispensation, but a parenthesis fixed in it on account of the perversity of the Jews; an inserted period, unknown to Old Testament prophecy, and set apart for the preparation of a heavenly, and not an earthly people.
> (Pentecost 1978, 138).

John F. Walvoord states, "Premillenarians who interpret prophecy literally, rather than figuratively, tend to distinguish believers in Christ in the present age from saints in the Old Testament" (Walvoord 1982, 17). J. Dwight Pentecost also wrote:

> Chafer has set forth twenty-four contrasts between Israel and the church which show us conclusively that these two groups can not be united into one, but that they must be distinguished as two separate entities with whom God is dealing in a special program.
> (Pentecost 1978, 201)

These are the great doctrinal distinctions on which dispensationalism is built.

DOES THE BIBLE TEACH THAT GOD HAS TWO CLASSES OF PEOPLE?

The Bible does not teach that God has two classes of people. Paul, who was raised as a strict Jew and called to be an apostle to the Gentiles, did not believe in two classes of people under God. In fact, he spoke to the contrary:

- Romans 2:11: "For there is no partiality with God." To claim the opposite would cast an aspersion on the Word of God.
- Romans 10:12: "For there is no distinction between Jew and Greek, for the same Lord over all is rich to all who call upon Him."

- Galatians 3:28: "There is neither Jew nor Greek, there is neither slave nor free, there is neither male nor female; for you are all one in Christ."
- Ephesians 2:13-14: "But now in Christ Jesus you who once were far off have been made near by the blood of Christ. For He Himself is our peace, who has made both one, and has broken down the middle wall of division between us."
- Acts 15:8-9: "So God, who knows the heart, acknowledged them by giving them the Holy Spirit, just as He did to us, and made no distinction between us and them, purifying their hearts by faith."

It was the blood of Christ that broke down the middle wall of partition that made the distinction between Jew and Gentile (Eph. 2:13-14). When we deny this truth, we deny an aspect of the atonement and find ourselves in the realm of the false cults that deny Christ shed His blood for this purpose. A doctrine that allows for two people of God builds up the wall that the blood of Christ tore down. This is heresy!

John Fort, in his book *God's Salvation, Epistle to the Romans*, states that God did away with the distinction between Jew and Gentile, but that these distinctions would be restored in the millennium. He writes, "In Acts 2:18, 33 and 10:45 God thus formally doing away with the natural distinctions between Jew and Gentile (distinctions formed by God himself, and in the Millennium to be re-established)...The middle wall of partition between Jew and Gentile, which had been broken down by God, (both in this present age being baptized into one body, Eph. 2:14), will also be restored" (Fort undated, 72,75). Is this not heresy? Does it not run counter to the atonement? The Bible teaches that it took the blood of Christ to break down the middle wall of partition (Eph. 2:14).

Nor can we who are saved and in the kingdom disassociate the Old Testament believers from the believers in the New Testament. Jesus made a strong statement when He said, "I say to you that many will come from east and west, and sit down with Abraham, Isaac, and Jacob in the kingdom of heaven" (Matt. 8:11). How then can there be two separate people of God?

Dispensationalism and its two-kingdom theory implies that the kingdom of *heaven* is for the Church and that the kingdom of *God* is for the

Jew. However, Jesus plainly stated that Abraham, Isaac and Jacob were all in the kingdom of *heaven*. Was Jesus wrong?

Furthermore, under the New Covenant, Scripture teaches that no one can get saved apart from Christ and the Church (Acts 4:11-12). Dispensationalism teaches that the nation of Israel will be saved when Christ appears at His second coming, but this would be contrary to Revelation 22:11-12. There will be no chance at that time to put on a religious garment. When the Bridegroom comes for the Bride, the door of salvation will be forever closed (Matt. 25:1-12; Luke 13:25). Is God's Word contradictory by saying something in one place and the opposite in another?

In answer to Chafer's comment, "The distinction between the purposes for Israel and the purposes for the Church is about as important as that which exists between the two testaments," how can we separate God's work in the Old Testament (which was the promise and preparation for the Son) from God's work in the New Testament (which is the advent and work of His Son)? Under the Old Covenant, the Son was promised in Eden (Gen. 3:15). Under the New Covenant, the Son is the Savior of the world (1 John 4:14).

THE GOSPEL WAS IN THE OLD TESTAMENT

In Galatians 3:8, Paul states that God Himself preached the gospel to Abraham: "And the Scripture foreseeing that God would justify the Gentiles by faith, preached the gospel to Abraham beforehand, saying, 'In you all the nations shall be blessed.'" This Paul calls the gospel of His Son, which was promised by the prophets in the Holy Scripture (Rom. 1:1-4). It was none other than justification by faith. In Romans 10:15-17, Paul states it was the gospel of salvation that was preached by Isaiah (Isa. 52:7; 53:1). Hebrews 4:2 indicates that this same gospel was preached during Moses' time and specifically states that he wrote of Christ (John 5:46-47).

It must also be said that the original promise to Abraham was not an earthly promise. Abraham looked for a city that had foundations and whose builder and maker was God (Heb. 11:9-10,13-16). Hebrews 13:14 states, "For here we have no continuing city but we seek one to come." Abraham's calling was to a heavenly city, of which the Church is now a part (Gal. 4:21-31; Heb. 12:22-24; Rev. 21:2, 9-10). This does not bespeak an earthly promise or an earthly inheritance for Israel. The book of Hebrews, which was written to Jews, says that they were partakers of the heavenly calling (Heb. 3:1). Should not this disqualify the position that Israel's calling was an earthly one?

DISPENSATIONALISM'S BASIS FOR TWO CLASSES OF PEOPLE

Dispensationalists cite 1 Corinthians 10:32, "Give no offense, either to the Jews or to the Greeks or to the church of God," as their proof of a distinction between the elect of Israel and the Church. Any Bible student knows that national or natural Israel is not the Church. But without denying biblical truth, the Church *is* "spiritual Israel," and it is expressed as such in Galatians 3:7-29 and 6:15-16, where even Gentile believers are called the "Israel of God." This shows that there is a carryover of the people of God from the Old Testament to the people of God in the New Testament.

In *Things To Come*, J. Dwight Pentecost cites 1 Corinthians 10:32 as proof that God makes a distinction between the Jews and the Church. He writes, "That the term Jew continues to be used as distinct from the church (1 Cor. 10:32) shows that the Gentiles do not supplant Israel in God's covenant program" (Pentecost 1964, 88).

Pentecost further asserts, "In citing the Abrahamic covenant, Peter, in Acts 3:25, applies only *the universal aspects* of the covenant to those to whom he speaks. The *national aspects* must await future fulfillment by the nation Israel" (Ibid., 90, emphasis mine). Peter makes no such distinction! Where in the Bible can such a distinction as being universal and national be verified? This is another false assumption that cannot be biblically proven. It is wrongly dividing the Word of Truth!

One of the first problems to deal with in any biblical text is context. The context of 1 Corinthians 10:32 is certainly one of cultural differences between a believer and a non-believer as to eating foods offered to idols, and so forth. Paul begins a discussion on such matters in Chapter 8 and carries it through to Chapter 10. The context thus has nothing to do with a covenant relationship of God with Israel that distinguishes it from the Church after the cross.

On the contrary, in Romans 15:8-9, Paul, writing to the Gentile church in Rome, states, "Jesus Christ has become a servant to the circumcision [Jews] for the truth of God, to confirm the promises made to the fathers, and that the Gentiles might glorify God for His mercy." Under the New Covenant, Christ has confirmed the promises made to the Jewish fathers and now applies them to the Gentiles in the New Testament Church. This truth is too obvious to be denied.

To further accentuate this idea, Paul says in Romans 15:27, "For if the Gentiles have been partakers of their spiritual things..." Is Paul not saying that the church in Rome has become heir of the spiritual promises of Israel—promises that are now confirmed to the believing Gentiles under the New Covenant? The Bible calls these truths the "spiritual things" of Israel. Does this not mean that the promises to Israel were spiritual in nature as opposed to literal?

In his commentary on 1 Corinthians 10:32, William Barclay states that the believer or Christian should "live in such a way that you will cause neither Jew nor Greek nor church members to stumble" (Barclay 1975, 93). Charles Hodge puts it this way: "'Give no occasion to sin,' or cause one to 'stumble.' The exhortation is to avoid being the cause of sin to others" (Hodge 1953, 202).

First Corinthians 10:31 is the key to the entire passage: "Therefore, whether you eat or drink, or whatever you do, do all to the glory of God." It must be said that the context does not deal with any covenantal distinction between Israel and the Church but speaks purely on the ground of cultural relationships. Dispensationalism has misrepresented 1 Corinthians 10:32.

Under the New Covenant, God makes no distinction between Jew and Gentile (Acts 15:6-9). Romans 10:12, Galatians 3:8, and Colossians 3:11 each speak to the fact that all are one in Christ. If the Jew is separate from this, he is not in Christ. In Colossians 3:12, Paul refers to the Colossians as the *elect* of God; therefore, the word *elect* cannot refer only to the Jew, per se. The national Jew is no longer in covenant relationship with God, because Christ has taken away the Old Covenant and has replaced it with His New Covenant (Heb. 10:9). Therefore, the Old Covenant that Israel was under no longer stands. The truth of this scripture is so plain there should be no argument!

According to Ephesians 2:14-18 and Colossians 2:14, every distinction between Jew and Gentile vanished at Calvary.

PAUL'S DISTINCTION BETWEEN JEWS AND JEWS WITHIN ISRAEL ITSELF

In 1 Corinthians 10:18, Paul states, "Observe Israel after the flesh." Who is this "Israel after the flesh"? In Romans 9:3, Paul is speaking of the natural Israel when he says, "My countrymen according to the flesh" and then makes a distinction within Israel itself: "For they are not all Israel who are of Israel" (v. 6). Paul is thus saying there are two Israels: one natural Israel (not the people of God) and one spiritual Israel (the people of God). Romans 9:8 plainly states, "Those who are the children of the flesh, these are not the children of God."

All of those who belonged to the national Israel were never the true Israel of God, even though they were circumcised (Rom. 2:28-29; 9:6). Furthermore, in Romans 11:5-7, Paul reminds us that in the Old Testament Israel there was always only a remnant according to the election of grace that constituted the true Israel. Just who are the children of God? Paul answers this in Galatians 4:21-31, and especially in verses 28-29: "Now we brethren, as Isaac was, are children of promise. But, as he who was born according to the flesh then persecuted him who was born according to the Spirit."

Does this not bespeak being born again of the Spirit (John 3:3-5)? There cannot be two people of God, the national Israel under the Old Covenant and the Church under the New Covenant. Since Calvary, there cannot be two covenants in effect at the same time (Heb. 10:9). Israel did not have any national promises under the Old Covenant that were not supplanted by the cross.

THE DISPENSATIONAL IDEA THAT THE CHURCH IS NOT REVEALED IN THE OLD TESTAMENT

Dispensational writers have said the doctrine of the Church is not found in the Old Testament, that the truth for our times is only found in Paul's epistles. It is difficult to see how passages in Zechariah, Daniel, Isaiah, and Ezekiel, for example, have no application or reference to the New Testament Church.

John MacArthur, Jr., says the following about dispensationalism:

> Its chief element is a recognition that God's plan for Israel is not superseded by or swallowed up in His program for the church. Israel and the church are separate entities, and God will restore national Israel under the earthly rule of Jesus as Messiah. I accept and affirm this tenet, because it emerges from a consistently literal interpretation of Scripture…And in that regard, I consider myself a traditional premillennial dispensationalist.
>
> (MacArthur 1988, 25)

Charles C. Ryrie affirms this position in his book *Dispensationalism Today* (Ryrie 1965, 43-47). Further, Ryrie quotes Ephesians 2:12-15 in his book *The Basis of Premillennial Faith* to prove that the Gentiles did not inherit Israel's promises. He states, "In this passage Gentiles are expressly said to be excluded from the blessings peculiar to Israel" (Ryrie 1978, 64). This is taking this scripture out of context. The context of this passage is Ephesians 2:11-22, in which Paul states that the Gentiles are no longer strangers and foreigners, but are *fellow citizens* with the saints and are called *the household of God*.

The "household of God" is what elect Israel was in the Old Testament and is into what saved Gentiles enter under the New Covenant. This tells us that the Gentiles were not excluded from the blessings that were peculiar to Israel, but they became one with them in the same household. Romans 15:27 states, "For if the Gentiles have been partakers of their spiritual things, their duty is to minister to them in material things." Does this not mean that the Gentiles have inherited Israel's spiritual status?

Scofield states, "Therefore, in approaching the study of the Gospels the mind should be freed, so far as possible, from mere theological concepts and presuppositions. It is especially necessary to exclude the notion—a legacy in Protestant thought from post-apostolic and Roman Catholic theology—that the Church is the true Israel, and that the Old Testament foreview of the kingdom is fulfilled in the Church…. Do not, therefore, assume interpretations to be true because familiar" (Scofield 1945, 989). Can we not then say that because dispensationalism "has become familiar," we should not assume that it is true? Yes! This is the stance that we are taking in this book.

In his book *The Rapture Question,* Walvoord states, "Not only do the Scriptures indicate that the church of the present age is a distinct body of believers, but there is good evidence that the age itself is a parenthesis in the divine program of God *as it was revealed in the Old Testament*" (Walvoord 1978, 23, emphasis mine). If this were biblically true, why did Peter at the inception of the Church in Acts 3:24 say, "Yes, and all the prophets from Samuel and those who follow, as many as have spoken have also foretold these days." Peter's words have to mean that the prophets had a revelation of the age of the Messiah and His Church. In Acts 2:22, Peter, speaking to the House of Israel, also uses another Jewish prophecy from Joel 2:28-32 and applies it to the Church.

L. Thomas Holdcroft makes the following comments regarding the outpouring of the Holy Spirit on the Day of Pentecost and says: "Peter explained, 'this is what was spoken by the prophet Joel' (Acts 2:16), for these happenings partially fulfilled Joel's prophecy (cf. Joel 2:28, 29). The larger fulfillment awaits the millennium" (Holdcroft 2001, 20).

Where is a "millennium" explicitly found in the text? Under divine inspiration, Peter did not hesitate to say, "This is that which was spoken by the prophet Joel." However, he did not say that this was a part of what Joel said! This meant that Joel's prophecy was for the Church, and that it was the beginning of the *last days.* The millennium has conveniently become a "glove compartment" that dispensationalists use to hide things for which they have no answer.

Holdcroft continues, "To say that Joel predicted the bestowment of the Spirit is not to say that he foresaw the church." When Peter said *this is that,* why deny the Church as not being in the picture? Holdcroft concludes, "To predict the fact of the Spirit's outpouring was not to predict God's application of that event." Is this not a direct denial of the text? Is Holdcroft not stating that Acts 2:16 is not correct and that God by divine inspiration should not have applied it to the Church? How brave can we become in our handling of the Word of God (2 Pet. 3:16; 2 Cor. 4:2)?

David also foresaw the Church Age in Psalm 110 when he prophesied of the Messiah being at the right hand of God. Peter used this psalm to show how it had been fulfilled by the resurrected Christ, who was now seated on David's throne (Acts 2:34-36). If these prophecies were not for the Church Age, why in the New Testament are they applied to the Church?

A BIBLICAL RESPONSE

The Bible answers the dispensational position of Walvoord, Pentecost and others on their statements that the term "Church" applies only to the New Testament Body of Christ and therefore distinguishes New Testament believers from Old Testament believers.

Where in Scripture does it indicate that the Church of the present age is a distinct body of believers separate from Old Testament believers? Did Jesus not deny this position in Matthew 8:11 when He said, "Many shall come from the east and the west and sit down with Abraham, Isaac, and Jacob in the kingdom of heaven"? This statement is in striking contrast to dispensationalism, as no two different bodies of believers or two kingdoms are found or implied by Jesus. Clearly, Jesus intended that everyone would be in the same kingdom.

Peter also denies any distinction between Jew and Gentile. In Acts 15:9, he states, "[God] made no distinction between us and them, purifying their hearts by faith." Likewise, in Acts 7:38, when Stephen gave the Israel of his day a lesson on their own history, he called Israel in their wilderness wanderings the "church in the wilderness" (τη εκκλησια εν τη ερημω).

Scofield admits, "In the wilderness Israel was a true church (Gr. *ecclesia* = called out assembly), but in striking contrast with the N. T. *ecclesia* (Matt. 16:18 note)" (Scofield 1945, 1158). Where in the Bible does it say that Israel quit being the true Church? Does the word *ecclesia*, "called out assembly," mean one thing in one place and another in another place? Were not all of Jesus' followers *called out*? How then can there be a striking contrast in being *called out*? In Acts 15:14-15, James, quoting Peter and referring to the New Testament Church, declares, "How God at the first visited the Gentiles to take out of them a people for His name. And with this the words of the prophets agree." Paul maintains this as the fulfillment of Amos 9:11-12. The word *visit* in Acts 15:14 means "to visit with a purpose," the purpose here being for God to take out a people for His name.

The dispensationalists affirm that the Church, the Body of Christ, is never spoken of in the Old Testament. While it is true that the phrase "Body of Christ" was not written out in the Old Testament, in Ephesians 3:6, Paul plainly states, "The Gentiles should be fellow heirs, *of the same body*, and partakers of His promise in Christ through the gospel" (emphasis mine). Since we do not have two gospels, this has to be the same gospel that God preached to Abraham (Gal. 3:8). Therefore, the Gentile church was inducted into the same body as that of Old Testament Israel.

This verse nullifies the dispensational view and proves that the Old Testament saints together with the New Testament saints belong to the same body. To say that Israel was not related somehow to Christ even in the Old Testament would be greatly misleading (1 Cor. 10:1-4). Ephesians 1:10 declares that God in Christ is gathering together in one all things in heaven and on earth. How then can it be said that God has two classes of people?

Furthermore, Ephesians 2:11-22 plainly states that the saints of the Old Testament and those of the New Testament are incorporated into "one and the same household of God, the same temple, the same building," as that of the Old Testament saints. There are no two distinct peoples of God found in the Bible. To say that there are two distinct peoples of God under the New Covenant is to cast an aspersion on God and His Word. Ephesians 3:11 states that the Church was God's eternal plan. Therefore, how could it not be foretold or foreseen in the Old Testament? Ephesians 3:15 also specifically states that God has only one family "from whom the whole family in heaven and earth is named." Israel is not one family and the Church another.

In the light of these Scriptures, how can we say that God has two distinct bodies of people, one from the Old Testament and another in the New Testament? Does the Bible tell the truth or not?

Referring back to the quote by Walvoord in *The Rapture Question*, "that the church of the present age is a distinct body of believers, but there *is good evidence* that the age itself is *a parenthesis* in the divine program of God as it was revealed in the Old Testament" (emphasis mine), I inquire: Where is the "good evidence" stated in the Old Testament that this age— the Church Age—is a "parenthesis"? And just where is this revealed in the Old Testament? This is another man-made assumption without biblical proof. It is a scheme superimposed on the Bible.

Walvoord continues, "Generally speaking, however, those who distinguish clearly between the church and Israel have recognized the present age as an *unexpected* and *unpredicted parenthesis* as far as the Old Testament prophecy is concerned" (Walvoord 1978, 23-24, emphasis mine).

Do you not see the contradiction Walvoord makes within his own argument? The Church cannot be both *revealed* in the Old Testament and at the same time be *unexpected and unpredicted*. In his first statement he is telling the truth; in the second, he is following dispensational lines. The statements made by dispensationalists should be backed up by Scripture—not just some theological speculation—before they can be held as tenable.

Walvoord continues to contradict himself by saying, "Nothing should be plainer to one reading the Old Testament than that the foreview therein provided *did not* describe the period of time between the two advents. This very fact confused even the prophets (cf. 1 Pet. 1:10-12)" (Ibid., emphasis mine). By "foreview," Walvoord means the period of time between the two Testaments, which would be the fulfillment of the sixty-nine weeks of Daniel 9.

Walvoord goes on to say that this "confused" the prophets. He quotes 1 Peter 1:10-12 to prove his point. Of course, Peter is certainly not saying that the prophets were confused, but that it was revealed to them that what they were writing was not for themselves but for us of the Church Age.

A June 1997 article in the magazine *Zion's Hope* states, "We believe that Israel is distinct from the Church (Rom. 10:1; 11:1), and that Israel's promises of future blessing will be literally fulfilled at the Messiah's second coming." The references given from Romans do not speak to this statement.

Dr. R. F. Suerig in *A Study of the Testimony* says, "The Church, which is the body of Christ, has no scriptural authority for preaching today, 'The Kingdom of Heaven is at hand'" (Suerig undated, 21). Suerig continues to say that the Son of God was rejected at His first advent "by His earthly people," but at the second advent "He will be accepted by that Nation" (Ibid., 38). This statement is contrary to Scripture. Jesus Himself gave the apostle John these words on the subject of His second coming: "He who is unjust, let him be unjust still; he who is filthy, let him be filthy still; he who is righteous, let him be righteous still; he who is holy, let him be holy still. 'And behold, I am coming quickly '" (Rev. 22:11-12).

Concerning Paul as a teacher of the Gentiles, Suerig makes the following comments on 1 Timothy 2:7:

To teach the Gentiles what? Did he proclaim the Kingdom of Heaven at hand? Not at all. He preached the grace of Christ. Through him Christ made known the new truth; the truth concerning this parenthetical dispensation; that which had been a mystery in former ages. To miss this is to remain in confusion.

(Suerig undated, 44)

It should be solemnly noted that in Acts 28:23-31, as late as A.D. 63 Paul was still preaching the kingdom of God. While Matthew talks about the kingdom of heaven, Mark (quoting the same parables) uses the phrase "kingdom of God." Therefore, the kingdom of heaven and the kingdom of God are biblically synonymous. This dividing of the Word of Truth into two kingdoms on the part of dispensationalism is certainly misleading.

In *Things to Come,* J. Dwight Pentecost writes, "The existence of an entirely new age, which only interrupts temporarily God's program for Israel, is one of our strongest arguments for the premillennial position. It is necessary for one who rejects that interpretation to prove that the church itself is the consummation of God's program" (Pentecost 1978, 136). How can over two thousand years be considered a temporary program? And where in the Bible does it say that the Church Age temporarily interrupts God's program for Israel? Pentecost must first of all scripturally prove his position. He makes a statement unsupported by the Bible and then expects us to take it as if it were gospel truth.

Pentecost continues, "It has been illustrated how this whole age existed in the mind of God *without having been revealed in the Old Testament*" (Ibid., 137, emphasis mine). There is disagreement here between Walvoord, who says the Church Age "was revealed in the Old Testament" and Pentecost, who says "this whole age existed in the mind of God *without* having been revealed in the Old Testament" (emphasis mine).

Pentecost continues, "Allowance was thus made for this present age, without its actual existence ever having been specifically revealed in the Old Testament" (Ibid., 138,193). Dr. Earl D. Radmacher, in a May 1974 article in *Moody Monthly,* states, "The church age is an unprophesied age, both with respect to Old Testament predictions and New Testament signs." These are contradictory statements from the same playing field. Which one is the truth?

Later in *Things to Come,* Pentecost says, "The mystery form of the kingdom, then, has reference to the age between the two advents of Christ"

(Ibid., 143). Where in the Bible does it speak about a "mystery form of the kingdom"? Jesus talked about the mysteries "of" (genitive case) that which pertains to the kingdom, but never that the kingdom itself was a mystery.

IS THE CHURCH FOUND IN ZECHARIAH?

Zechariah testifies in Zechariah 11:4-14 that the Messiah was betrayed, sold, and crucified for thirty pieces of silver. Matthew 26:15 and 27:9 both verify this fact as being fulfilled in Christ. This is a picture of Christ dying for our sins under the New Covenant, which is proof that the Church was prophesied in the book of Zechariah.

In Ephesians 5:25, Paul writes, "Christ loved the church and gave Himself for her." How can we escape the fact that Zechariah was talking about the New Testament Church, for which Christ died? If Zechariah was not talking about the Church, then for whom did Christ die? The Bible says that the Jews were blinded to this fact and that in the reading of the Old Testament they still have the veil over their heart, but when they turn to the Lord the veil will be taken away (2 Cor. 3:14-16). Those who profess to know Christ and do not see Christ's death for the Church in Zechariah still have not had the veil taken away.

If Christ died for the Church (Eph. 5:25), then He had to die for the Old Testament saints as well. This means that they must also belong to the Church, or He did not die for them. The following references state that Christ died for the saints under the Old Covenant, whose sins had previously been passed over:

- Rom. 3:24-25: "Being justified freely by His grace through the redemption that is in Christ Jesus, whom God set forth as a propitiation by His blood, through faith, to demonstrate His righteousness, because in His forbearance God had passed over the sins that were previously committed."
- Hebrews 9:15: "And for this reason He is the Mediator of the New Covenant, by means of death, for the redemption of the transgressions under the first covenant, that those who are called may receive the promise of the eternal inheritance."

Does this not prove that Christ's death was for the Old Testament saints as well as for the Church? Christ did not die to make two separate bodies of people. Peter, on the day of Pentecost in which three thousand were converted into the Church, quoted from the Psalms twice and once from Joel, which shows that God's New Testament Church originated from the Hebrew Scriptures. In each of these cases, no literal interpretation of the Old Testament was offered by Peter. The scriptures were interpreted spiritually and are fulfilled in what is now called the New Testament Church. The Church in the New Testament was the fulfillment of the Jewish Scriptures and is one body with the elect of Israel of the Old Testament.

WHEN DID THE NEW TESTAMENT ASPECT OF THE CHURCH ORIGINATE?

Dispensationalists tell us that the Church did not start until the Day of Pentecost, and that all that went on before that time was still under the law of the Old Testament. However, Jesus says differently. In Luke 16:16, He stated, "The law and the prophets were until John. Since that time the kingdom of God has been preached and everyone is pressing into it." In Matthew 11:13, Jesus said, "For all the prophets and the law prophesied until John."

The law ended with John the Baptist and the beginning of Christ's ministry, which was the foundation of the New Testament Church. "For no other foundation can anyone lay than that which is laid, which is Jesus Christ" (1 Cor. 3:11). Therefore, the New Testament Church had to begin before Pentecost. If it did not, it would mean that none of the teachings of Jesus belong to the Church and, according to dispensationalists, are still a part of the Old Covenant. This would be ludicrous.

If Christ died for the Old Testament saints, they must also constitute the Church. Furthermore, in Hebrews 11:40, we are told that the Old Testament saints could not be made perfect apart from the New Testament believers. Is this not the blending of the people of both covenants together as one body? Secondly, is it not true according to Hebrews 9:15 that the eternal inheritance of the saints under the Old Covenant also depended on Christ's death? It is too bad that the New Testament writers did not know that these Jewish promises did not belong to the New Testament Church before they so applied them!

Jesus further sanctioned this position in Matthew 8:11-12 when He spoke with the centurion, a Gentile who had put his faith in Christ, saying, "Many will come from the east and the west, and sit down with Abraham, Isaac, and Jacob in the kingdom of heaven." What Jesus joined together let no man put asunder!

To say that the Church did not begin until the Day of Pentecost and that Matthew 8:11-12 therefore does not apply to the Church is arbitrary. How could Adam, being a type of Christ (Rom. 5:14) and one for whom Christ died, not be in the Church? The Church did not begin on the Day of Pentecost. It was baptized by the Holy Spirit on that day.

Recall that Stephen said Israel in the wilderness was called the Church, the *ekklesia:* "This is he, that was in the church in the wilderness" (Acts 7:38 KJV). How then can we say that the Church is not found in the Old Testament? In 1857, Joseph Angus wrote:

> The distinction between Jew and Gentile is formally abolished, and that our dispensation is spiritual; thinking, moreover, that the description in prophecy, if taken literally, would lead to a belief in the restoration of Judaism, and in the introduction of a system adapted to the infancy rather than the maturity of the church; finding that these descriptions, so far as the re-establishment of the Jews is concerned, are not repeated in the New Testament, and that many prophecies which seem to apply to them as a nation, are referred in the New Testament to the church, or to the conversion of the Jews, Acts 2:17-21; Rom. 11:26; they conclude that a spiritual interpretation of the whole series is most consistent with the tenor of Scripture.
>
> (Angus 1857, 297)

It is interesting that Rev. Edward Bickerseth, a premillennialist, believed and used Old Testament Scriptures to prove that "the Jews are visibly called into the church (Dan. 9:27; Ezek. 20:32-34; Isa. 49:9-12; 62:1)" (Ibid., 299). Likewise, F. W. Farrar in his exposition on Daniel said, "That ideal Israel which is composed, not of Jews, but of Gentiles. Then faith and hope have never found even an ideal of approximate fulfillment save in Christ and in His kingdom, which is now, and shall be without end" (Farrar 1908, 163).

From Acts 1–13, the Early Church was nearly made up of all Jews who had been converted to Christianity. Therefore, *these saved Jews constituted the New Testament Church in Jerusalem.* Why then are these New Testament saved Jews different from the elect Jews of the Old Testament? No doubt these are the same individuals mentioned by Paul in Romans 11:7 that constituted the elect and that had obtained the promises of God to Israel in the Old Testament. Because the Church in the New Testament is called the "Israel of God" (Gal. 6:15-16), how can there be another Israel that has not been purchased by the blood of Christ—one that is waiting for a salvation at the second coming?

The imagery of the tabernacle and the temple in the Old Testament were fulfilled and elevated to a higher and more spiritual frame by Jesus Christ, who came to fulfill the law and the prophets. John 1:14 states, "Christ dwelt [tabernacled] among us." Romans 10:4 says, "Christ is the end of the law." These verses specifically state that Jesus Christ fulfilled and brought the Old Testament types to an end, which included the covenanted law of Moses (Rom. 7:6-7; 2 Cor. 3:3-13; Heb. 10:9).

Luke 24:25-27 tells us that Jesus fulfilled all that Moses and the prophets said concerning Him. Likewise, on the Day of Pentecost, Peter stated the same when he said, "All the prophets that have spoken from Samuel and those who follow, as many as have spoken, have also foretold of these days" (Acts 3:24). How can there be other days beyond Christ's New Covenant when they are here applied as fulfilled?

AS TO THE CHURCH NOT FOUND
IN THE OLD TESTAMENT

Paul, in his address to the church at Rome, proved that the gospel he preached and by which he established churches came straight from the Old Testament. In fact, Paul quotes the Old Testament eighty-four times in Romans, which would seem to necessitate the Church as being prefigured therein: "Paul, a servant of Jesus Christ, called to be an apostle, separated to the gospel of God, which He promised before through His prophets in the Holy Scriptures, concerning His Son Jesus Christ our Lord, who was born of the seed of David according to the flesh, and declared to be the Son of God with power, according to the Spirit of holiness, by the resurrection from the dead" (Rom. 1:1-4).

According to His divine nature, Christ is declared to be the Son of God. As to His human nature, He is seed of the woman, the Messiah, and appears as such in Paul's gospel. Peter and Paul both connect the kingship of David with the kingdom and kingship that Jesus the Messiah instituted at His first advent (Acts 2:29-36; 13:26-41). Therefore, the kingdom of Christ was prefigured in the Old Testament.

The righteousness that Christ brought was foretold and witnessed to in the law and the prophets of the Old Testament. This is stated in Romans 3:21-22: "But now the righteousness of God apart from the law is revealed, being witnessed by the Law and the Prophets, even the righteousness of God, through faith in Jesus Christ, to all and on all who believe. For there is no difference."

Jeremiah spoke of the righteousness that the Messiah, the branch of David, would bring when He came, and that His name would be called "The Lord Our Righteousness" (Jer. 23:5-6). In 1 Corinthians 1:30 and 2 Corinthians 5:21, Paul states that the believer has been made the righteousness of God in Christ. How can there be a righteousness apart from the righteousness of God given to us in Christ?

Because Christ died for the Old Testament saints and is the foundation of the Church (1 Cor. 3:11), the Church is inseparable from the Old Testament saints. Paul's gospel came from the prophets of the Old Testament. In all of Paul's writings, he quotes or alludes to the Old Testament 167 times. Does this not tell us from where Paul got his message for the Church? In particular, there are four times in the New Testament that specifically state that the gospel was in the Old Testament:

1. In Romans 1:1-2, Paul states he was set apart for *the gospel of God,* which God promised through His prophets in the Holy Scripture.
2. In Romans 10:16, Paul lays out the principles of how an individual may be saved. He calls "being saved" as hearing and *obeying "the gospel" (vv.* 6-17). In verse 16, Paul quotes Isaiah 52:7 and 53:1 as *"the gospel."*
3. In Galatians 3:8, Paul says the Scripture foreseeing that God would justify the heathen by faith preached *"the gospel"* to Abraham. As proof, he quotes Genesis 12:3, which indicates that to Paul, the gospel began in the Pentateuch.
4. In Hebrews 3:1–4:2, the author states that *the gospel* was preached to Israel, but it was not mixed with faith in them that heard it. The writer of Hebrews includes Psalm 95:7-11 in this section as part of that *gospel.*

By comparing the Old Testament predictions with the New Testament fulfillment, it is clear that the New Testament Church is the fulfillment of the Old Testament Jewish Scriptures.

OLD TESTAMENT PREDICTIONS	NEW TESTAMENT FULFILLMENT
Israel is a kingdom of priests, Ex. 19:6	The church is a kingdom of priests, 1 Pet. 2:9–12
The Passover lamb, Ex. 12	Christ is our Passover, 1 Cor. 5:7
Gentiles are not God's people, Hosea 1:10; 2:23	Gentiles can become God's people, Rom. 9:22–26
The rebuilding of the tabernacle of David, Amos 9:11–12	Saved Gentiles admitted into the New Testament church which is God rebuilding the tabernacle of David, Acts 15:15–18
New Covenant promised Jer. 31:31–34	New Covenant established, Luke 22:14–20; Heb. 8:7–13; 10:15–17; 13:20
Messiah's forerunner, Isa. 40:1–3	Fulfilled, Luke 3:1–5
The rejected stone, Ps. 118:22–26	The rejected Stone is Jesus, Eph. 2:20; Matt. 21:42, Rom. 9:32–33
All nations were included in the Abrahamic promise, Gen. 12:1–3	Believing Gentiles are Abraham's seed, Gal. 3:7–29

To say that the Church was unforeseen in the Old Testament is quite the opposite of what the New Testament teaches.

It is a fundamental principle of orthodoxy that all biblical doctrines are built on the basis of *sola scriptura*, the Scripture alone. The Scripture alone gives legitimacy to any doctrine. Apart from Scripture, we are left with nothing but man's own authority, which is of human origin. That which God has put together let no man put asunder.

The book of Hebrews teaches that Jesus Christ is the Messianic fulfillment of prophet, priest, and king as found in the Old Testament. The New Testament interprets Christ's death as that of the Passover lamb (John 1:29, 35; cf. Lev. 16:16-17, which describes the Day of Atonement). In 1 Corinthians 5:7, Paul states, "Christ, our Passover, was sacrificed for us." His interpretation of Mark 14:24-25 in 1 Corinthians 11:23-26, "This is the cup of the New Covenant in My blood," is that these verses are the fulfillment of the New Covenant promised in Jeremiah 31:31-34 and Exodus 24:8.

NEW TESTAMENT AFFIRMATIONS OF ONE WORK OF GOD	
including both Jews and Gentiles under the Covenant that Christ instituted	
One building	Eph. 2:21; 1 Cor. 3:9, God does not have two buildings.
One foundation	Eph. 2:20; 1 Cor. 3:11, God does not have two foundations.
One household	Eph. 2:19; 1 Tim. 3:15; Heb. 3:1–6, God has only one household.
One temple	Eph. 2:21; John 2:19–21; 1 Cor. 3:16; 6:19; 2 Cor. 6:16; Acts 17:24, both believing Jew and Gentile form one temple.
One people of God	1 Pet. 2:10; Hos. 1:10; 2:23, God does not have two peoples.
One cornerstone	Eph. 2:20; Matt. 21:42; 1 Pet. 2:6, Christ is that cornerstone.
One family	Eph. 3:15, God has only one family in heaven and on earth.
One body	Eph. 2:16; 1:22–23; 3:6, saved Gentiles have come into the "same body" with Israel; then this body was in existence prior to the New Testament church. This is a startling fact for dispensationalists. It annuls the position of God having two bodies of people!
One hope of calling	Eph. 4:4; 1 John 3:1
One holy priesthood	1 Pet. 2:5
One royal priesthood	1 Pet. 2:9
One holy nation	1 Pet. 2:9
One Lord	Eph. 4:5
One faith	Eph. 4:5
One baptism	Eph. 4:5
One God	Eph. 4:6
One fold	John 10:16, One flock and one shepherd does not sound like two different flocks of sheep when there is only one fold!

Paul, a preacher to the Gentiles, stated that he was being judged for the hope of the promise made to the Jewish fathers (Acts 26:6, 22-23). From where did he draw his preaching and conclusions when he said he only spoke of those things that Moses and the prophets said would come? Paul's preaching to the Gentiles and his desire to bring them into the Church was based entirely upon the Jewish Old Testament. Yet we are told by dispensationalists that the Old Testament does not foresee the Church, when in fact the Church was born out of the preaching of the Old Testament.

The psalmist certainly spoke of the Church when he wrote, "You have ascended on high. You have led captivity captive; You have received gifts among men" (Ps. 68:18). Paul equated this with his words in Ephesians 4:7-11 concerning the gifts that Christ bestowed on the Church. That which the psalmist indicated of Israel also speaks of the New Testament Church.

Likewise, in 1 Corinthians 10:1-11, Paul uses another incident in Israel's history in antiphony of the relationship to the Gentile church at Corinth. He tells the Corinthian church that they are now spiritually related to Israel's fathers (1 Cor. 10:1) and that on the way to their promised land they should take heed not to tempt Christ as Israel did. It is interesting that in verse 4, Paul says that Christ was with Israel when they went through their wilderness experience.

For the Galatian church, which was Gentile, Paul used Jewish terminology and then applied it to the Galatians to show how they were citizens of the Jerusalem that was from above, the mother of us all (Gal. 4:21-31). How could a Jewish Scripture be applied to a Gentile church if that church were not the heir of Old Testament Israel and her promises?

Genesis 9:27 states, "May God enlarge Japheth, and may he dwell in the tents of Shem." This indicates that the Gentiles (Japheth) would one day dwell in the tents of Shem. Is this not an Old Testament prophecy that the Gentiles would come into the inheritance with Israel?

There can be no question that Christ reconstituted Old Testament Israel as the New Testament Church and called it the Israel of God (Gal. 6:16). Jesus chose twelve disciples to take the place of the twelve tribes of Israel. He sent out the seventy, who were to take the place of the Sanhedrin. When He closed the book of Revelation, the apostles were established as the foundation and Israel as the gates of the heavenly Jerusalem (Rev. 21:13-14). The Bible does not teach that Israel has an earthly calling but that, as gates of the heavenly Jerusalem, they are a part of a heavenly calling.

God's redemptive work in the world goes on through the Church. The central theme of the New Testament is that the inheritance of Israel was now fulfilled in the Church. All nations would enter the Church through the salvation that was in Christ (Acts 4:11-12; Eph. 2:1-22), outside of which there was no salvation. The Gentile was now in the "household of God," as Israel was in the Old Testament. The Church of which Paul spoke in Ephesians was called God's eternal purpose (Eph. 3:11). Therefore, the Church was a *prolepsis*—that is, it was anticipated in the Old Testament.

In *The Rapture Question*, Walvoord asks, "Does the term 'church' include the saints of all ages?" (Walvoord 1978, 19). Comparing scripture with scripture, the Bible clearly answers this question with a resounding "yes":

- John 11:52: Caiaphas prophesied that Christ was to die not only for that nation but to gather in *one* nation all the children of God who were scattered abroad.
- Romans 1:1-16: Paul says he was separated to the gospel of God, which God promised before through His prophets in the Holy Scripture.
- Romans 2:28-29: Paul states a Jew is not a Jew unless his praise is of God (cf. Gen. 49:8; Phil. 3:3).
- Romans 4:13-14: Abraham was to be heir of the world, not just of Palestine. He became the father of us all—both Jew and Gentile—who now constitute the Church. The Church is God's eternal purpose.
- Romans 10:8-17: The covenant in Deuteronomy 29–32 is now applied to New Testament salvation—thus making believers under both covenants one!
- Romans 15:8-27: Christ, a minister of the circumcision (the Jewish people), came to confirm the Jewish promises to the Gentiles of the New Testament Church.
- Romans 16:25-26: Paul states that his preaching of Christ came from the prophetic Jewish Scriptures and was made known to all nations.
- Galatians 3:7-29: The gospel preached to Abraham by God was that the Gentiles would be justified by faith and become one with Abraham as his seed.
- Galatians 4:21-31: The Gentiles belong to the Jerusalem above (cf. Heb. 12:22, 24; Rev. 22:2).
- Galatians 6:15-16: The Gentile Church is called the Israel of God.
- Revelation 21:2, 9-27: The New Jerusalem is composed of all God's people from both the Old and New Testaments.
- Genesis 9:27: Japheth was to live in the tents of Shem, a prophecy that indicates the Gentiles would come into the house of Shem and form one household under God.
- Genesis 22:17: The blessing of Abraham was to make all people one in God.
- 1 Corinthians 10:1-4: Corinthian Gentile believers had *Jewish fathers,* which thus made them spiritually related to Old Testament believers.

- 2 Corinthians 6:2: Quoting Isaiah 49:8, Paul states that *the acceptable time* of salvation included the Corinthian Gentiles in this Jewish prophecy.
- Genesis 15; 17; 22: These three chapters reveal that Abraham saw Christ's day (cf. John 8:56). This does not imply a diversity of God's people.
- Acts 3:19-26: The blessing of Abraham was first of all for the forgiveness of sins, which was justification by faith (cf. Gal. 3:14), and second that they might receive the promise of the Spirit by faith.
- Acts 10:43: The Jewish Old Testament prophets said, "That whoever believes through His name will receive the remission of sins." Peter applied this to Cornelius, a Gentile.
- Acts 15:15: According to Peter, Paul, and James, the rebuilding of the *tabernacle of David* was the receiving of Gentile converts into the New Testament Church (cf. Amos 9:11-12).

In all of these references, Jesus, Peter, and Paul were tying together the fact that from all of eternity, there was only *one people of God*. Jesus, in establishing the New Covenant, made everything new:

- A new covenant (Luke 22:20; Heb. 10:9; 13:20).
- A new sacrifice (1 Cor. 5:7, Heb. 10:5; 13:15-16).
- A new temple (John 2:18-21; Acts 17:24; Eph. 2:21; 1 Cor. 3:16; 6:19; 2 Cor. 6:16).
- A new kingdom (John 3:3-5; 18:36; Matt. 8:11; 16:19; Luke 22:29).
- A new creation (2 Cor. 5:17).
- A new Israel, redeemed from all nations (Gal. 6:16; Rev. 5:9).
- A new priesthood (1 Pet. 2:5, 9).
- A new Jerusalem (Gal. 4:21-31; Heb. 12:22-24; Rev. 21:2). The present Jerusalem is now as seen in Revelation 11:8.
- A new people of God (1 Pet. 2:10).
- A new city (Heb. 11:16; 13:14; Rev. 3:12).
- A new way of worship (John 4:21-24; Heb. 10:18-22).
- A new name given (Rev. 2:17).
- A new age, the last age of human history (Heb. 9:26).

- A new heaven and a new earth (2 Pet. 3:10-14).

THE CHURCH, GOD'S NEW TESTAMENT ISRAEL

The arguments presented in Ephesians 2:11-22 and the book of Galatians prove that God does not have two separate groups of people. In Christ, both saved Jews and Gentiles compose the one Body, the one household, and the one family of God (Eph. 2:19; 3:15; Gal. 3:8-29). The Gospels proclaimed the prophetic aspects of Old Testament Israel as now being fulfilled:

- Luke 1:32-33: Jesus was born king in the house of David.
- Luke 1:68-79: Zechariah's prophecy about the salvation promised under the Old Covenant (called the Holy Covenant) was now fulfilled in Christ's covenant (Luke 24:46-47).
- Malachi 3:1: The messenger of the covenant was Christ.
- Matthew 1:21: The angel bore witness to the Messiah saving His people from their sins.
- Luke 2:30-31: Simeon's prophecy of this salvation was for *all* people.

These references are a direct assertion that the Old Covenant was being fulfilled by the Messiah and now composed the New Testament Church. Romans 11:5-7 affirms that Jesus Christ, the apostles, and the New Testament Church came out of the faithful remnant of the Old Testament saints.

There is no place in Scripture that says God is or will be dealing with national Israel separate from the Church under the New Covenant, because Christ's covenant is the last and eternal one (Heb. 13:20). Yet this is a major doctrine of dispensationalism—a man-made and Judaistic eschatology built on an assumption not warranted by Scripture.

THE CHURCH HAS INHERITED ISRAEL'S PROMISES

In the economy of God, the New Testament church is considered to be God's new Israel. National Israel has been rejected from her position. Daniel 9:24 states, "Seventy weeks are determined for your people," which indicates that something was to happen to Israel before the end of the seventy weeks.

Acts 13, which tells of the beginning of Paul's ministry, indicates in verse 46 that a direct change to the Gentiles had been made. In 1 Thessalonians 2:16, Paul states that God's wrath had come on Israel to the utmost. Jesus had warned the nation of Israel about this in Matthew 23:32 when He said, "Fill up the measure of your fathers' guilt." Furthermore, God had warned Israel about this from the time of Moses (in relation to the curses) up to the time of Isaiah, Amos, Hosea, and Jeremiah. Both Paul and Peter affirmed this in their writings (Rom. 9; 1 Pet. 2:8).

Israel stumbled, "being disobedient to the word, to which they also were appointed." In addition, Jesus took the kingdom away from Israel (Matt. 21:33-45). The Gentiles, in their conversion to Christ, would now be the circumcision of Christ (Col. 2:11). The Philippians are told that they are now the circumcision (Phil. 3:3). Circumcision was a Jewish rite that put an Israelite into the camp of God's people.

Paul ascribed Jewish covenant promises as being inherited by the New Testament Church:

1. The Gentiles were not circumcised under the Old Covenant (Eph. 2:11).
2. As such, they were without Christ (v. 12).
3. They were aliens from the commonwealth of Israel (v. 12).
4. They were strangers to the covenants (v. 12).
5. They had no hope and were without God in the world (v. 12).
6. Now in Christ they would be brought near (*eggus*), into, and with Israel (v. 13).
7. This was accomplished through the blood of Christ (v. 13).
8. Christ broke down the middle wall of partition between Jews and Gentiles (v. 14).
9. Christ abolished the law of commandments (v. 15).
10. He thereby made one new man and peace (v. 15).
11. Christ reconciled Jew and Gentile into *one body* (v. 16). The elect Jews were already in that body (1:22-23; 3:6).
12. Christ put to death the enmity between Jew and Gentile (2:16).
13. Christ came and preached peace to both Jew and Gentile (v. 17).
14. Christ created access for both Jews and Gentiles to God (v. 18).
15. Gentiles were no longer strangers and foreigners (v. 19).

16. Gentiles would be fellow citizens with the saints and members of the household of God (v. 19).
17. The foundation is the apostles, prophets, and Christ (v. 20).
18. This constitutes God's entire building (v. 21).
19. This is God's temple and dwelling place of the Holy Spirit (v. 22).

Peter affirms the truth that New Testament born again converts are God's elect. Peter ascribes Israel's covenant promises to the Church no less than fifteen times:

1. The Church is the elect of God (1 Pet. 1:2).
2. The Church has been born of the Spirit, as Isaac (v. 23; cf. Gal. 4:29).
3. Christ is the living stone (2:4).
4. The believers are also living stones (v. 5).
5. The Church is a spiritual house (v. 5).
6. The Church is a holy priesthood (v. 5).
7. The believers are an elect generation (v. 9).
8. They are a royal (kingly) priesthood from Exodus 19:6 (v. 9).
9. They are a holy nation (v. 9).
10. They (Gentiles) are God's special people (v. 9; cf. Deut. 7:6-8; 1 Pet. 2:9-10)
11. They were once not a people (v. 10; cf. Hos. 1:6-10; 2:23; Rom. 9:26).
12. They are now the people of God (v. 10).
13. They are now to show forth God's praises (v. 9; cf. Gen. 49:8; Rom. 2:28-29; Heb. 13:15; Isa. 43:20-21).
14. They are now sojourners and pilgrims in the earth (v. 11).
15. They are now to offer up spiritual sacrifices (v. 14).

These were attributes of Israel under the Old Covenant, but under the New Covenant they are attributed to the Church. To deny this is tantamount to denying the Scriptures and divine inspiration. God does not have people saved outside of Christ and the New Covenant (Acts 4:11-12; Luke. 22:20; Heb. 13:20). Paul states that the reception of the Jew would be life from the dead (Rom. 11:15), which is what every sinner has when he comes to Christ. They were dead in trespasses and sins, but are now made alive in Him.

To conclude, the Bible teaches that the elect Israel of the Old Covenant and the Church of the New Covenant are one and the same people of God. This is without distinction, and therefore both have the same destiny.

Chapter 7

THE TABERNACLE OF DAVID

Theologically, much ado has been made over *what* is the tabernacle of David and *when* it is to be rebuilt. Is it to be rebuilt in the future, or has this already been fulfilled? The main Scriptures that must be dealt with regarding this issue are Amos 9:11-12 and Acts 15:15-18:

> On that day I will raise up the tabernacle of David, which has fallen down, and repair its damages; I will raise up its ruins and rebuild it as in the days of old: that they may possess the remnant of Edom, and all the Gentiles who are called by My name, says the Lord who does this thing.
>
> (Amos 9:11-12)

> And with this the words of the prophets agree, just as it is written; "After this I will return and rebuild the tabernacle of David, which has fallen down; I will rebuild its ruins, and I will set it up; so that the rest of mankind may seek the Lord, even all the Gentiles who are called by My name," says the Lord who does all these things, known to God from eternity are all His works.
>
> (Acts 15:15-18)

The context of both of these chapters should be held in view. Dispensationalists would have us believe that in Acts 15:6-18, the Church council was discussing the prophetic future instead of a present pressing problem that needed to be resolved at that time. Would not this be reprophesying a prophecy? This is an unheard of hermeneutic in interpreting Scripture.

In this passage in Acts, James was answering the problem at hand as to whether the Gentiles who were being saved could be a part of the Church without circumcision and the keeping of the law of Moses. To solve this problem, the Holy Spirit through James used the prophecy of Amos as the answer to the question at hand.

Peter had just spoken Acts 15:14 that God had visited the Gentiles and taken out of them a people for His name. James then verifies Peter's statement as the answer to the problem at hand by saying, "And with this the words of the prophets agree" (v. 15). From this context, it is evident that the receiving of the Gentiles into the Church apart from circumcision and the keeping of the law was God rebuilding the tabernacle of David.

Under the Old Covenant, a Gentile who wanted to become a member of God's kingdom would first have to be circumcised and become a proselyte in the Jewish faith. Under the New Covenant, those who wanted to enter the kingdom of God had to be born again (John 3:3-5; Col. 1:13). This is what the argument in Acts 15 was all about.

Furthermore, the declaration that was read was the answer to the present situation in all the churches, and "they rejoiced over its encouragement" (v. 31). The churches certainly did not rejoice over something that did not apply to them or that was to occur two thousand or more years into the future. They rejoiced in something that was apropos to themselves at that time.

Dispensationalists would have us believe that James was reprophesying a prophecy (their own hermeneutic) about a future date in the millennium as the fulfillment of Amos 9:11-12. However, according to the context of both Amos 9 and Acts 15, this is absurd. In Acts 15:19, James was answering the present situation when he said, "I judge that we should not trouble the Gentiles who are turning to God." James was not reprophesying a prophecy, but making a present application of Amos 9:11-12.

Scofield says the following on Acts 15:15-17: "Dispensationally, this is the most important passage in the New Testament" (Scofield 1945, 1169). Scofield further states:

"After this [viz. the out-calling] I will return." James quotes from Amos 9:11-12. The verses which follow in Amos describe the final regathering of Israel, which the other prophets invariably connect with the

fulfillment of the Davidic Covenant (e.g. Isa. 11:1, 10-12; Jer. 23:5-8)…
And will build again the tabernacle of David, i.e. re-establish the Davidic
rule over Israel.

(Ibid., 1170)

Scofield maintains that the Davidic covenant is the thousand-year millennium and thus does not connect Acts 15:15-17 to the church as being
the rebuilding of the tabernacle of David. However, we cannot bypass his
use of Isaiah 11:1,10 and Jeremiah 23:5-8 as being millennial, because the
New Testament writers ascribe both of these references relating to Christ
as having been fulfilled in Christ's New Covenant. In Romans 15:12, Paul
applied Isaiah 11:1,10 to show that Christ was the Root of Jesse and that
He was resurrected to reign over the Gentiles.

Likewise, the fulfillment of Jeremiah 23:5-8, in which the Messiah
is called "the Lord Our Righteousness," was applied by Paul to Christ
under the New Covenant (1 Cor. 1:30; 2 Cor. 5:21). How then can it be
said that these passages are millennial? A prophecy thus fulfilled cannot
be applied again as yet unfulfilled.

Scofield says, "The Dispensation of the Kingdom (2 Sam. 7:16) begins with the return of Christ to earth, runs through the 'thousand years'
of His earth-rule and ends when he has delivered up the kingdom to the
Father (1 Cor. 15:24)" (Ibid., 1341). Scofield puts 1 Corinthians 15:24
as occurring at the end of the millennium, whereas 1 Corinthians 15:21-
24 states that Christ will turn the redemptive kingdom over to the Father
at the time of the resurrection "when He puts an end to all rule and all
authority and power."

According to dispensationalists, the resurrection *precedes* both the tribulation and the millennium. Scofield has just said that the kingdom will be
turned over to the Father after the thousand years, whereas 1 Corinthians
15:21-24 states that it will be at the time of the resurrection. How could
Christ turn over a redemptive kingdom at the resurrection (the rapture;
see 1 Thess. 4:16; 1 Cor. 15:21-24) before the tribulation and then again
after the millennium? You cannot have it both ways.

Scofield calls Amos 9:11-12, "Future kingdom blessing: (1) The Lord's
return and the re-establishment of the Davidic monarchy" (Ibid., 940).
Scofield is saying that James is reprophesying the prophecy of Amos as
occurring in the millennium. How can you reprophesy a prophecy? To

preserve his dispensationalism, he has to do it, which just shows how far they will go in misapplying Scripture.

The biblical truth of Acts 15 is that the Messianic reign of Christ began at His first advent and that the coming of the Gentiles into the Church was God rebuilding the tabernacle of David.

WHAT IS THE TABERNACLE OF DAVID THAT WAS TO BE RAISED UP?

Certainly, the rebuilding of the tabernacle was not just about the fact that the Gentiles were coming into covenant relationship with God. It also had to do with the kingship line of David that had fallen. There had been no king of David's line on the throne since 586 B.C., when Nebuchadnezzar destroyed Jerusalem and its temple. Something had to happen to restore the Davidic kingship. The event that occurred was that the Messiah came and took on Himself the kingship of David, as prophesied in the Old Testament.

David's descendants were the reigning kings until Judah went into Babylonian captivity. Other prophets had predicted the downfall of the Jewish kingdom, which was the overthrow of the tabernacle of David. Hosea had prophesied, "For the children of Israel shall abide many days without king or prince, without sacrifice or sacred pillar, without ephod or teraphim. Afterward the children of Israel shall return and seek the Lord their God and David their king. They shall fear the Lord and His goodness in the latter day" (Hos. 3:4-5).

Hosea prophesied about 750 B.C. Shortly after this time, both Israel and Judah were taken captive into Assyria and Babylon. David's house fell when Judah went into captivity. At that point, the line of kings of David's dynasty ended. Therefore, Hosea's prophecy dealt with the time of the Babylonian captivity and the latter days as being the end of the Old Covenant. It was at this time that they would seek the Lord and David, their King, which was the Lord Jesus Christ, as David had been dead for about three hundred years by this time.

Amos 9:11 states that "in that day" God would raise up the tabernacle of David that had fallen down. *What day?* The phrase "in that day" in prophetic writings often refers to the day of the Messiah. In Acts 15, the whole discussion centers on the fact that the Messiah had come and on the changes taking place that were a result of His coming. Amos 9:11 unequivocally states that when this came to pass, the Gentiles would be admitted into the realm of God's people. This is what James gives answer to in Acts 15:15-18.

What do other scholars say about Amos 9:11-12 and Acts 15:15-17? George E. Ladd, a classical premillennialist, puts it this way:

> The conference was brought to a decision by the speech of James, the brother of Jesus, who had become the spiritual head of the Jerusalem church. He recalled Peter's experience at Caesarea when the Gentiles were obviously brought into the family of faith. Then he said, "With this the words of the prophets agree, as it is written, 'After this I will return and will rebuild the dwelling of David...that the rest of men may seek the Lord, and all the Gentiles who are called by my name.'" (15:15-17). James cites the prophecy of Amos 9:11-12 to prove that Peter's experience with Cornelius was a fulfillment of God's purpose to visit the Gentiles and take out of them a people for his name. It therefore follows that the "rebuilding of the dwelling of David," which had resulted in the Gentile mission, must refer to the exaltation and enthronement of Christ upon the (heavenly) throne of David and the establishment of the church as the true people of God, the new Israel.
>
> (Ladd 1974, 355)

Ladd is saying here that Amos 9:11-12 was fulfilled in the Church by the admission of the Gentiles. He also states that Christ's exaltation and enthronement in heaven was that He is on the throne of David, which exempts a future millennium. This also established the New Testament Church as the true people of God, the new Israel.

Richard Watson, in his sermon "Christ the Branch," says, "After a life of suffering, He was exalted to 'the throne of His father David.' And thus a Prince of that royal line is now 'Prince of the kings of the earth'" (Lane and Tippett 1848, 388, 1848).

Conybeare and Howson make this statement:

> The passages which the Holy Spirit has caused to be recorded for our instruction are those which relate to the Apostles themselves...The triumphant entry of Jesus into Jerusalem, was the "Kingdom of David ushered in by Jesus" (Mark 11:1-11; Matt. 21:1-11; with Zech. 9:9; Luke 19:29-38; John 12:12-15)...James turns to the ancient prophets,

and adduces a passage from Amos to prove that Christianity is the fulfillment of Judaism. And then he passes to the historical aspect of the
subject, contending that this fulfillment was predetermined by God
himself, and that the Jewish dispensation was in truth the preparation
for the Christian.

(Conybeare and Howson 1863, 216)

F. F. Bruce says:

The terms in which James summarized Peter's speech—"how first God
visited the Gentiles, to take out of them a people for his name"—have
been misused in the interests of modern dispensationalism. If it is true
as the *Scofield Reference Bible* says (*ad loc.*) that "dispensationally, this is
the most important passage in the N.T." it is strange that it would have
come from the lips of James —"austere, legal, ceremonial," as the same
work elsewhere calls him (p. 1306). James meant that God had clearly
shown His pleasure that the new community which was to display His
glory in the world should be drawn from the Gentiles as well as from
the Jews. And in this he found the fulfillment of the prophetic words
of Amos 9:11 .... But James's application of the prophecy finds the
fulfillment of its first part (the rebuilding of the tabernacle of David)
in the resurrection and exaltation of Christ, the Son of David, and the
reconstitution of His disciples as the new Israel, and the fulfillment of
the second part in the presence of believing Gentiles as well as believing
Jews in the Church.

(Bruce 1998, 309-310)

Because the New Testament affirms that Acts 15:15-17 is the fulfillment of Amos 9:11- 12, how can it be said that it is yet to occur in the
future? The Holy Spirit cannot be the author of two diverse views on the
same text. Did not the apostles in Acts 15 know what they were saying?

James answered the problem by saying that the Gentiles coming into
the Church was God rebuilding the tabernacle of David. Peter had just
said in Acts 15:14 that God through him had visited the Gentiles and
taken out of them a people for His name. James verifies this action by
quoting the passage from Amos 9—that the salvation of the Gentiles was
God building the tabernacle of David that had fallen down.

In this passage in Acts, James declares the work of Paul, Barnabas, and
Peter among the Gentiles to be the fulfillment of the words not only of

the prophet from whom he quoted but also of the prophets (plural; v. 15), thus indicating that other prophets so agreed. In the *New Commentary on Acts of the Apostles,* McGarvey makes this statement on Acts 15:13-21:

> The argument is that the statements of Peter, and of which those made by Barnabas and Paul, were in fulfillment of prophecy concerning the Messiah's reign; and it supplied all that was lacking to convince the brethren. The prophet had in previous verses predicted the downfall of the Jewish kingdom, which would be the overthrow of the tabernacle or house of David, whose descendants were the reigning kings; and in the verses quoted he predicts the rebuilding of the same, which could occur only by some descendant of David again ascending the throne. But after that downfall, no man of David's race became a king until Jesus was enthroned in heaven. This, then, was the rebuilding of the ruins, and it was to be followed by "the residue of men." That is, the Gentiles, seeking after the Lord, as Gentiles had been doing ever since Peter's visit to the house of Cornelius.
>
> (McGarvey 1872, 66)

E. Earl Ellis puts it this way: "In Acts, James (Acts 15:16ff) explicitly connects the rebuilt 'tabernacle' with the inclusion of the Gentiles" (Ellis 1975, 91). In his pamphlet "Christians Believe," Cecil J. Lowry, Ph.D. D.D. writes:

> We believe that God spoke to David through the Prophet Nathan (2 Sam. 7:12-13), saying that after David's death and burial, but before the Second Advent and General Resurrection, one of David's sons, the Greater David or true Messiah, would die and be resurrected to sit upon the throne of David over Israel forever; We believe that God plainly taught Israel that David's throne was actually God's throne in that it represented God's seat of authority over Israel; We believe that both David and his throne were typical of the true David, Christ, and His throne; We believe as true types both were temporary and destined to give place forever to Christ and His eternal throne; We believe that the Holy Ghost has given us a fuller revelation of the Davidic Covenant in the Prophets and Psalms; We believe that a fundamental tenet of the Davidic Covenant is that his Son, the Savior-king, would ascend to Heaven to be seated at the right hand on the true Mount Zion, in the Heavenly Jerusalem, as King over the united Israel of God, the Church triumphant and the Church militant; We believe that there is not one

single verse in either the Old or the New Testament that places the Messiah's throne in temporal Jerusalem; We believe that Jesus was the true fulfiller of the Law and the Prophets; We believe that our Lord Jesus Christ was the promised Son who was born and died while David's body was still in the grave, before the Second Coming and General Resurrection, and was resurrected to sit upon God's throne in Heaven as King over the true Israel, His Church, forever; We believe that on the Day of Pentecost Saint Peter pointed out to natural Israel the fact that Jesus was not only the promised Son, but that His Resurrection, Ascension and Exaltation at God's right hand as the eternal Head of His Church was the true fulfillment of the Davidic Covenant; We believe that Saint Peter also clearly showed Christ's death, Resurrection and New Testament Economy to be the true fulfillment of the Abrahamic Covenant.

(2 Sam. 7:1-16; 1 Chron. 29:23; 17:4, 9-15; 28:4-8;
2 Chron. 9:8; 1 Kings 9:3-7; Acts 2:29-36; Rev. 1-5; 3:7)

The center of biblical theology is God, not Israel! God is His own center in all He does. Salvation under the New Covenant is dependent on grace, not race. God's purposes stand according to election, not on the Jewish people.

SCRIPTURES TEACH THAT CHRIST IS KING AND IS PRESENTLY ON THE THRONE OF DAVID

Revelation 5:1, 6 states that the occupants of the throne in heaven are the Father and the Son, both having but one and the same throne! As to the classical dispensational argument that states Christ postponed the kingdom because of the rejection by the Jews, Psalm 2:1-3,6 speaks to the exact opposite: "Why do the nations rage, and the people plot a vain thing? The kings of the earth set themselves, and the rulers take counsel together, against the Lord and against His Anointed, saying, 'Let us break their bonds in pieces and cast away Their cords from us'…Yet I have set My King on My holy hill of Zion."

In Acts 4:25-26 Peter uses Psalm 2:1-2 to affirm that in spite of national Israel's rejection of Christ, God set up Christ as His king. Psalm 45:6 states, "Your throne, O God, is forever and ever; a scepter of righteousness is the scepter of Your kingdom." Hebrews 1:8-9 declares that Psalm 45 has been fulfilled in the person of Christ. Because Christ's throne and kingdom is forever and ever, it could not have been postponed or delayed.

In Romans 1:1-4, Paul affirms that what the prophets of the Old Testament wrote was the *gospel of God,* and that the gospel of God concerned His Son Jesus Christ who proceeded from the seed of David according to the flesh. In Romans 15:8-27, Paul concludes that Christ is reigning from the throne of which Isaiah had prophesied, "He would rise to reign over the Gentiles" (v. 12), which is the fulfillment of Isaiah 11:1,10. Therefore, Isaiah 11 has been fulfilled by Christ's first coming and cannot apply a second time to the millennium.

Isaiah 9:6-7 states, "The increase of His government and peace there will be no end, upon the throne of David and over His kingdom, to order it and establish it with judgment and justice from that time forward, even forever." In other words, Isaiah prophesied that there would be no break in Christ's kingdom once it was started. It was to be from that time forth forever (v. 6). Christ could not sit on the throne of David unless He was king!

In Matthew 21:5, Jesus says, "Tell the daughter of Zion, 'Behold, your King is coming to you, lowly, and sitting on a donkey, a colt, the foal of a donkey.'" This verifies the fact that Christ was king and is the fulfillment of Zechariah 9:9-10. Luke 19:38 cites the same reference and states, "Blessed is the king who comes in the name of the Lord." Mark 11:10 expresses it this way: "Blessed is the kingdom of our father David." What further proof of Christ as king do we need?

Hebrews 1:8 states, "But of the Son He says, 'Your throne, O God, is forever and ever, a scepter of righteousness is the scepter of Your kingdom.'" Surely this was the prophetic fulfillment of 2 Samuel 7:13. The Book of Hebrews closes with the fact that "we are receiving a kingdom which cannot be shaken" (12:28). The author of Hebrews knows nothing of a postponed kingdom as the dispensationalists claim! Christ was presently king of the kingdom and was on the throne of David.

The throne of David, the house of David, and the kingdom of David all speak to one and the same aspect of the tabernacle of David. You cannot have one without the other. It has all been fulfilled in the New Testament Church, which is the fullness of Him that fills all in all (Eph. 1:22-23). Outside of this Church, there is no room for any more fullness.

THE LAND AND ITS PEOPLE

A main premise of dispensationalism is that in the Old Testament, Israel never literally occupied all the land promised to Abraham and his descendants. Dispensationalists say that Israel's possession of the land is an unfulfilled prophecy that has yet to be fulfilled. Is this what the Scripture teaches? Consider the following five questions to clarify the controversy over this issue of the land promised to Abram:

1. Was the land promised to Abraham's literal seed forever?
2. Did the promise have anything to do with Abraham's spiritual seed, Christ?
3. Did Israel under the Old Covenant fully posses the land that was promised?
4. Does modern Israel have a claim on the land that was promised to Abraham?
5. Was the land something other than just Palestine?

Since the time dispensationalism was developed around 1830, there has been an ongoing controversy in theology concerning the land promised to Abraham and his descendants. In Galatians 3:15-16, Paul affirms that Abraham's seed (descendant) is Christ. Most theologians affirm that Christ fulfilled the Abrahamic covenant. On this basis, it can be said that according to the New Testament, no part of that covenant was left unfulfilled.

DISPENSATIONALIST THEORIES ON THE LAND ISSUE

Scofield states, "It is important to see that the nation has never as yet taken the land under the unconditional Abrahamic covenant, nor has it ever possessed the whole land (cf. Gen. 15:18 with Num. 34:1-12)" (Scofield 1945, 250).

John F. Walvoord wrote, "The promise to Abraham was realized through the nation Israel, though the ultimate possession of the land and the restoration of Israel are unfulfilled as the Old Testament closes" (Walvoord 1982, 16). J. Dwight Pentecost states, "The promises in the Palestinic covenant concerning the possession of the land are fulfilled by Israel in the millennial age (Isa. 11:11, 12; 65:9; Ezek. 16:60-63; 36:28-29; Hos. 1:10-2:1; Mic. 2:12; Zech. 10:6). These references to the possession of the land promise fulfillment of the Palestinic covenant" (Pentecost 1978, 477).

Dispensationalists claim that Isaiah 11 is a millennial chapter. But what does this chapter in Isaiah really say? Isaiah 11:10 says, "In that day." What day? "And in *that day* there shall be a Root of Jesse, who shall stand as a banner to the people" (v. 10, emphasis mine). Revelation 5:5 states that Jesus was the Root of Jesse. Therefore, "that day" has to refer to the days of Christ, the Messiah.

In Romans 15:10, Paul states that Isaiah 11:10 was fulfilled in Christ. Therefore, Isaiah 11 cannot be a millennial passage.

In *The Basis of the Premillennial Faith*, Charles C. Ryrie says, "Israel must yet come into possession of that land, for she has never fully possessed it in her history" (Ryrie 1978, 49). In his book *Final Countdown*, Ryrie states, "In all her history, Israel has never occupied all the land given in God's original promise" (Ryrie 1989, 47).

Ryrie further states the following regarding the unconditional covenant promised to Abraham: "If the covenant is unconditional, then the national aspect of it must yet be fulfilled, and premillennialism is the only system of interpretation which makes a place for a national future for Israel in which she possesses her land" (Ibid., 52).

This is certainly saying that the basis for the millennium is the Jews having the land covenant fulfilled, even if it takes the millennium to do it. There is not one scripture in the New Testament that affirms such a position. It must be said that the references thus given can be proved to be already fulfilled in Christ's—the Messiah's—New Covenant. None of these verses can apply in any sense to a so-called millennial age.

Students of the Bible who are yet unlearned in the Scripture take what Scofield and his followers say as the supreme gospel on the subject. It was the mistaken hope of many who had been trained in the dispensational school that Israel, on becoming a nation in 1948, would gain control of the land originally promised to them. Because dispensationalists claim to be literalists in their interpretation of the Bible, they also claim that the nation of Israel today owns all the land by a promise of God to Abraham.

Dispensationalists also believe that Israel is in Palestine today on the basis of fulfilled prophecy. The scriptures they use concerning Israel's return to the land are those that have already been fulfilled by their return from Babylonian captivity and thus cannot have a second fulfillment in the millennium (the books of Ezra and Nehemiah answer to this, as do Ezekiel 37:15-28 and Zechariah 11:7,14). To use scriptures that have already been fulfilled is to call for a double fulfillment of prophecy.

Dispensationalists have used such "double reference" prophecy as their hermeneutic to prove their claims. However, in his book *Biblical Hermeneutics,* Milton Terry proves that double reference prophecy is untenable (Terry undated, 493-500). If a case can be made for a double fulfillment prophecy, a case can then also be made for a double fulfillment of Isaiah 7:14, "Behold, the virgin shall conceive and bear a Son." Dispensationalists would never agree to this, but then they have left the door open. So, where does it stop?

It is interesting to note that in his tape *Through the Bible,* J. Vernon Magee, a dispensationalist, declares that Israel is not in the land today as a result of fulfilled prophecy. So, there is a division in their own camp. Which side is right?

THE LAND PROMISED, FROM ABRAHAM TO JOSHUA

Are dispensational writers biblical or not? Their writings and assumptions are not correct in that they say the land promise has not been fulfilled. References that they associate with the land covenant as being fulfilled in the millennium are misapplied. The following biblical references prove that the land promised to Abraham was literally fulfilled in the Old Testament. The Scripture will be our sole premise of defense.

In Genesis 12:1-7, God promised to give the land to Abram's descendants. Verse 7 states, "Then the Lord appeared to Abram and said, 'To your descendants I will give this land.'" The extent of the land that was given is referenced in Genesis15:18: "In the same day the Lord made a covenant with Abram, saying: 'To your descendants I have given this land, from the river of Egypt unto the great river, Euphrates'" [cf. with Numbers 34:1-12, where a full description is given].

In Genesis 17:7-8, God incorporates the *land* into an *everlasting covenant:* "And I will establish My covenant between Me and you and your descendants after you in their generations for an everlasting covenant, to be God to you and your descendants after you. Also I give to you and your descendants after you the land in which you are a stranger, all the land of Canaan, as an everlasting possession; and I will be their God." Adam Clarke states the following regarding this passage:

> It is literally true that the Israelites possessed the land of Canaan till the Mosaic dispensation was terminated in the complete introduction of that of the Gospel. But as the spiritual and temporal covenants are both blended together, and the former was pointed out and typified by the latter, hence the word even here may be taken in its own proper meaning, that of ever-enduring, or eternal; because the spiritual blessings pointed out by the temporal covenant shall have no end. (Clarke undated, 112)

In Deuteronomy 34:1-5, God showed Moses the land that He swore to Abraham:

> Then Moses went up from the plains of Moab to Mount Nebo, to the top of Pisgah, which is across from Jericho. And the Lord showed him all the land of Gilead as far as Dan, all Naphtali and the land of Ephraim and Manasseh, all the land of Judah as far as the Western Sea, the South, and the plain of the Valley of Jericho, the city of palm trees, as far as Zoar. Then the Lord said to him, "This is the land of which I swore to give Abraham, Isaac, and Jacob. Saying, I will give it to your descendants. I have caused you to see it with your eyes, but you shall not cross over there."

In Joshua 1:1-6, Joshua takes command of Israel after the death of Moses. God defines the land to him in verse 4: "From the wilderness and this Lebanon as far as the great river, the River Euphrates, all the land of the Hittities, and to the Great Sea toward the going down of the sun, shall be your territory."

The land was fully defined from Abraham to Joshua.

DID ISRAEL POSSESS ALL OF THE LAND?

Joshua 11:23 states, "So Joshua took the whole land, according to all that the Lord said unto Moses; and Joshua gave it for an inheritance unto Israel according to their divisions by their tribes. And the land rested from war."

Joshua 21:43-45 states, "So the Lord gave to Israel all the land of which He had sworn to give to their fathers, and they took possession of it and dwelt in it. The Lord gave them rest all around, according to all that he had sworn to their fathers. And not a man of all their enemies stood against them; the Lord delivered all their enemies into their hand. Not a word failed of any good thing which the Lord had spoken to the house of Israel. All came to pass."

Joshua, at the age of 110, said to Israel, "Behold, this day I am going the way of all the earth. And you know in all your hearts and in all your souls that not one thing has failed of all the good things which the Lord your God spoke concerning you. All have come to pass for you; not one word of them has failed" (Josh. 23:14).

Are these scriptural references not divinely inspired? Or was Joshua not telling the truth when he made these statements? No! Joshua knew the situation and the language, and he understood the Covenant. Therefore, what Joshua said has to be the truth. Have Scofield and his followers never read this part of the Bible? How can there be any further doubt as to whether Israel really possessed the land? But there is more:

- 1 Kings 4:21: "So Solomon reigned over all kingdoms from the River to the land of the Philistines, as far as the border of Egypt. They brought tribute and served Solomon all the days of his life." This is the literal fulfillment of Genesis 15:18 concerning the totality of the land that was promised to Abraham: "To your descendants I have given this land, from the river of Egypt to the great river, the River Euphrates."

- 1 Kings 8:56: "Blessed be the Lord, who has given rest to His people Israel, according to all that He promised. There has not failed one word of all His good promise, which he promised through His servant Moses."
- 1 Kings 8:65: "At that time Solomon held a feast, and all Israel with him, a great congregation from the entrance of Hamath to the Brook of Egypt."
- 2 Chronicles 9:26: "So he [Solomon] reigned over all the kings from the River to the land of the Philistines, as far as the border of Egypt."

This was the full geographical extent of the land that was originally promised to Abraham. Therefore, under David and Solomon, the land promise was literally fulfilled. All that remained to fulfill the covenant promises was that which pertained to the Messiah, the branch and seed of David, which was to be accomplished by bringing in the everlasting covenant. This is the motif of Christ's new and everlasting covenant (Heb.13:20). This covenant was promised to Abraham in Gen. 17:7 and was finalized by Christ's atoning death.

WHAT DID JEHOSAPHAT AND NEHEMIAH SAY ABOUT THE LAND PROMISE?

As late as 805 B.C., Jehosaphat said the following about the land promise to Israel: "Are You not our God, who drove out the inhabitants of this land before Your people Israel, and gave it to the descendants of Abraham Your friend forever?"

Around 450 B.C., Nehemiah declared, "You are the Lord God, who chose Abram, and brought him out of Ur of the Chaldeans, and gave him the name Abraham; You found his heart faithful before You, and made a covenant with him to give the land of the Canaanites, the Hittites, the Amorites, the Perizzites, the Jebusites, and the Girgashites—to give it to his descendants. You have performed Your words, for You are righteous" (Neh. 9:7-8).

In Nehemiah 9:22, he states, "Moreover You gave them kingdoms and nations, and divided them into districts, so they took possession of the land of Sihon, The land of the king of Heshbon, and the land of Og king of Bashan."

In Nehemiah 9:24-25, the prophet adds, "So the people went in and possessed the land; You subdued before them the inhabitants of the land, the Canaanites, and gave them into their hands with their kings and the people of the land, that they might do with them as they wished. And they took strong cities and a rich land, and possessed houses full of all goods, Cisterns already dug, vineyards, olive groves, and fruit trees in abundance. So they ate and were filled and grew fat, and delighted themselves in Your great goodness."

Lest Israel think that they by their might and ingenuity took possession of the land, the psalmist writes by divine inspiration:

> We have heard with our ears, O God, our fathers have told us, the deeds You did in their days, in days of old: You drove out the nation with Your hand, but them You planted: You afflicted the peoples, and cast them out. For they did not gain possession of the land by their own sword, nor did their own arm save them; but it was Your right hand, Your arm, and the light of Your countenance, because You favored them.
>
> (Psalm 44:1-3)

All these biblical references provide evidence that Israel did literally possess all the land that God originally promised. So why is it so hard for dispensationalists to believe what the Bible says? Yet some even outright deny that the land promise was fulfilled. How many times does the Bible have to say something before it is true?

WHAT DID JESUS SAY ABOUT THE LAND PROMISE OF THE OLD COVENANT?

There is another aspect of biblical truth to consider: The Old Covenant was abrogated, taken away, by Christ when He established His New Covenant. This is seen in Hebrews 10:9, "Behold, I have come to do Your will, O God." Jesus takes away the first Covenant that He may establish the second.

Since Calvary, no two Covenants have been in effect at the same time. Nothing from the Old Covenant is binding under the New Covenant that is not specifically restated. There is not one reference in the New Testament that affirms the land to Israel! Christ's everlasting covenant is the only one now in effect (Heb. 13:20).

Jesus Himself affirmed this when He said, "From the days of John the Baptist until now the kingdom of heaven suffers violence, and the violent take it by force. For all the prophets and the law prophesied *until* John" (Matt. 11:12-13, emphasis mine). By "the prophets," this means *all* the prophets. Luke also affirms, "The law and the prophets were *until* John. Since that time the kingdom of God has been preached, and everyone is pressing into it" (Luke 16:16, emphasis mine).

WHO REALLY OWNS THE LAND OF PALESTINE?

"Now let me sing to my well-beloved a song of My Beloved regarding His vineyard: My Well-beloved has a vineyard on a very fruitful hill. He dug it up and cleared out its stones, and planted it with the choicest vine. He built a tower in its midst, and also made a winepress in it; so He expected it to bring forth good grapes. 'And now, O inhabitants of Jerusalem and men of Judah, judge please, between Me and My vineyard. What more could have been done to My vineyard that I have not done in it? Why then when I expected it to bring forth good grapes, did it bring forth wild grapes? And now, please let Me tell you what I will do to My vineyard: I will take away its hedge, and it shall be burned; and break down its wall, and it shall be trampled down. I will lay it waste; it shall not be pruned or dug, but there shall come up briers and thorns. I will also command the clouds that they rain no rain on it.' For the vineyard of the Lord of hosts is the house of Israel, and the men of Judah are His pleasant plant. He looked for justice, but behold, oppression; for righteousness, but behold, a cry for help" (Isa. 5:1-7).

The "vineyard" mentioned in Isaiah 5:7 was Israel. Psalm 80:8 states, "You have brought a vine out of Egypt; You have cast out the nations and planted it." There can be no question as to who the vine represented. Isaiah had already spoken of the figure of the vineyard as being under God's judgment: "The Lord will enter into judgment with the elders of His people and His princes; For you have eaten up the vineyard; the plunder of the poor is in your houses" (Isa. 3:14). Isaiah put this parable into a song and sang it to Israel to get their attention (Isa. 5:1).

Jesus used this parable of the vineyard three times in the New Testament when referring to Israel's downfall (Matt. 21:33-46; Mark 12:1-12; Luke 20:9-19). Is it not peculiar that Matthew, in presenting the Messiah to Israel, states four specific references to Israel's fate?

1. In Matthew 3, God used Christ's forerunner, John the Baptist, to announce that *"even now the axe is laid to the root of the trees"* v. 10). Israel was one of those trees. The only tree left is "the tree of life," Christ Jesus.

2. In Matthew 8:10-12, Jesus Himself received a Gentile centurion into the kingdom "Assuredly, I say to you, I have not found such great faith, not even in Israel." Jesus then announced that the children of the kingdom were to be cast into outer darkness, where there would be weeping and gnashing of teeth.

3. In Matthew 21:18-20, Jesus next cursed the fig tree (which represented Israel) and said, "Let no fruit grow on you ever again" (τον αιωνα, eternally).

4. In Matthew 21:33-45, Christ followed that statement with the parable of Israel having been God's vineyard. He takes the kingdom away from Israel and gives it to a nation bearing the fruits of it.

Consider the following synchronization of Matthew 21:33-46 with Isaiah 5:1-7:

1. The landowner is God (Matt. 21:33).
2. God planted a vineyard on a very fruitful hill (Isa. 5:1).
3. Israel is God's vineyard (Isa. 5:7).
4. God set up a hedge around it (Matt. 21:33).
5. He dug a winepress in it (Matt. 21:33).
6. He built a tower in it (Matt. 21:33; Prov. 18:10).
7. He gathered out the stones (Isa. 5:2).
8. He planted it with the choicest vine (Jer. 2:21).
9. God did all He could do to the vineyard (Isa. 5:4).
10. He then leased the vineyard out to tenant vinedressers (Matt. 21:33) on the basis of crop sharing that he would receive his portion of the fruits in their season (v. 34).
11. The landowner then went into a far country (Matt. 21:33).
12. At harvest time God sent messengers to gather his portion of the fruit (Matt. 21:34). These were the prophets.
13. The tenant leaders beat one, killed one, and stoned another (Matt. 21:35).
14. The landowner sent others of his servants (Matt. 21:36).

15. Finally, the landowner sent his own son to gather the vintage (Matt. 21:37, see also Matt. 21:18-19).

16. The tenants killed the son in order to seize the inheritance (Matt. 21:38-39).

17. The landowner himself came and called them to account (Matt. 21:40).

18. The tenant vinedressers, unaware of the direction of Jesus' parable, unknowingly pronounced their own judgment (Matt. 21:41).

19. Jesus' replied to the vinedressers, the chief priests, and the Pharisees to whom He was speaking (Matt. 21:42-43) that because the vineyard belonged to God, He had the right to do with it that which He pleased.

    • In Matthew 21:42, Jesus called Himself the *stone* that the builders (Israel) rejected, which now would become the chief cornerstone of the Church (Eph. 2:19-22; 1 Pet. 2:6).

    • Jesus took the kingdom of God away from Israel and gave it to a nation bringing forth the fruits, that nation being the New Testament Church composed of Gentiles (Matt. 8:11-12; Acts 13:46; 18:6; 28:28; 1 Pet. 2:4-10).

    • In Matthew 21:44, Jesus referred to Himself as the *stone* (the one rejected in verse 42) and that now, whoever fell on Him would be broken—that is, saved from their past sins—but those who do not fall on Him (neglect His salvation, Heb. 2:3) would be ground to powder.

    • In Acts 3:23, Peter, speaking of the prophet who replaced Moses, quoted Deuteronomy 18:15,18-19 and applied it to Christ: "And it shall be that every soul who will not hear that Prophet shall be utterly destroyed from among the people."

This takes away all the supposed rights that Israel had in their position under God. Therefore, the vineyard belonged to God all the time. He merely had leased it to Israel. Does God not have a right to do whatever He wants with something He owns?

THE NEW TESTAMENT WRITERS CONFIRM
THE LAND PROMISE AS FULFILLED

If the literal land was meant in the promise to Abraham, why then in Acts 7:5 does Stephen say, "And God gave him [Abraham] no inheritance in it, not even enough to set his foot on"? If we are to understand that the promise made to Abraham was that he would literally inherit the earthly land, Abraham must then return to fulfill the promise.

Dr. Charles Halph states, "Jesus is coming back to resurrect Abraham, Isaac, and Jacob and give them the land" (Halph, *The Christian Jew Hour*, March 26, 1993). Where in the New Testament does it teach that this must occur before the promise can be literally fulfilled? Did Stephen speak out of order, or was the Spirit of Truth not speaking through him? This is a serious question that the dispensationalists must answer scripturally. They must also consider whether their position destroys biblical inspiration because of the way that the New Testament writers interpreted the covenant made to Abraham.

Stephen says God brought Joshua "into the land possessed by the Gentiles, whom God drove out before the face of our fathers until the days of David" (Acts 7:45; cf. 2 Chron. 9:26). Paul affirmed the same when he said, "And when he had destroyed seven nations in the land of Canaan, he distributed their land to them by allotment" (Acts 13:19).

Who is telling the truth, the biblical prophets or the prophets of dispensationalism? Would not accepting the dispensational view deny biblical truth and the inspiration of Scripture? Furthermore, as to the land issue, we have the support of the following scriptures: Psalm 78:55; 105:9-44; 135:12; Jeremiah 32:22-23; Acts 13:19. When is enough, enough? Should not the Scripture speak for itself?

HOW DOES PAUL INTERPRET THE
LAND PROMISE IN ROMANS?

The promise God made to Abraham was on the basis of faith—the faith of Abraham! God's promise that he would be the heir of the world was not made to Abraham or to his seed through the law but through the righteousness of faith (Rom. 4:13).

The true heirs of the Covenant promise were those who had the faith of Abraham (Rom. 4:9-13,16). Is this not what Paul tells us in Romans 4:13, that the "land of Canaan" represented the whole world? Was this not also the way God chose to fulfill the Covenant promise to Abraham that he would be *the father of many nations*, and that through him all the families of the earth would be blessed (Gen. 12:3; 17:4)? This would naturally include the Gentiles that compose the *many nations*. Did Noah not prophesy this in Genesis 9:27 when he said, "May God enlarge Japheth, and may he dwell in the tents of Shem"? The Gentiles were descendants of Japheth, and the Israelites were descended from Shem.

Nor let us forget what Ezekiel 47:21-23 says: "Thus you shall divide this land among yourselves according to the tribes of Israel. It shall be that you will divide it by lot as an inheritance for yourselves, and for the strangers who dwell among you and who bear children among you. They shall be to you as *native-born* among the children of Israel; they shall have an inheritance with you among the tribes of Israel. And it shall be that in whatever tribe the stranger dwells, there you shall give him his inheritance, says the Lord God" (emphasis mine).

In the same Covenant, not only was the land in question but also the people to whom the promise was given. What is spiritually true of the people must also be true of the land. In Romans 9:3, 6-8 Paul fully declares himself on the subject as to who the true seed of Abraham is. He says Abraham's seed is actually divided into two classes. Some are of the flesh (v. 3), and these are not the children of God (v. 8). In verse 7, Paul says only the children of the promise of Isaac are the children of God and to be counted as seed.

In 1 Corinthians 10:18, Paul says there is an Israel according to the flesh. Under the New Covenant Israel, the descendants of Abraham according to the flesh do not comprise the children of God (Rom. 9:8). This is strong language, but it is God's Word. If the Bible is correct, this must apply not only to Israel of today but also the Israel of that time as well. This then leads us back to Paul's argument in Romans 4 that only those who have the *faith of Abraham are his true seed or descendants* (vv. 4-13).

In Romans 9:27, Paul states that even though Israel would become as the sand of the sea, only "the remnant will be saved." In this verse, Paul quotes from the prophecy in Isaiah 10:22. This remnant is established in Romans 11:7: "What then? Israel has not obtained what it seeks; but the elect have obtained it, and the rest were blinded." The promise being fulfilled in the elect people also had to include the land, because the two are inseparable.

HOW DOES PAUL INTERPRET THE LAND PROMISE IN GALATIANS?

In Galatians, Paul avers to the principle he already laid down in Romans; namely, that the fulfillment of the covenant promises to Abraham were based on faith and that the elect had become the heirs of all the promises that God made to Abraham.

Furthermore, we are told by Paul that all the spiritual descendants of Abraham (including the saved Gentiles) are heirs of Abraham and therefore a fulfillment of the covenant promise made to him that in him all nations would be blessed (Gal. 3:7-9, 29; 4:1-7). From this, there can be no doubt that all the promises to Israel were based on their ultimate fulfillment of faith in the Messiahship of Jesus Christ, the true seed or descendant of Abraham, which included Gentiles outside of the camp of Israel.

In Galatians 3:7-9, Paul states, "Therefore know that only those who are of faith are sons of Abraham. And the Scripture foreseeing that God would justify the Gentiles by faith, preached the gospel to Abraham, beforehand, saying, 'In you all the nations shall be blessed.' So then those who are of faith are blessed with believing Abraham."

Christ's gospel was preached to Abraham in 2000 B.C. This was the gospel Christ came and fulfilled and in which all the Gentile nations would be blessed or justified by faith in Christ. Galatians 3:16,19 confirms that the promise of Abraham was not to his literal seed but to Christ, the seed to whom the promise was made. "And if you are Christ's then you are Abraham's seed, and heirs according to the promise" (Gal. 3:29).

Paul further accentuates this fact in Galatians 4:1-7. Paul specifically states that the Galatians do not come under the servitude of guardians, as Christ has come. They are now to be counted as sons, and thus heirs of God through Christ. Gentiles would now be heirs of the Abrahamic covenant:

> Now I say that the heir, as long as he is a child, does not differ at all from a slave, though he is master of all, but is under guardians and

stewards until the time appointed by the father. Even so we, when we were children, were in bondage under the elements of the world. But when the fullness of the time had come, God sent forth His Son, born of a woman, born under the law, to redeem those who were under the law, that we might receive the adoption as sons. And because you are sons, God has sent forth the Spirit of His Son into your hearts, crying out, "Abba, Father!" Therefore you are no longer a slave but a son, and if a son, than an heir of God through Christ.

(Gal. 4:1-7)

In Galatians 4:21-31, Paul repeats this same argument when he says that the children of the promise are those who are born of the Spirit as Isaac was (v. 29). This puts the Jews in the same category in which Jesus put Nicodemus in John 3. They must be born again! Nicodemus, a Jew, needed to be born again of the Spirit in order to enter the kingdom of God.

Since the covenant of Abraham found its spiritual fulfillment in Christ and the New Testament Church, how could the land, which was a part of that same covenant, require a literal fulfillment?

CANAAN WAS A TYPE OF HEAVENLY LAND AND HEAVENLY CITY

Hebrews 11:8-10 and 13-16 tell us that when God promised Canaan to Abraham and his descendants, it was not the literal land that was meant:

By faith Abraham obeyed when he was called to go out to the place which he would receive as an inheritance. And he went out, not knowing where he was going. By faith he dwelt in the land of promise as in a foreign country dwelling in tents with Isaac and Jacob, the heirs with him of the same promise. For he waited for the city which has foundations, whose builder and maker is God....These all died in faith, not having received the promises, but having seen them afar off were assured of them, embraced them and confessed that they were strangers and pilgrims in the earth. For those who say such things declare plainly that they seek a homeland. And truly if they had called to mind that country from which they had come out, they would have had opportunity to return. But now they desire a better, that is, a heavenly country. Therefore God is not ashamed to be called their God, for He has prepared a city for them.

These references plainly tell us that Canaan was a type of heaven itself. The patriarchs sought a heavenly country instead of literal Canaan. Thus, God had more than just the physical land of Canaan in sight when He gave the original promise. This New Testament application certainly cancels out the literal dispensational position that the land was an end in itself.

Hebrews 12:18-29 contrasts the place in which Israel in the Old Testament came with the place in which the New Testament saints come. Israel of the Old Testament came to Mount Sinai, while the believer in the New Testament comes to Mount Zion. According to 1 Peter 2:6, Mount Zion is the Church in which the foundation Stone, Jesus Christ, was laid. This is a direct quote from Isaiah 28:16 that is now being applied to the Church.

Since this is the case, the church had to be a subject of Old Testament prophecy and the fulfillment of Old Testament Zion. According to the hermeneutic that the Old Testament prophecy is interpreted by New Testament fulfillment, these verses show us that Canaan was a type which is now fulfilled in the antitype, both as to the land (Rom. 4:13) and to the people (Rom. 11:7). Furthermore, in Matthew 21:42 Jesus says that He is the *stone* of the Old Testament prophets (see also Ps. 118:22-23; Acts 4:11; 1 Pet. 2:7 and appendices B and C in this book).

Hebrews 12:22-24 provides us with clear evidence that Canaan was typical of a heavenly country and a heavenly city: "But you have come to Mount Zion and to the city of the living God, the heavenly Jerusalem, to an innumerable company of angels, to the general assembly and church of the firstborn who are registered in heaven, to God the Judge of all, to the spirits of just men made perfect, to Jesus the Mediator of the New Covenant, and to the blood of sprinkling that speaks better things than that of Abel" (Heb. 12:22-24).

The New Testament believers come to Mount Zion, not Mount Sinai. Mount Zion is the city of the living God. Mount Zion is the heavenly Jerusalem, the general assembly and Church of the firstborn who are registered in heaven. God is the judge of all and the spirits of just men made perfect. It is Christ the mediator of the New Covenant and the blood that speaks better things than that of Abel.

The author of the book of Hebrews calls the Church, "Mount Zion." Therefore, Old Testament Zion is replaced by the New Testament Church. Peter confirms this in 1 Peter 2:6, which states that the foundation stone of the Church is the stone of Isaiah 28:16, which is Jesus Christ. He is now the chief cornerstone of the Church, where the foundation stone was laid. There can thus be no doubt as to Old Testament Zion being fulfilled in and by the New Testament Church.

Galatians 4:21-31 gives us the same analogy as that in Hebrews. Mount Sinai speaks of the present earthly city of Jerusalem, which is in bondage with her children and is represented by Hagar, the Old Covenant. But the New Covenant believer is born of the Spirit as Isaac was (v. 29) and is represented by Sarah, the mother of us all, the Jerusalem that is above. This is the same as the heavenly Jerusalem in Hebrews 12:22.

This is also the fulfillment of Isaiah 60:14, "And they shall call you The City of the Lord, Zion of the Holy One of Israel." Jesus' statement as to the present and physical Jerusalem is seen in Revelation 11:8.

Micah 4:2 states, "For out of Zion the law shall go forth, and the word of the Lord from Jerusalem." This was surely fulfilled in Acts 1:8, where Jesus commanded His disciples to preach the gospel first in Jerusalem, then in Judea, Samaria, and the end of the earth. Acts 2:1-39 states this was an immediate fulfillment: verse 5 says there were people "from every nation under heaven."

The final fulfillment of this promised city and land will be completed in the new heavens and the new earth (2 Pet. 3:10-13). All New Testament believers will be a part of it, as is seen in Hebrews 13:14: "For here we have no continuing city, but we seek the one to come." In Revelation 3:12, Jesus promises to the overcomer that He will "write on him the name of the city of My God, the New Jerusalem, which comes down out of heaven from My God." As John closes the book, he adds, "Then I, John saw the holy city, New Jerusalem, coming down out of heaven, from God, prepared as a bride adorned for her husband" (Rev. 21:2) and "Come, I will show you the bride, the Lamb's wife. And he carried me away in the Spirit to a great and high mountain, and showed me the great city, the holy Jerusalem descending out of heaven from God" (Rev. 21:9-10).

This is the ultimate picture of the city for which Abraham looked and which Jesus Christ is preparing for all those who love Him and His appearing. Because the Bible teaches that the present Jerusalem is in bondage with her children (Gal. 4:25) and is spiritually called Sodom and Egypt (Rev. 11:8), there can be no earthly Jerusalem to come. It has been replaced by the New Jerusalem from above, which is the bride of Christ, the city of the living God. Therefore, the New Testament interpretation of the Old Testament shows that Canaan was typical and is now fulfilled in the antitype, both to the land and to the people.

WHICH IS RIGHT: DISPENSATIONALISM OR THE BIBLE?

A. B. Davidson has this to say on the subject of the land: "The patriarchs sought a heavenly country (Heb. 11:16) and looked for the city that hath foundations, the heavenly Jerusalem (Heb. 11:10, 16; 12:22). And the 'house of God' is one throughout all history (Heb. 3:1)." (Davidson 1950, 99). He further states:

> That such representations are true to the spirit of the Old Testament religion might seem implied in calling it a religion. The mere land of Canaan was never in itself all that was understood either by those to whom it was promised or by God who promised it, when it was named as Israel's heritage...It was regarded as a settled place of abode with God, where He would be fully present, and where they would find repose in His fellowship.
>
> (Ibid.)

In his commentary on Hebrews 11:10, Lenski says, "The earthly land of promise is only the earthly type and symbol of the heavenly Canaan" (Lenski 1946, 391). William R. Newell says that it was a revelation to Abraham of the city of Rev. 21:19-20 (Newell 1947, 381). Wickliff says, "To Abraham and to his lineage, God promised to give the land of promise by which is understood the land of bliss, that is heaven" (Wickliff undated, 61).

Ezekiel 37:15-28 refers to the spiritually restored Israel and about making them one nation under one king, "David, my servant" (v. 22). This king is none other than Jesus, the resurrected son of David. David had been dead for some four hundred years, so the text could not be speaking of him. The New Testament states that this prophecy was fulfilled in David's greater son, the Lord Jesus (Matt. 15:22), who was resurrected to sit on David's throne (Acts 2:29-31). Jesus Himself claims that He is on the throne (Rev. 3:21) and that on the throne He is the root and offspring of David (Rev. 4:1-3; 5:5-6). Ezekiel 37:24 says that this king was to be a shepherd. Jesus called Himself that shepherd (John 10:11) and the One who would make the sheepfold one (John 10:16). Jesus does not have sheep in two different folds, the Church and national Israel.

Luke 1:31-33 states that the promise to David the king was fulfilled in the person of Christ, the Messianic king, the head of the New Testament Church. Because the king is associated with the *land* (Ezek. 37:22, 25), we must take it that the land is also related to Christ and His Church—with the land now being the world (Rom. 4:13-17).

Ezekiel 37:26 states that the covenant was to be an everlasting covenant of peace. Jesus' covenant was an everlasting covenant (Heb. 13:20) and a covenant of peace (John 14:27; Acts 10:36; Eph. 2:14, 15, 17). The covenant that Christ made is the fulfillment of the one that Ezekiel was talking about.

In Acts 3:24-26, Peter preached to Israel and told them that they had killed the Prince of life, but that if they repented, they would be forgiven. Now, he avers that all the prophets from Samuel on have foretold of *these days.* If the prophets spoke of *these days* as referring to Abraham's seed (Christ), then to what other days could the prophecy apply? These were the sons of these prophets and of the covenant that God made with Abraham, saying, "And in your seed all the families of the earth shall be blessed" (Gen. 12:3).

In Acts 3:26, Peter states what the blessing of Abraham was: God had sent His servant Jesus "to bless you, in turning away every one of you from your iniquities." The blessing of Abraham was the forgiveness of sins. Too much is made of the blessing of Abraham that has nothing to do with New Testament fulfillment.

In conclusion, the land promise was fulfilled literally, typically, and spiritually. Israel's only hope and salvation was in the Messiah, the Lord Jesus Christ. God is now gathering into one all things under Christ's headship (Eph. 1:10). Because the Church is the fullness of Him who fills all in all, God can have nothing outside of this fullness. Otherwise, the Church would not be called His fullness (Eph. 1:22-23).

WILL ALL ISRAEL BE SAVED?

"All Israel will be saved" at Christ's second coming—or so the dispensation-alists teach based on Romans 11:26-27. Is this what the Bible teaches?

J. Dwight Pentecost, using these verses, states, "This salvation (v. 26) is the salvation that was promised to Israel in the Old Testament which was to be realized when the Messiah instituted the millennial reign" (Pentecost 1978, 468). But where in the Old Testament is the salvation of Israel waylaid until the millennium? Where in the Old Testament is a millennium explicitly spoken of?

James Hastings says, "The doctrine of the millennium is not found in the Old Testament" (Hastings 1908, 3:370). There is thus a problem as to the millennium. The following eight references teach that Jesus provided salvation by His death on the cross for the nation of Israel and also opened the door to the Gentiles:

1. The angel of the Lord said, "You shall call His name Jesus, for He shall save His people [the elect from both Jew and Gentile] from their sins" (Matt. 1:21).
2. John the Baptist declared the same (Matt. 3:1-12).
3. It is seen in the song of Mary (Luke 1:54-55).
4. Zechariah prophesied it (Luke 1:68-70,72-73,77-79).
5. John declares it (John 1:11-13).
6. John the Baptist announced it (John 1:29).

7. Peter preached it (Acts 2:14, 22, 38-41; 3:18-26).
8. Paul declares it (Acts 13:24, 46; 26:20).

How can these scriptures not be counted for the salvation of Israel in the present age? Furthermore, why does the Bible announce that the message of salvation was for "the Jew first" (Acts 3:26; 11:19; 13:46; 26:20; Rom. 1:16; 2:9-10)? The answer was to call the elect Jews out of the apostate nation into the Church.

Jesus Himself said that He was sent *to the lost sheep of the house of Israel* (Matt. 10:6; 15:24). Were not all of Christ's disciples from among Israel? The blessing of the Abrahamic covenant that Christ fulfilled was for the sins of Israel (Acts 3:24-26; 5:31; 13:23, 26, 38, 46). For this purpose, Christ died and commissioned His disciples to preach it to all nations (Luke 24:46-47).

Concerning John 11:50-52, where does the nation of Israel fit in? In verse 50, Caiaphas was prophesying and said, "Nor do you consider that it is expedient for *us* that one man should die for *the people*, and *not* that the *whole nation* should perish" (emphasis mine).

Why does dispensationalism bypass these references about Christ's present salvation for the nation of Israel when He died for the nation at His first advent? The Early Church was comprised of saved *Jews*—probably millions of them by the time of Acts 21:20 when Paul says many myriads of Jews believed. A "myriad" means ten thousand and there were many tens of thousands. It was with these Jews that the New Covenant of Christ was made and literally fulfilled (Jer. 31:31-34; see also Heb. 8:8-13). It was also to this group, the New Testament Church, to which the Gentiles were added and became a part with the Jews. To say salvation was not provided for Israel by the deliverer, Christ, when He came the first time is to explicitly falsify the revelation of truth that was given to these New Testament authors. To do so would be dispensing with the Word of God.

Since when did reprophesying an Old Testament prophecy become a hermeneutic? Is this not what dispensationalists are doing with Romans 11:26-27 when they take a prophecy in Isaiah 59:20-21 that Paul applied to Israel in his day and then reprophesy it for the Jew in the millennium?

Scofield in his comments on Zechariah 13:1 goes so far as to say that the fountain that opens for the house of David and the inhabitants of Jerusalem for sin and for uncleanness will not open for Israel until the millennial kingdom (Scofield 1945, 976). The phrase "that day" in Zechariah 13:1 has to be the same day as that in Zechariah 11:11, in which Christ was sold for thirty pieces of silver and placed on the cross for Israel's sins. Does not Scofield's statement deny forgiveness for Israel until the millennium? Does not 2 Corinthians 5:19 declare that God in Christ has reconciled the entire world to Himself? It does not say that Israel was omitted.

If salvation for the Jewish people is in the millennium after Christ returns, is not this teaching a dual form of salvation? Where in the Bible is such a dual form of salvation taught? Does this not put the present Jewish people in a holding pattern that never will find resolution? Does the Bible say Christ did not die for the salvation of the Jewish nation when He came the first time? Why does the Bible command the preaching of the gospel in every nation and to the Jew first if the Jews were not included at the time?

WHO IS THE ISRAEL OF ROMANS 11:26 THAT IS SUPPOSED TO BE SAVED?

Paul previously stated, "They are not all Israel who are of Israel" (Rom. 9:6). Which Israel then is Paul talking about in Romans 11:26 when he says, "All Israel will be saved"? When was that salvation to be accounted to them? Why does the Bible distinguish Jew from Jew and Israel from Israel in the following passages? And what is meant by the word *Israel* or *Jew* as Paul uses them?

First, Paul designates an Israel that is not Israel, but which is Israel after the flesh:

- Romans 2:28: "He is not a Jew which is one outwardly."
- Romans 9:6: "They are not all Israel who are of Israel."
- Romans 9:3: Paul speaks of "my countrymen according to the flesh."
- 1 Corinthians 10:18: Paul speaks of an "Israel after the flesh."
- Romans 9:7: "Nor are they children because they are the seed of Abraham."
- Romans 9:8: "Those who are the children of the flesh, these are not the children of God."

- Romans 11:7: "Israel has not obtained what it seeks."
- Rev. 2:9; 3:9: Jesus said there were "those who say they are Jews and are not, but lie."

Paul then designates an Israel within Israel that is of the Spirit:

- Romans 2:29: "But he is a Jew which is one inwardly."
- Romans 9:8: "But the children of the promise are counted as the seed."
- Galatians 3:7: "Therefore know that only those who are of faith are sons of Abraham."
- Romans 11:7: The remnant is within Israel, "but *the elect has obtained it*" (emphasis mine).
- Romans 9:7: "In Isaac your seed shall be called."

Why was the true Israel to be found in Isaac? Paul answers this question in the following verses:

- Galatians 4:28: "Now we brethren, as Isaac was, are the children of the promise."
- Galatians 4:29: "Him who was born according to the Spirit."

These are His people, as found in Matthew 1:21. As to the designation of the name "Israel," it should carry us back to its origin. The name was pronounced upon Jacob after he wrestled with God and became a "prince with God" (Gen. 32:28). According to the law of first precedence, the meaning of the name "Israel" consistently means *one whose life and character has spiritually been changed by God*. Adam Clarke translated Genesis 32:30 this way: "I have seen Elohim face to face and my soul is redeemed." This should answer who a true Israelite is. Does Isaac being born of the Spirit in Galatians 4:28-29 depict John 3:3-5?

Is there a salvation apart from the cross and separate from the *elect* that did obtain the promises (Rom. 11:5-7)? If not, salvation is only through Jesus Christ and what He has already accomplished by the cross (Acts 4:11-12). The Bible does not teach that another deliverer will come out of Zion with another salvation apart from the Lord Jesus Christ, who has already reconciled the world to Himself (2 Cor. 5:19).

Furthermore, was not Paul's ministry also for the nation of Israel? In Romans 10, Paul's prayer and ministry to Israel was that they might be saved. In Romans 11:14, he said he wanted to provoke those of his own flesh that he might "save some of them." Why did Paul on all his missionary journeys go first into the synagogues and preach to the Jews that Jesus was their Messiah if salvation did not apply to national Israel at that time?

In Romans 11:26-27 Paul, quoting from Isaiah 59:20-21, says, "And so all Israel will be saved as it is written: 'The Deliverer will come out of Zion and He will turn away ungodliness from Jacob; for this is My covenant with them, when I take away their sins.'" The question is, What was prewritten on the subject of Israel's salvation? Furthermore:

- When was this salvation to take place?
- Why does the Bible use the word *covenant* in this verse?
- Who is the deliverer that was to come out of Zion, and when?
- Old Testament Messianic prophecies spoke of Israel's salvation.

Note that Israel's salvation would be in the deliverer who would come out of Zion. Isaiah, when speaking to Israel, told them that the Messiah would be given as a covenant (Isa. 42:6; 49:8). Christ's covenant (Matt. 26:26-29) was that covenant (Heb. 8:7-13). Hebrews 13:20 says Christ's covenant is the eternal covenant. When Christ came the first time, He *was* that deliverer out of Zion. Apart from Him there is no salvation (Acts 4:11-12).

There are four major views on the phrase "all Israel." Here is a paraphrase of Dr. David L. Hocking's view on the subject from *Guidelines on Romans:*

- All the elect of Jews and Gentiles.
- All the elect only of Israel.
- The whole nation of Israel, every individual member.
- Israel as a nation, but not necessarily every individual (Hocking 1983, 121).

If the word *Israel* is to be used literally (as dispensationalists suggest), every single individual Israelite would have to get saved. According to Acts

13:45-46 and 1 Thessalonians 2:14-16, this can never be true. Did not Jesus teach that some Jews would not escape the damnation of hell (Matt. 23:33)? However, if the words *Jew* or *Israel* are to be taken spiritually (as in Romans 2:28-29 and 9:6), then the Bible is not talking about every individual Israelite but only those who were true Israelites within the nation of Israel. There can be no doubt that these are whom Paul calls the "elect" in Romans 11:5-7. This is the essence of Romans 9–11. Because of Christ's New Covenant of salvation by faith, all believers—both Jew and Gentile—become the true descendants of Abraham and are called the "Israel of God" (Gal. 6:16).

According to Rabbi Morris N. Kertzer in his book, *What Is a Jew*, "A Jew is one who accepts the faith of Judaism…. An important part of any valid definition must also include what a Jew is not. The Jews are not a race" (Kertzer 1978, 3). Kertzer further states, "In 722 B.C.E. a disaster of major proportions occurred: Israel, the kingdom of the ten tribes, was destroyed by the imperial power of Assyria. That marked the end of Hebrew history and the beginning of Jewish history. The word, Jew, is simply an abbreviation of Judean" (Ibid., xx).

From this, we gather that a Jew is one who has a certain type of religion. This stance can be seen as far back as the book of Esther. It was probably around 475 B.C., when Persia was the world ruling nation, that Esther, a Jew, became queen to Ahasuerus. Persia ruled over 127 different provinces from India to Ethiopia. It was at this time that a religious conspiracy was set up against the Jews that Nebuchadnezzar had taken captive into Babylon. Haman, Ahasuerus's right hand man, wanted all the Jews destroyed, because Mordecai, a Jew, would not bow or pay homage to him.

However, in the meantime, Esther, the queen, interceded to God for her people. Haman's decree was reversed and fell on his own head, as he went to the gallows instead of Mordecai. At this time, the Jews had a great time of rejoicing and gladness, and "many of the people of the land became Jews, because fear of the Jews had fallen upon them" (Esther 8:17).

How could a Persian (or any other nationality) become a Jew? They could do so by changing their religion. This is the essence of Romans 2:28-29; 9:6. Therefore, due to the biblical and historical account, these references as to the words *Jew* or *Israelite* cannot be taken literally in Romans 11:26.

A modern example of the same: Sometime after Israel became a nation, a Jew who had converted to Catholicism and become a priest wanted to migrate to Israel, because he was a Jew. However, the Jewish courts would not admit him, as he had changed his religion. They determined that he was no longer a Jew.

THE MESSIAH IS THE TRUE "ISRAEL"

The Bible teaches in Isaiah 49:1-8 that the Messiah is called Israel. Verse 3 states, "You are My servant, O Israel." In verse 6, it says of the servant, "I will also give You as a light to the Gentiles, that You should be My salvation to the ends of the earth." Matthew 4:16 applies Isaiah 49:1-8 as being fulfilled in Christ. Therefore, Jesus, the Messiah, is the true Israel. This was foreseen in Exodus 4:22, Hosea 11:1, and Matthew 2:15. Isaiah says that the Messiah would be given as a covenant to the people (Isa. 49:8). What other covenant could this be than the one to which Matthew 26:26-29 and Romans 11:27 is referring?

Let it be affirmed again that the Bible teaches Christ's death was for the sins of Israel. Immediately after Pentecost, the apostles preached forgiveness of sins to the people of Israel and called them to repentance. Peter, speaking to Israel, verifies this fact:

- Acts 2:14: Peter spoke to "men of Judea."
- Verse 22: He spoke to the "men of Israel."
- Verse 36: He spoke to "all the house of Israel."
- Verse 41: Of these, three thousand repented.
- Acts 3:17-19: Peter called Israel to repentance and conversion on the basis of the prophets and Jesus' fulfillment of the Abrahamic covenant (vv. 25-26).
- Acts 4:8,11-12: Peter, using their own scriptures, called Jesus the stone that the builders rejected (Ps. 118:22), outside of which there was no salvation.
- Acts 5:31: He said of Christ, "Him God has exalted to His right hand to be Prince and Savior, to give repentance to Israel and forgiveness of sins." Peter was here alluding to Psalm 110, where Christ, the Messiah, was to be exalted to the right hand of God.

Paul, speaking to Israel in Acts 13:22-24, verifies Christ's death was for the forgiveness of Israel's sins:

- Verses 22-23: Paul said that Christ, the king from David's seed, had come, died, and been resurrected by God to be "for Israel a Savior—Jesus."
- Verse 26: "Men and brethren, sons of the family of Abraham, and those among you who fear God, to you the word of this salvation has been sent."
- Verse 38: "Through this man is preached to you the forgiveness of sins."
- Acts 20:21: Paul testified to the Jews about "repentance toward God and faith toward our Lord Jesus Christ."
- Acts 26:19-21: Paul, in testifying before King Agrippa, said that his preaching to the Jews was "that they should repent, turn to God, and do works befitting repentance."

Do not these scriptures concerning Christ's new and eternal covenant negate the theory of a future covenant and a future method of salvation for the nation of Israel? Romans 11:26-27 assures us Israel's salvation was included in the covenant Christ made. Paul avers in Acts 13:22-39 that God in Christ provided salvation for Israel. Verses 22 and 26 specifically state that God raised (resurrected) a Savior for Israel and that this word of salvation was sent to them. For proof of this, this chapter in Acts refers to the Old Testament Jewish Scriptures five times (vv. 33-35, 41, 47). Therefore, Israel's salvation was foretold in the Old Covenant and fulfilled in the New Covenant that Christ inaugurated. If the Jews are saved in the future simply because they are Jews by nationality, it would require a different gospel of salvation than the one purchased by the cross. Whereas Matthew 1:21 states, "You shall call His name Jesus, for He will save His people from their sins." It would be heresy to say differently.

Romans 11:32 states that there are no special privileges for Israel as God "has committed them all to disobedience." Paul introduced this truth in Romans 3:9-18. Both Jew and Gentile now stand in the same relationship to God. Both are under sin; therefore, Christ brings salvation to both on the same ground. Israel is not to be saved apart from Christ and His present salvation. Thus, salvation for Israel must take place within the Church, as the Church is the fullness of Christ, who fills all in all. It cannot be both ways.

As to Romans 11:26, "All Israel will be saved," we must in all honesty use the rest of the quotation, "just as it is written." The question is what was thus written? It is certainly not the unbiblical assumptions that all Israel will be saved at the second coming of Christ. The text does not say that! "All Israel will be saved, just as it is written" must refer to something *already written*, which would be the Messianic texts of the Old Testament. There are no other biblical writings. Christ is the Messianic deliverer who came out of Zion and reconciled the world to Himself (2 Cor. 5:19). It cannot be a salvation at a post-coming of Christ. Jesus Himself denies this in Revelation 22:11-12.

According to dispensationalists, Christ is to make the covenant of Jeremiah 31:31-34 with the Jews after His second coming. However, if this is case, then according to Hebrews 9:16-17, He would have to die again, because a covenant demands the death of the testator. Hebrews 9:26 tells us that Christ died "once to put away sin by the sacrifice of Himself." Christ died *once* for sin and cannot and will not die again (Rom. 6:10). Death no longer has dominion over Him (Rom. 6:9). In Isaiah, God cried out to a willfully sinning Israel, "What more could have been done to My vineyard that I have not done in it" (Isa. 5:4)? What does God have to do apart from what He has already done in Christ to forgive Israel's sins?

In Acts 4:11-12, there is no other name under heaven whereby anyone can get saved. There is no other mediator (1 Tim. 2:5). There can be no other covenant! Nor is there any other sacrifice to be offered (Heb. 10:18)! Christ's sacrifice was the once and forever saving act, and it will never be repeated. The statement that Christ died "once" is repeated too many times in Hebrews to be ignored! Earl F. Palmer puts it this way in *Salvation by Surprise*:

> On the one hand the continuity with Abraham, David, and Moses is unbroken, yet the newness of that fulfillment is so wholesale that the old Israel must itself now be fitted into the new reality by faith. Israel must trust in this fulfillment and obey the claim of God's authority in Christ. If Israel does not trust in Jesus Christ, her Lord, that denial amounts to the rejection of the very fulfillment of the Old Testament people [national Israel]. The result of unbelief is discontinuity for that part of Israel which does not believe in God's word.
>
> (Palmer 1978, 118)

As to Palmer's statement, in Acts 3:22-23, Peter declared that those who would not listen to Christ the prophet who had been raised up like Moses would be destroyed from among the people—the "people" here being Israel! Did Jesus not state this same truth in Matthew 8:11-12?

WHAT IS MEANT BY "LIFE FROM THE DEAD"?

What is the meaning of Romans 11:15 in which it says, "What will their [Israel's] acceptance be but life from the dead?" The Bible declares that every sinner is dead in trespasses and sins but that when they come to Christ, they are spiritually resurrected, saved, and made alive (John 5:24-25; Eph. 2:1,5). What biblical interpretation can be put on these verses other than the fact that Israel's acceptance by Christ in salvation is "life from the dead," which is to be born again?

As to Romans 9–11, the chapters from which the dispensationalists draw their picture of a future salvation for Israel, the following must be said:

- These chapters say nothing about Israel getting their land back.
- These chapters say nothing about God returning the kingdom to Israel that He took away from them in Matthew 21:43.
- This passage says nothing about Israel having a different destiny from the Church.
- These chapters also say nothing about Israel having a separate salvation apart from the Church in the future.

ISRAEL AND THE OLIVE TREE

Contrary to the idea that Israel will have a destiny and salvation different from that of the Church, Paul presses home the picture of the olive tree (Rom. 11:16-24) from which unbelieving Israel was broken off as branches. In his pamphlet "The Good Olive Tree" on Romans 11:26, Dr. George B. Fletcher writes, "The 'good olive tree' is not the nation of Israel. Paul is speaking of that good olive tree into which believing Gentiles were grafted among the natural branches, believing Jews, and with them partaking of the root and fatness, 11:17. Believing Gentiles were not grafted into the nation of Israel, so they cannot be the good olive tree" (Fletcher 2001, 2]). Note the following:

- Israel was not the "olive tree"; they were branches broken off from the olive tree (Rom. 11:17).
- Israel was broken off because of unbelief (Rom. 11:20).
- If Israel did not continue in unbelief, they would be grafted back on to the olive tree (Rom. 11:23) from which they were broken off.
- This is the same olive tree into which the Gentiles were grafted (Rom. 11:17), and they thereby inherit that from which unbelieving Israel was cut off.

The believing Jew and Gentile become one as grafted into the same "olive tree." Israel's salvation, then, does not have a destiny separate from the Church. In Romans 11:26, the phrase "and so" means "in this manner" Israel is to be saved. Not in some other manner.

Romans 10 states that the salvation Jesus brought was for both the Jew and the Gentile, which was drawn from the Hebrew Scriptures. Paul begins this chapter in Romans with a prayer for Israel's salvation in his time. He then proceeds to give the plan of salvation as seen in the Jewish scriptures of the Old Testament. In Romans 11:14, Paul's ministry was that he might *save some*. Therefore, the salvation that he was talking about was a salvation then and there for Israel, not in some distant millennium. Thirteen times in Romans 10–11 and in just 11 verses, Paul draws his point of salvation for Jew or Gentile from the Old Testament:

- Romans 10:5 from Leviticus 18:5.
- Romans 10:6 from Deuteronomy 30:12-14.
- Romans 10:7 from Deuteronomy 30:13.
- Romans 10:8 from Deuteronomy 30:14.
- Romans 10:11 from Isaiah 28:16.
- Romans 10:13 from Joel 2:32.
- Romans 10:15 from Isaiah 52:7; Nahum 1:15.
- Romans 10:16 from Isaiah 53:1.
- Romans 10:18 from Psalm 19:4.
- Romans 10:20 from Isaiah 65:1.
- Romans 10:21 from Isaiah 65:2.

Why does Paul use the Jewish Scripture to prove God's salvation for Israel if it did not apply to them? Is this not also the same way Gentiles become saved? How then can we say the Church is not found in the Old Testament? Is this not proof that the Church has inherited Israel's promises and is therefore the fulfillment of those promises? Then the "all Israel" of Romans 11:26 is the elect both of the Jew and the Gentile.

As to Israel's future salvation, George B. Fletcher says, "And so, when the natural branches, which were broken off through unbelief, shall be grafted in again, it will not be into Moses, but into Christ; not into the nation of Israel erected at Sinai, but into that which is built upon the foundation of the apostles and prophets, Jesus Christ himself being the true cornerstone, namely, the Church" (Ibid., 2).

The Bible does not hold out a future salvation for Israel apart from the present redemption provided in Jesus Christ for His Church, which is His Body, the fullness of Him who fills all in all. There is no fullness outside of the Church (Eph. 1:22-23).

In conclusion, it must be noted as someone has said that the Jews do not need Christ to come to them for salvation, they need to come to Christ! This is because the Redeemer has already come to Zion.

Chapter 10

THE COVENANTS FROM ABRAHAM TO JEREMIAH

L. Thomas Holdcroft states, "The church and national Israel are fundamentally different bodies, with each existing under its own covenant. Nevertheless, to those Jews not under the New Covenant, the old Abrahamic covenant still stands" (Holdcroft 2001, 20).

Does the Bible not state that Christ fulfilled the Abrahamic covenant by His New Covenant as it was applied to the Church in Acts 3:22-26, Galatians 3:8-29, 4:21-31, and Hebrews 12:22-24? Also, the Bible states that Christ took away the first covenant under which all other covenants were operating when He came the first time: "Sacrifice and offering you did not desire [this was a practice from the Adamic to the Mosaic covenant] but a body You have prepared Me. Behold, I have come to do Your will O God, He takes away the first that He may establish the second" (Heb. 10:5, 9).

From the time of Calvary, there never have been two covenants in operation at the same time. It is explicit in the New Covenant that there is only one mediator, "the Man Christ Jesus" (1 Tim. 2:5-6). Christ brought in the *everlasting covenant,* which is now the only covenant of salvation in existence (Acts 4:11-12). The Mosaic covenant was the redemptive mediation of all previous covenants, and Moses was the mediator. However, according to Hebrews 3:1-6, Christ replaced Moses in God's house, because Christ is the "Mediator of a better covenant" (Heb. 8:6).

CHRIST, THE SEED OF ABRAHAM, IS THE FULFILLMENT OF THE ABRAHAMIC COVENANT

Genesis 12:1-3 states that God's promise to Abraham was "in you all the families of the earth would be blessed." In Genesis 17:7, God promised that He would establish an everlasting covenant in Abraham's descendants (seed). The seed of Abraham in the New Testament was interpreted as being Christ and His followers (Gal. 3:16, 29). The blessing of Abraham is the salvation Christ purchased for the forgiveness of sins (Acts 3:25-26), specifically Israel's. In other words, this is the covenant Christ inaugurated when He came in the first advent. Hebrews 13:20 declares this to be the eternal covenant.

The covenant promise to Abraham was based on God's oath to assure all the heirs of the promise of the immutability of His word (Heb. 6:13-20). Paul says the covenant of Abraham was the gospel God Himself preached to Abraham "and the Scripture foreseeing that God would justify the Gentiles by faith, preached the gospel to Abraham beforehand, saying, 'In you all the nations shall be blessed'" (Gal. 3:8). The act of circumcision did not alter the gospel message, because the promise was given to Abraham while he was yet uncircumcised (Rom. 4:11).

The essence of this gospel is justification by faith (Rom. 4:1-5), not of the law of works! Jesus said, "This is the work of God, that you believe in Him whom He sent" (John 6:29). We are now justified by faith in Christ (Rom. 3:21-28). This Abrahamic promise of justification by faith was seen by Paul as being fulfilled to the Galatians who were Gentiles (Gal. 3:8,14). Paul states that this brought the saved Gentiles under the promise of the Abrahamic covenant: "In you all nations shall be blessed" (v. 8). God calls the Galatian believers "Abraham's seed and heirs according to the promise" (v. 29).

Paul, a missionary to the Gentiles, further elucidates on this covenant promise by declaring that he was called out and "separated to the gospel of God which He promised before through His prophets in the Holy Scriptures, concerning His Son Jesus Christ our Lord, who was born of the seed of David according to the flesh, and declared to be the Son of God with power according to the Spirit of holiness, by the resurrection from the dead" (Rom. 1:1-4).

Peter, preaching to Israel after the lame man was healed, declared, "You are sons of the prophets, and of the covenant which God made with our fathers, saying to Abraham, 'And in your seed all the families of the earth shall be blessed. To you first, God having raised up His Servant Jesus, sent Him to bless you, in turning away every one of you from your iniquities'" (Acts 3:25-26). This confirms the fact that the blessing of Abraham was first and foremost the forgiveness of Israel's iniquities. In Acts 2:39, Peter pleads with the people by saying, "The promise *is to you* and as many as the Lord our God will call" (emphasis mine).

Paul affirms that the Gentiles being justified by faith and filled with the Spirit was a part of the Abrahamic covenant so that "the blessing of Abraham might come upon the Gentiles in Christ Jesus, that we might receive the promise of the Spirit through faith" (Gal. 3:14).

Dispensationalists say national Israel (the physical seed of Abraham) and the Church are two separate and distinct people under God and the promises to Israel were earthly while the promises to the Church are heavenly. This again is a man-made theology that does not bear up under the scrutiny of Scripture. If Israel's promises were earthly, why in Hebrews 11:10, 13, and 16 does it state that Abraham looked for a city (a heavenly one) whose builder and maker was God, while at the same time during his earthly journey, he was only a stranger and pilgrim? If Abraham's calling was earthly, why did he desire a heavenly country? If Israel's promises were earthly, it would be a direct negation of Abraham's faith. Who has their wires crossed? Certainly not the biblical authors!

The Covenant of Abraham was renewed in Isaac: "Dwell in this land, and I will be with you and bless you, for to you and your descendants I give all these lands, and I will perform the oath which I swore to Abraham your father. And I will make your descendants multiply as the stars of heaven; I will give to your descendants all these lands; and in your seed all the nations of the earth shall be blessed" (Gen. 26:3-4).

The same Covenant was renewed in Jacob: "And behold, the Lord stood above it and said: I am the Lord God of Abraham your father and the God of Isaac; the land on which you lie I will give to you and your descendants, Also your descendants shall be as the dust of the earth; you shall spread abroad to the west and the east, to the north and the south; and in you and in your seed all the families of the earth shall be blessed" (Gen. 28:13-14).

The same Covenant was renewed with Moses (Ex. 6:2-8). In Exodus 6:8, God said to Moses, "And I will bring you into the land which I swore to give to Abraham, Isaac, and Jacob; and will give it to you as a heritage: I am the Lord." In giving the law to Moses, God did not annul the covenant with Abraham. He merely added the law to it until Christ the Messiah, the Seed of Abraham, would come (Gal. 3:16,19).

In Hebrews 4:1-2, when the Children of Israel were about to enter the Promised Land, God spoke to them about entering into His rest: "For indeed the gospel was preached to us as well as to them: but the word which they heard did not profit them, not being mixed with faith in those who heard it." The gospel was not only in the covenant of Abraham but also inherent in the law.

Scofield makes the following comment on Exodus 19:8: "The Dispensation of Promise (the covenant of Abraham) ended when Israel rashly accepted the law" (Scofield 1945, 20). This is not biblical truth according to Galatians 3:17-19, where Paul specifically states that the promise to Abraham was not annulled; rather, the law was added to the promise until Christ, the Seed, would come. Therefore, the promise to Abraham continued to be in force after the law was given. God did not make any promises to the Jews as a race. He made it with the covenanted community within Israel, the ones who had the faith of Abraham. This is proved by Romans 9.

In Isaiah's time, God called Israel back to the righteousness of the faith of Abraham (Isa. 51:1-6). Abraham's relationship to God was always one of faith (Heb. 11:8). The Abrahamic covenant promises were later renewed to David (2 Sam. 7:1-29; 1 Chron. 28:1-8). David's covenant was to be an everlasting covenant (Isa. 55:3). In these passages, additions to the Abrahamic covenant relate to the kingship of the seed of Abraham that God promised to him (Gen. 17:6). David's kingship (2 Sam. 23:1-5) was a type of the kingship of the Messiah and how He would rule over His people. Isaiah 9:6-7 reaffirms David's seed, the Messiah, to be king:

> For unto us a Child is born, unto us a Son is given; and the government will be upon His shoulder, and His name will be called Wonderful, Counselor, Mighty God, Everlasting Father, Prince of Peace. Of the increase of His government and peace there will be no end, upon the throne of David and over His Kingdom, to order it and establish it with judgment and justice from that time forward, even forever. The zeal of the Lord of hosts will perform this.

David was a descendant of Abraham through the line of Judah. This prophecy attaches itself to the Abrahamic covenant in the sense of the royal dignity of David's kingship. This covenant was promised to Israel while they were under the law of Moses. According to Paul in Romans 4:6-7 (taken from Psalm 32:1-2), the same blessedness was promised in the Abrahamic covenant. The blessing was the forgiveness of sins (Acts 3:25-26). Therefore, David's covenant was an extension of the Abrahamic covenant.

The promise that David would never lack a man on his throne (Jer. 33:17) was fulfilled in David's seed, the Messiah, the "branch" that would grow out of his roots. Romans 1:1-4 relates that Jesus was the "seed of David"; the one who would fulfill all the Davidic promises by the gospel as promised in the Old Covenant. Furthermore, Jesus Himself said, "I am the Root and the Offspring of David" (Rev. 22:16).

The fact that Jesus was the fulfillment of the Davidic covenant is stated throughout the New Testament. Matthew alone refers to Jesus as "the Son of David" nine times (Matt. 1:1; 9:27; 12:23; 15:22; 20:30-31; 21:9, 15; 22:42). In this last verse in Matthew, Jesus Himself affirms that He is the Son of David and David's Lord as predicted in the Old Testament.

Furthermore, in Acts 13:32-39, Paul, speaking of the promises of David in the Old Testament, said, "God has fulfilled this for us their children, in that He has raised up Jesus. As it is also written in the second Psalm: 'You are My Son, today I have begotten you.' And that he raised Him from the dead, no more to return to corruption, He has spoken thus: 'I will give you the sure mercies of David.'" In this passage, Paul quotes from Psalm 2:7, and 89:28 and Isaiah 55:3. Several hundred years after David, Isaiah had reaffirmed the covenant of David as being an everlasting covenant.

Christ was the fulfillment of the Davidic covenant, the Greater Son of David, the Branch. Peter said that the resurrected Christ is on the throne of David (Acts 2:29-36). He is king of the kingdom, ruling His Church from a heavenly perspective (Rev. 3:21). Jesus' oversight and instructions to the seven churches in Revelation 2–3 verifies this fact.

The prophet Ezekiel called the covenant of David an everlasting covenant of peace (Ezek. 37:24-26). Jesus, the seed of David, inaugurated the everlasting covenant (Heb. 13:20). Jesus' covenant was the covenant of peace (John 14:27; Acts 10:36; Eph. 2:14-17).

Arno Gaebelein says, "Messiah, the Christ was thus cut off and did not receive that Kingdom which is promised Him as the Son of David according to the flesh" (Gaebelein 1911, 154). Where in Scripture is it stated that Jesus did not receive the kingdom promised to Him? Where is the scriptural promise that Jesus would rule according to the flesh?

Jesus said He was from above and His kingdom was not of this world (John 18:36). Isn't that enough to tell us His own interpretation of His kingdom? It was predicted that Christ, who came in the flesh as the seed of David, would be resurrected to sit on David's throne (Ps. 132:11). This was fulfilled (Acts 2:30). After the resurrection, Christ had a glorified body, and in that state He sat on David's throne to rule. David, "foreseeing this, spoke concerning the resurrection of Christ" and that He would be seated at "the right hand of God" (Acts 2:31, 33).

According to the Old Testament prediction in Psalm 2, the "nations rage and the people plot a vain thing," in spite of which God will set up His king on the holy hill of Zion (vv. 2, 6). The New Testament fulfillment of this in Acts 4:25-28 affirms that God has set Jesus as His king on His holy hill of Zion, which Peter says is the Church. 1 Peter 2:6-8 states that Jesus, the chief cornerstone, was laid in Zion as the foundation stone. This also fulfills the prophecy of Isaiah 8:14, and 28:16 and Psalm 118:22.

Paul affirms that Jesus, the risen Christ, the root of Jesse, is presently ruling on the throne of David: "There shall be a root of Jesse; And He who shall rise to reign over the Gentiles, In Him the Gentiles shall hope" (Rom. 15:12). Paul quotes this as the fulfillment of Isaiah 11:1,10. On the other hand, dispensationalists say that Isaiah 11 is not yet fulfilled, but will be fulfilled at the millennium.

In speaking to the New Testament Church, Paul said Christ "gave Himself for us, that he might redeem us from every lawless deed and purify for Himself His own special people, zealous for good works" (Titus 2:14). Peter, likewise, speaking of the New Testament Church in 1 Peter 2:9, said, "You are a chosen generation, a royal priesthood, a holy nation, His own special people." Was this not foreshadowed in Deuteronomy 14:2? It was prophesied in the Old Testament that Gentiles would become the people of God (Hos. 1:10; 2:23, see also 1 Pet. 2:9-10). According to the New Testament, all Old Testament redemptive covenants pointed to Christ and were completely fulfilled in Him.

ALL OLD TESTAMENT REDEMPTIVE COVENANTS WERE TYPES OF AN EVERLASTING COVENANT TO COME

It is quite remarkable that all Old Testament redemptive covenants were types of an eternal covenant:

- Genesis 17:19: Abraham's covenant was a type of an *everlasting covenant.*
- Exodus 31:16: The covenant of law to Moses was a type of an *everlasting covenant.*
- Isaiah 55:3: The Davidic covenant was a type of an *everlasting covenant.*
- Jeremiah 31:31-34 and 32:40: God promised a New Covenant that would be the *everlasting* or eternal covenant.

Has the everlasting covenant of Jeremiah been inaugurated? This is a hotly debated subject, especially by dispensationalists who say this covenant has not yet come but will be made with Israel in the millennium.

DISPENSATIONAL AUTHORS ON THE JEREMIAH COVENANT

Clarence Larkin wrote, "This covenant has not yet been made. It is to be made with Israel after they get back to their own land. It is promised in Jer. 31:31-37. It is unconditional and will cover the Millennium and the New Heaven and New earth." (Larkin 1920, 51).

J. Dwight Pentecost, in his book *Things to Come,* says the following of the Jeremiah Covenant:

- "Its period of fulfillment is yet future" (Pentecost 1978, 118).
- "The covenant guarantees salvation to the nation Israel...this covenant was made with Israel the physical seed of Abraham according to the flesh, and with them alone" (119).
- "It must be viewed as yet future, for this covenant can not be realized by Israel until God has effected her salvation and restoration to the land" (120).

- "This covenant must follow the return of Christ at the second advent" (120).
- "This covenant will be realized in the millennial age" (121).
- "The covenant stands as yet unfulfilled and awaits a future literal fulfillment" (125).
- "The gospel is not a covenant, but the revelation of the salvation of God. It proclaims the great salvation. We enjoy indeed all the essential privileges of the New Covenant, its foundation being laid on God's part in the blood of Christ, but we do so in spirit, not according to the letter...In the New testament it has no reference whatever to the church in this age" (122).

Since when is the gospel not a covenant? The gospel of Christ is the fulfillment of the Abrahamic covenant, which Paul in Galatians 3:8 calls the gospel preached by God Himself. It is the gospel Paul proclaimed (Rom. 1:16; 4:1-4). In Acts 3:19-26, Peter says that it was the covenant that God made with Abraham. Christ Himself preached this gospel (Mark 1:14-15), and in Luke 22:20, He calls it His New Covenant: "This cup is the New Covenant in my blood, which is shed for you." Hebrews 13:20 confirms that Christ's blood is the blood of the everlasting covenant. What other covenant, then, was Christ's gospel?

Furthermore, Hebrews 8:7-13 and 10:15-18 verify that Christ is the fulfillment of the Jeremiah covenant. The problem with dispensationalism is that it circumvents the New Testament passages that declare the reality and fulfillment of the Old Testament and then puts those passages in the millennium. Covenants cannot be displaced by dispensations and still have the harmony of the ongoing redemptive work of God that culminates in Christ's New Covenant.

JEREMIAH'S NEW COVENANT

Dispensationalists claim that the covenant in Jeremiah 31:31-34 is for Israel only and that the Church has no part in it:

> Behold the days are coming says the Lord, when I will make a New Covenant with the house of Israel and with the house of Judah—not according to the covenant that I made with their fathers in the day that I took them by the hand to lead them out of the land of Egypt, My covenant which they broke, though I was a husband to them, says the Lord. But this is the covenant that I will make with the house of Israel after those days, says the Lord: I will put My law in their minds and write it on their hearts, and I will be their God, and they shall be My people. No more shall every man teach his neighbor, and every man his brother, saying, "know the Lord," for they all shall know me from the least of them to the greatest of them, says the Lord. For I will forgive their iniquity, and their sin I will remember no more.

Regarding the fulfillment of Jeremiah's covenant, J. Dwight Pentecost states that it is a covenant yet to be made with the nation of Israel in the millennial age (Pentecost 1978, 121). Pentecost continues by saying, "The covenant can only be fulfilled literally by those with whom it is made and, since the church is not Israel, the church can not fulfill that covenant... the covenant stands as yet unfulfilled and waits a future literal fulfillment" (Ibid., 123, 125).

As to the literalism of dispensationalism, it certainly falls apart in this prophecy. According to Jeremiah 31:32, was it God's *literal* hand or His *spiritual* hand that led Israel out of Egypt? Likewise, was God a *literal* husband or a *spiritual* husband to Israel? The answer is self-defining. Literalism can never be used as a true inclusive scriptural hermeneutic!

Pentecost further states, "The covenant guarantees salvation to the nation of Israel...this covenant was made with Israel the physical seed of Abraham according to the flesh, and with them alone" (Ibid., 119). However, the Bible never says that the salvation of the nation of Israel according to the flesh is guaranteed. Who is the true seed of Abraham according to Romans 9:6-8 when it says, "All Israel is not Israel and those who are children of the flesh, these are not the children of God?" Therefore, Abraham's seed according to the flesh are not the true Israel!

Pentecost also claims, "In the New Testament it [the Jeremiah covenant] has no reference whatever to the church in this age" (Ibid., 122). If this is true, why does Hebrews 8 and 10 quote and apply the Jeremiah covenant as fulfilled by Christ's New Covenant? Besides this, Hebrews 10:9 states that when Christ came, He took away the first covenant to establish the second. Therefore, the covenant that Israel was under was taken away by Christ when He made His New Covenant. Because Christ took away the first covenant, there have not been two covenants in operation at the same time.

Paul, a Jew who knew the covenants, was given a direct revelation from Christ (Gal. 1:11-12) that recognized only two covenants (Gal. 4:24). One was from Mount Sinai (the Old Covenant) that genders to bondage; the other was from Jerusalem, which is "above" and "the mother of us all" (v. 26).

Paul tells us plainly in 2 Corinthians 3:3-16 that the covenant of law written on tablets of stone has been taken away by coming to Christ (v. 16). In the same context, he says God has made him a "sufficient minister of the New Covenant" (v. 6). Hebrews 9:12 says that by this covenant, Christ purchased eternal redemption for us. If it is eternal, there never can be another form of redemption to come later for the Jews. This is the covenant under which the Church is operating, which dispensationalists deny.

If dispensationalism is correct in asserting that Christ did not fulfill the New Covenant of Jeremiah but took away the Old Covenant

(Heb. 10:9), then Israel has to wait until the millennium to be in a covenant relationship with God. What happens redemptively to Israel in the meantime? If the Jeremiah covenant does not apply to the Church (as Pentecost says), there is no salvation for Israel until the millennium. But if Christ did fulfill the New Covenant that Jeremiah spoke of when He came, and if He provided eternal redemption, there cannot be a separate form of salvation later for the nation of Israel. There is no other conclusion that can be reached. Besides, what does this do to the atonement that Christ purchased for all mankind?

WITH WHOM DID CHRIST MAKE HIS COVENANT?

Was it not Christ's New Covenant that He instituted with Israel? Were not His disciples all Israelites with whom He made His New Covenant? According to Galatians 3:7-29, are not all believers Abraham's seed and constitute the Israel of God (Gal. 6:16)? Peter calls Gentile believers "God's chosen [elect] people" (1 Pet. 2:9-10). Furthermore, why did Jesus choose twelve disciples if it were not to replace the twelve tribes of Israel? Why did He choose the Seventy unless He was replacing the Sanhedrin? Was not Jesus' cabinet all Israelites? How then can it be said that Christ did not make His covenant with Israel?

Concerning the Jeremiah covenant, J. Dwight Pentecost says, "If the church fulfills this covenant, she may also fulfill other covenants made with Israel and there is no need for an earthly Millennium" (Ibid., 116). In these statements, Pentecost apprehends the truth of the scriptures, but because of his stance on the millennium and literalism, he does not accept the New Testament interpretation and fulfillment of the Jeremiah covenant as found in Hebrews 8 and 10. Why does he accept Matthew 1:23 as the fulfillment of Isaiah 7:14 but not Hebrews 8 and 10 when the book of Hebrews uses the same principle of fulfillment concerning the Jeremiah covenant? As previously stated, can we expect a second fulfillment of Isaiah 7:14?

According to Galatians 6:15, the people of the New Covenant are "a new creation." In verse 16, this new creation is called "the Israel of God." This new creation cannot be different than the "new creation" of 2 Corinthians 5:17—that of born-again believers. The Bible never speaks of two new creations under the New Covenant.

Time-wise, Pentecost says of the Jeremiah covenant, "This covenant must follow the return of Christ at the second advent…This covenant will be realized in the millennial age" (Ibid., 120-121). As you may recall, Clarence Larkin wrote that this covenant has not yet been made. Of course, we can expect all dispensationalists to say the same thing.

However, the author of Hebrews declares that the Jeremiah covenant was fulfilled by Christ and applied to the Church. In fact, the exact words of Jeremiah are quoted by the author of Hebrews:

> But now he has obtained a more excellent ministry, inasmuch as he is also Mediator of a better covenant, which was established on better promises. For if the first covenant had been faultless, then no place would have been sought for a second. Because finding fault with them, he says: "Behold the days are coming, says the Lord, when I will make a New Covenant with the house of Israel and with the house of Judah—not according to the covenant that I made with their fathers in the day when I took them by the hand to lead them out of the land of Egypt because they did not continue in My covenant, and I disregarded them, says the Lord. For this is the covenant that I will make with the house of Israel after those days says the Lord: I will put My laws in their mind and write them on their hearts; and I will be their God, and they shall be My people. None of them shall teach his neighbor, and none his brother, saying, 'Know the Lord,' for all shall know Me, from the least of them to the greatest of them. For I will be merciful to their unrighteousness, and their sins and their lawless deeds I will remember no more." In that He says, "A new covenant," He has made the first obsolete. Now what is becoming obsolete and growing old is ready to vanish away.
>
> (Heb. 8:6-13)

In Hebrews 10, the author says, "'Behold I have come to do Your will, O God.' He takes away the first that He may establish the second" (Heb. 10:9).

Furthermore, Hebrews 10 argues that the Old Testament sacrifices were insufficient to purify the conscience and take away sins (Heb. 10:1-10). Hence, God sent a new sacrifice in the person of Christ to replace the Old Covenant and establish the New Covenant (Heb. 10:9-18). In verses 16-17, the author uses the verses from Jeremiah 31:31-34 as the basis for the prophetic fulfillment of Jeremiah's covenant by Christ and His New Covenant, to which, according to verse 15, the Holy Spirit bore witness.

"'This is the covenant that I will make with them after those days, says the Lord: I will put My laws into their hearts, and in their minds I will write them,' then He adds, 'Their sins and their lawless deeds I will remember no more'" (Heb. 10:16-17).

Pentecost says that the Jeremiah covenant has to be fulfilled literally by those with whom it was made; therefore, the Church cannot fulfill that covenant. To the contrary, the book of Hebrews declares the Jeremiah covenant was fulfilled by Christ, to which the Holy Spirit gave witness (Heb. 10:15). It would be heresy and a blatant denial of biblical inspiration to deny its fulfillment in the Church.

The dispensationalist position caused such a problem to practitioners that Lewis Sperry Chafer speaks of two New Covenants (Pentecost 1978, 124). Chafer must have seen in the book of Hebrews the answer to the problem, which is probably why he speaks of two New Covenants. However, would this not be adding to God's Word, which is taking the place of God Himself?

Alfred Edersheim, writing about a problem of biblical history, states the following:

> I have endeavored to discuss them as fully as the character of this work allowed. Whether or not I may always succeed in securing the conviction of my readers, I can at least say, that, while I have written what was not in accordance with my own conscientious conviction, *nor sought to invent an explanation merely in order to get rid of a difficulty,* my own reverent belief in the authority of the Word of God has not in any one case been the least shaken. (Edersheim undated, 4:vii, emphasis mine)

Pentecost saw the point of the fulfillment of the Jeremiah covenant when he said, "If the church fulfills this covenant, she may also fulfill other covenants made with Israel and there is no need for an earthly millennium" (Pentecost 1978, 116). This is a very gracious consent.

As mentioned previously, Abraham's covenant was a type of an "everlasting covenant" (Gen. 17:19); the law, as Moses' covenant, was a type of an "everlasting covenant" (Ex. 31:16); the Davidic covenant was called an "everlasting covenant" (Isa. 55:3); and Jeremiah's covenant, when instituted, is also called an everlasting covenant (Jer. 32:40). These covenants bespoke Christ's New Covenant as that everlasting covenant (Heb. 13:20), which was now fulfilled in the Church. Therefore, the Jeremiah covenant cannot be yet future in any sense of the word.

Pentecost says, "Amillenarians use the New Testament references to the New Covenant to prove that the church is fulfilling the Old Testament promises to Israel. Thus there would be no need for future earthly millennium inasmuch as the church is the kingdom" (Ibid., 119). How true! The best biblical hermeneutic is Old Testament biblical prophecy with New Testament fulfillment. This is the proper method of interpreting Scripture. George B. Fletcher, D.D., speaks to this fact when he says, "Whatever Christ taught by His Holy Spirit through the Apostles is final, authoritative, and infallible" (Fletcher 1971, 1).

Pentecost maintains that his reasons are incontrovertible. Have not the New Testament references proven that they are controvertible? Why try to argue away prophecy and fulfillment as stated in the Bible? Pentecost's argument is fallacious because, as in other like passages in which the New Testament becomes the fulfillment of Old Testament prophecies, he accepts prophecy with its fulfillment (e.g., Isa. 7:14, Matt. 1:23). Why does he not do the same here instead of trying to argue away that which the book of Hebrews states is the prophecy of Jeremiah fulfilled in Christ's New Covenant?

Pentecost also talks about the time of the fulfillment of the New Covenant: "It must be viewed as yet future, for this covenant can not be realized by Israel until God has effected her salvation and restoration to the land…This covenant must follow the return of Christ at the second advent" (Pentecost 1978, 120). In other words, Pentecost is saying that God has not yet effected the salvation of Israel, which can only happen at the return of Christ at the second advent. This is the same argument Scofield made in his comments on Zechariah 13:1, where he stated that the fountain open for sin and uncleanness has not yet come to pass for Israel but will at the second coming (Scofield 1945, 976). However, the Gospels and the entire book of Acts is based on the salvation that Christ provided for Israel "to the Jew first and then to the Gentile."

The following references state that the salvation Christ provided by His death on the cross was for Israel:

- Matthew 1:21: Jesus came to die for the sin of His people (the Jews) (cf. Luke 1:54-55, 68-70, 72-73, 77-79).

- John 1:11-13, 29: Jesus' death was for the sin of the world (Acts 2:14, 22, 38-41; 3:18-26). The blessing of Abraham is called "the turning of them away from their iniquities" (cf. Acts 4:1,11-12; 5:31; 13:23, 26, 38, 46).

How many scriptures do we need to prove that God in Christ has already provided salvation for Israel? Paul in Romans 3:24-26 declares that Christ died for the sins of Israel under the Old Covenant (see also Heb. 9:15). Therefore, it is a façade, a cover-up, to evade divine truth.

Edwin Prince Booth has this to say regarding the Jeremiah covenant:

> Of all Israel's prophetic interpreters the one who felt Yahweh's covenant bond with Israel most keenly and grasped it most profoundly was Jeremiah. Jeremiah looked forward still to a yet more adequate realization and expression of this covenant in a period which lay beyond his own day. In that New Covenant, which Yahweh would initiate there would be nothing of politics or of Jewish nationalism. Israelite laws, once essential to secure the faithfulness of the people of Yahweh, would no longer be necessary, for obedience to Yahweh's will would be spontaneous, instinctive and universally present in every Jewish heart (Jer. 7:23; 31:31-34). Then came Jesus, who stood in the full stream of covenant ideas, and whose very being is an incarnation of them. Jesus fastened upon Jeremiah's concept of the covenant, and linked it to himself with unique concreteness as "the New Covenant in my blood." By it he bound himself to the Christian community, the new Israel, and the Christian community to himself.
>
> (Booth 1942, 13)

In conclusion, biblically, the Jeremiah covenant has been fulfilled and ratified by the blood of Christ. If the Jews (Israel) are ever to be saved, they must come under Christ's New Covenant, for there is no salvation outside of that covenant (Acts 4:11-12).

THE RAPTURE OF THE CHURCH AND THE SECOND COMING OF CHRIST

In this chapter, I will seek to prove that the rapture (*parousia*) and the revelation (*apokalupsis*) of Christ's second coming are not two separate comings, but are one and the same event. First, in 1 Thessalonians 4:13-18, Paul states:

> But I do not want you to be ignorant brethren, concerning those who have fallen asleep, lest you sorrow as others who have no hope. For if we believe that Jesus died and rose again, even so God will bring with Him those who sleep in Jesus. For this we say to you by the word of the Lord, that we who are alive and remain until the coming of the Lord will by no means precede those who are asleep. For the Lord Himself will descend from heaven with a shout, with the voice of an archangel, and with the trumpet of God and the dead in Christ will rise first. Then we who are alive and remain shall be caught up together with them in the clouds to meet the Lord in the air. And thus we shall always be with the Lord. Therefore comfort one another with these words.

From this passage, dispensationalists teach that the Church (including the righteous dead) will be resurrected or taken out of the world in a secret rapture before the tribulation begins. To them, the wicked dead will not be resurrected until seven or 1007 years later. I believe this is an error in the use of Scripture.

In *The Approaching Advent of Christ,* Alexander Reese refers to the dispensational view of this passage and states, "The suggestion of Darby, backed by vigorous efforts of Kelly and others, to prove from this most magnificent passage in 1 Thess. 4 that a secret coming, a secret resurrection, and a secret rapture are portrayed, followed by the rise and reign of Antichrist, is among the sorriest in the whole history of freak exegesis" (Reese 1934, 146).

Jesus Himself stated that the righteous would be resurrected at "the last day," not seven or 1007 years after the last day (John 6:39, 40, 44-54; 11:24). Jesus also taught that judgment for all would occur "in the last day" (John 12:48). The coming of Christ in a secret rapture violates what these scriptures teach. Furthermore, Peter, Paul, and John all agree that both the righteous and the wicked will be judged at the same time, not seven or more years apart (Acts 10:42; 2 Tim. 4:1; 1 Pet. 4:5; Rev. 11:18). To say otherwise is to pervert these scriptures.

First Thessalonians 4:13-18 is Christ's coming (*parousia*) rapture of His church. The text states the following:

- The *Lord Himself* descends from heaven.
- It will be with *a shout.*
- It will be with the *voice of the archangel.*
- It will with the *trumpet of God.*
- The dead in *Christ will be resurrected.*
- Christ will bring *with Him* those who have died.
- Then all believers will be *caught up together with the Lord.*
- Christ will come *in the clouds.*

Dispensationalists claim 1 Thessalonians 4:13-18 teaches that a secret rapture will culminate the Church Age. Then there will be a seven-year tribulation period, which is postulated on the false premise of the postponement of the seventieth week of Daniel that is to take place after the Church has been raptured. However, there is nothing secret about anything in the text. One must ask, where in Scripture are these things implicitly stated?

In *A Theology of the New Testament,* George Eldon Ladd, referring to Walvoord's statements in his 1957 edition of *The Rapture Question,* states, "In fact, Walvoord goes so far as to admit that 'pretribulationism,' i.e. a coming of Christ before the great tribulation for the church, is not explicitly taught in Scripture" (Ladd 1974, 556). Ladd says this was deleted from his later printings.

As to Daniel's seventieth week, Daniel 9:26 states that the Messiah was to be cut off *after* the sixty-ninth week, which would be in the seventieth week. If God has postponed the seventieth week, then the Messiah was not yet cut off. On the other hand, if Scripture teaches that Christ has been cut off in Daniel's seventieth week and that the seventieth week has been fulfilled, then the dispensational position cannot be biblical.

In a May 1974 article in *Moody Monthly,* Dr. Earl D. Radmacher, president of the Western Theological Seminary in Portland, Oregon, says:

> The prophetic signs that precede the second coming of Christ to earth to set up his kingdom and the imminent, or any moment, return of Christ, *for* His raptured Church, Dispensational students of prophetic Scripture understand that these two events to be separate and distinct. The Second Advent is preceded by signs (cf. Mt.24:3) but the rapture of the Church is without any necessary signs and may, therefore, occur at any moment…No signs, as such were promised to notify the Church before He comes in the air and the "blitzkrieg" of tribulation begins. In this sense, then, we live in a "signless" age, that is a period of prophetic silence. The Church age is an unprophesied age, both with respect to Old Testament predictions and New Testament signs. The Church today is simply told to "wait for his Son from heaven."

In his book, *The Rapture Question,* John F. Walvoord states:

> The doctrine of the church has been rightly considered by theologians of all points of view as being an integral and important aspect of theology as a whole. Systems of theology can often be characterized by their ecclesiology. The premillennial system of interpretation has especially relied upon a proper understanding of the doctrine of the church as a body distinct from Israel and from saints in general. What is essential to premillennialism becomes an indispensable foundation in the study of pretribulationism. It is safe to say that pretribulationism depends upon a particular definition of the church, and any consideration of pretribulationism which does not take this major factor into consideration will be largely beside the point.

(Walvoord 1978, 19)

Walvoord continues, "If the term *church* includes saints of all ages, then it is self-evident that the church will go through the tribulation, as all agree that there will be saints in this time of trouble. If, however, the term *church* applies only to a certain body of saints, namely, the saints of this present dispensation, then the possibility of the translation of the church before the tribulation is possible and even probable. Decision therefore as to the exact nature of the church, is prerequisite to the discussion which follows" (Ibid.)

Is this not an admission by dispensationalists that without their particular man-made definition of the Church (which is outside of biblical bounds), there would be no secret rapture or seven-year tribulation period? To them, because the Bible does not affirm their definition of the Church, it has to be out of harmony with biblical truth.

Dispensationalists teach that the Church is Christ's Body and does not include Israel from the Old Testament, as they were not a part of Christ's Body. Therefore, the Old Testament saints will not be caught up in the rapture. Is this biblically true? To the contrary, in Ephesians 3:6, Paul states that the saved Gentiles will become fellow heirs of the *same Body* as Old Testament Israel. Therefore, the elect of Israel were also called a Body: "The Gentiles should be fellow heirs, of the *same body*, and partakers of His promise in Christ through the gospel." Jesus stated the same in Matthew 8:11: "And I say to you that many will come from east and west, and sit down with Abraham, Isaac, and Jacob in the kingdom of heaven." This means the dispensational view is unscriptural and therefore invalid.

The question is: Where in the Bible are either of these positions found in the text; that is, the *rapture* being a separate event from the second coming of Christ? Exegetically, these positions are not there. They are theories superimposed upon the text and unsupported by scripture. In fact, they are part of the dispensational scheme of interpreting the Bible.

This scheme officially came into existence about 1830 when it was introduced into Christianity by the Plymouth Brethren movement, a new doctrine that represented claims that had not been stated by the Church in the previous seventeen centuries. John Nelson Darby was its promoter. He introduced the idea of a "secret rapture" in 1883 at a Powerscourt session. Then in 1908, C. I. Scofield put this theology into his Bible notes, which served to promote the dispensational ideals. Scofield was the first to put it into print as a way of interpreting the Bible. W. E. Blackstone also wrote a book called *Jesus Is Coming* in which he further promoted the system. It is said, however, that before his death, Blackstone recanted this position.

Concerning the *Scofield Reference Bible*, E. Schuyler English wrote, "Most theologians credit J. N. Darby, a Plymouth Brethren scholar, with the first systematizing dispensational theology in the middle of the 19th century. But the work of Darby, humanly speaking, would have been lost or forgotten had it not been for a lawyer-turned-preacher: C. I. Scofield. In 1908, the first edition of his now famous *Scofield Reference Bible* was published" (*Christian Life Magazine,* September 1956).

Is Mr. English not saying that Darby was the originator of this theory as we have it today, but that it would have been lost were it not for C. I. Scofield? By saying that this doctrine would not have been known today had the *Scofield Reference Bible* notes not been written, English basically assures us of its recent origin in the history of the Church.

Tregelles, a Greek scholar and a member of the Plymouth Brethren in those days, says the idea of a secret rapture at a second coming of Christ had its origin in an utterance in Edward Irving's church, and this was taken to be the voice of the Spirit. Tregelles continued, "It was from that supposed revelation that the modern doctrine and the modern phraseology respecting it arose. It came not from the Holy Scriptures, but from that which falsely pretended to be the Spirit of God" (G. Eldon Ladd 1864, 41).

In 1842, B. W. Newton of Plymouth published a book entitled *Thoughts on the Apocalypse* in which he taught the traditional view that the Church would go through the tribulation. H. A. Ironside said that Newton considered Mr. Darby's dispensational teaching as the height of speculative nonsense. (G. Eldon Ladd 1864, 41).

Before proceeding further, let us present a diagram of the dispensational view of the rapture and the tribulation period.

THE DISPENSATIONAL POSITION				
• Christ's appearing in the air • Called the rapture or parousia • Christ coming FOR His saints			• Second coming of Christ • Called the revelation, apokalupse • Christ coming WITH His saints	
Church Age	**Seals**	**Trumpets**	**Vials – Bowls**	**Millennium**
	This time frame is supposed to be Daniel's seventieth week. It is also supposed to be Revelation 6–19. They call this period of time "the day of the Lord." Known as the seven-year tribulation period. When the seals, trumpets, and vials are poured out. When the Bridegroom comes for the bride. When Christ comes as a thief in the night. Supposed to be the time of Jacob's troubles, Jer. 30:7. Begins with the resurrection of believers who had died.			
A RESURRECTION				

Does the dispensational chart above not demonstrate that the dispensational position also predates the second coming of Christ? Dispensationalists set the second coming seven years after the so-called rapture, yet Jesus says that no man knows the day or the hour of His coming (Matthew 24:36).

As to whether the rapture is pre-, mid-, or post-tribulation, those who believe either position must prove by direct and explicit Scripture that there will be a seven-year tribulation period. As to Daniel's seventieth week, if the Bible teaches that the seventieth week is already fulfilled, there can be no basis whatever for a seven year tribulation—period!

In *The Rapture Question,* Walvoord starts his thesis on the rapture by stating that those who do not believe his position on the rapture are "liberals and neo-orthodox and that they contribute nothing to the rapture question" (Walvoord 1978, 8). He continues, "The liberals, who deny the scriptures by their premises are insulated from any real understanding of the doctrinal problems which relate to the rapture" (Ibid.).

Certainly, there are doctrinal problems with the rapture, and the students who read Walvoord for the first time will gather from it that he considers those not in his camp as liberals and neo-orthodox. In other words, a person is to read the Bible through Walvoord's glasses, or they fall under one of these labels. What a great way to turn off your students from any questions about the rapture! While we do not agree with all that Keirkegaard says, one thing he states is certainly true: "When you label me you negate me." Many a good theologian has been negated by such labeling. This means that we are not to question the rapture theory, or we will be labeled.

Walvoord continues, "It is as impossible to discuss the questions pertinent to the time of the rapture without *assuming* the authority of the Scripture as it is to solve a problem in mathematics without accepting the normal meaning of numbers. *With these proper assumptions*, however, the Scriptural revelation casts a broad shaft of light on the entire problem of the rapture" (Ibid, p. 8, emphasis mine).

It is not the normal meaning of numbers or the authority of Scripture that is at stake but the *assumptions* these dispensationalists have made in order to prove their point. One of their *assumptions* is transferring patterns of time stated in one period and then, without scriptural warrant, transferring them to another period of time to which the scriptures do not speak. By this, I mean the canceling out of Daniel's seventieth week from its immediate-following sixty-ninth week, as the sixty-ninth week so followed the sixty-eighth week. By this *assumption* dispensationalists produce a seven-year tribulation period beginning with a secret rapture of the Church.

Because Daniel's seventieth week has been biblically and historically fulfilled, there can be no seven-year period of tribulation to come. This, then, automatically eliminates a secret pre-tribulation rapture. On the other hand, the scriptures that dispensationalists apply to the secret rapture really belong to the second coming. This means that Christ will come back only once instead of twice, as the dispensationalists teach.

EVENTS DISPENSATIONALISTS TEACH ARE SUPPOSED TO HAPPEN AT THE TIME OF THE RAPTURE

Dispensationalists teach that the rapture is Christ coming *for* His saints at the beginning of the tribulation, as opposed to His coming *with* them seven years later. However, 1 Thessalonians 4:14 states that at the time Christ comes *for* His saints, He will bring *with* Him those who sleep. Additionally, 1 Thessalonians 3:13 states that when He comes in the rapture (*parousia*), He will come *with* all His saints. Since this happens at the rapture, it cannot happen seven years later at the revelation of Christ. This destroys the theory of the two future comings of Christ.

Dispensationalists also teach that the rapture is the resurrection of all dead believers in Christ (1 Thess. 4:16). This is the same time when all believers will be changed in a moment in a twinkling of an eye at the last trumpet (1 Cor. 15:51-55). It is the same event as John records in Revelation 11:15-19, which is the last trumpet when Christ comes to reign eternally. However, Jesus said believers would be resurrected at the last day (John 6:39-40, 44-54), not seven years later.

Furthermore, dispensationalists claim that at the rapture (*parousia*) believers will be caught up in the clouds to meet Jesus in the air (1 Thess. 4:17; Matt. 24:29-30). The rapture is the Bridegroom coming for His Bride, the Church (Matt. 25:1-13; Luke 13:25). When this takes place, the door of salvation will be closed and no one will get in (Rev. 22:11-12). There can be no salvation after Jesus comes, period. The rapture is Christ coming as a thief in the night (Matt. 24:42-43) and is supposed to be Christ's coming before the tribulation.

But consider these questions about the 1 Thessalonians 4:13-18 text:

- Does 1 Thessalonians 4:13-18 teach a secret rapture of the Church?
- Does it teach a secret coming of Christ?
- Does it teach that the Church will be taken prior to a tribulation?
- When does the text say this event will take place?
- Is the rapture "Jesus coming as a thief in the night"?
- Is this the same as the Bridegroom coming for the Bride?
- Has something been read into the text that is not there?

So, what does the Bible say will happen when Jesus comes "as a thief in the night"?

- Christ will come *with* His saints (1 Thess. 3:13).
- It is called the "day of the Lord" (1 Thess. 5:2).

- In 1 Thessalonians 5:2, Paul uses "day of the Lord" to refer to the second coming of Christ (when he will come as a "thief").
- In 2 Thessalonians 2:1-2, Paul says the "day of the Lord" is the same as Christ's coming (*parousia*), or rapture.
- Likewise, Peter uses "day of the Lord" when he refers to Christ's coming as a "thief" at the end of the age, when all elements shall melt with fervent heat and burn up and when the new heaven and the new earth will be ushered in creating eternity (2 Pet. 3:10). How then can this occur at the beginning of the tribulation?
- It is called the *parousia* and the "day of the Lord" in 2 Thessalonians 2:1-2.

Note that in 2 Peter 3:10, Christ's coming as a *thief* is called the "day of the Lord." In 2 Peter 3:4, this coming of Christ is called the *parousia* or rapture. In 3:7, it is the day of judgment and perdition of ungodly men. In 3:10-11, it is when the earth and heavens are dissolved. In 3:12, it is called the coming of the day of God. In 3:13, it is when we look for and enter the new heavens and a new earth. Also, consider that according to 2 Peter 3:10, Christ comes as a thief. How can there be a tribulation and a millennium after the present heavens and earth are dissolved?

Concerning Peter and the rapture, Hal Lindsey says, "The Apostle Peter lived in the first century and faithfully looked for the possibility of the Rapture occurring in his time." (Lindsey 1976, 184-185). Lindsey then quotes 1 Peter 4:7-11 as his proof. Lindsey continues, "Peter knew the prophecies concerning the Rapture, but even this great apostle didn't have the insight into prophecy that the diligent believer can have today through the Holy Spirit."

Where in 1 Peter 4:7-11 does Peter imply a rapture in his time? Rather, he states just the opposite in 2 Peter 3:10-13. Did Peter reverse himself in his own writings? Was the Holy Spirit fallible when He inspired Peter to write? Is Hal Lindsey saying that he has an infallible inspiration and Peter did not? Better read 2 Peter 3:16!

In Revelation 16:15, Jesus says, "Behold I am coming as a thief." He says this during the sixth vial, which is supposed to occur near the end of the tribulation. Jesus is saying that He has not yet come as a thief! Yet dispensationalists claim Christ's coming as a thief was to take place at the beginning of the tribulation period. This is also opposite to what Christ stated in Matthew 24:29. This surely makes the Bible contradict itself.

All of these references bespeak a resurrection. First Corinthians 15:54-55 states that at the resurrection, death will have ended. It will be swallowed up by victory and after this, no one will die. Yet dispensationalists have people dying during both the tribulation and the millennium. Who is right, the Bible or dispensationalists?

Matthew 24:29-31 asserts that Christ's coming will occur immediately after the tribulation, and then the sign of the son of man will appear. All will see Him, and the tribes will mourn (Rev. 1:7; Zech. 12:10-14). Then they will see the son of man coming in clouds of heaven with power and great glory. Angels will sound a great trumpet and gather together God's elect from one end of heaven to another. There is nothing secret about this event.

These scriptures speak of the rapture (*parousia*), or the second coming of Christ, as one and the same event. They therefore prove that the rapture, as such, cannot be a secret coming of Christ. None of these references teach that there will be a secret coming of Christ to gather His elect, but rather that it will be visible, with the sound of a trumpet and the voice of an archangel. Every eye shall see Him and all the tribes of the earth will mourn because of Him.

The dispensationalists say that the rapture (*parousia*) is Christ coming *for* His saints at the beginning of the tribulation, and then coming *with* them seven years later during the revelation [*apokalupsis*]. None of this is found in the texts—it is something that has been added by dispensationalists. God warns us not to add to His Word. (See Appendix A: You Shall Not Add to the Word of God.) In Matthew 15:6, Jesus said we make the Word of God of non-effect by adding to it. Jesus also said it would be His Word that would judge us in the last day (John 12:48). How carefully then should we handle God's Word lest we be judged!

In his book *The Blessed Hope*, George Eldon Ladd says this about the rapture (or the *parousia*) of Christ:

> The parousia will be a glorious event. Christ will destroy the Man of Lawlessness by the breath of his mouth and "by the manifestation (literally, "epiphany" or "outshining") of his parousia" (2 Thess. 2:8). The rendition of the King James version is not wrong: "by the brightness of the coming." This epiphany will be a glorious event for Paul speaks of "the epiphany of the glory of our great God and our Saviour" (Titus 2:13).... We find the same teaching of a glorious visible parousia in Jesus'

words. "For as the lightning comes forth from the east, and is seen even unto the west; so shall be the parousia of the Son of man" (Matt. 24:27). It will be like a bolt of lightning, glorious, visible, evident to all.

(Ladd 1956, 63-64)

Alexander Reese, a premillennialist, has this to say about the new theory of a secret rapture:

It is a sentimental delusion that a secret Rapture, or a pre-tribulation Rapture, is the hope of the Church. Scripture, on the contrary, asserts in the clearest manner that the Glorious Appearing of Christ is the definite hope of Christians (Tit. 2:13) and with the terrible inconvenience of theorists, locates it at the Day of the Lord. From Matthew to the Book of Revelation the Lord and His Apostles set no other hope before the Church. The Rapture is a mere incident of the Appearing, spoken of in order to show the relation of sleeping to the living saints at the one Advent in glory, and especially that the saints who survive till the Advent will have no advantage at all over the dead in Christ. It is a stupid obsession to make the Rapture the touchstone of everything. Yet this is what is universally done.

(Reese 1934, 266)

Reese says both Sir Robert Anderson and R. A. Torrey gave up the secret rapture idea (Ibid., 27, 148).

WHAT DOES 1 CORINTHIANS 15:51-52 TELL US?

In 1 Corinthians 15:51-52, Paul states, "Behold, I tell you a mystery; we shall not all sleep, but we shall all be changed in a moment, in the twinkling of an eye, at the last trumpet. For the trumpet will sound, and the dead will be raised incorruptible, and we shall be changed."

What the text is saying is that a change will take place in the body of the living believer, which is a mystery. This change will take place in the living believer at the "last trumpet," which will occur at the resurrection, as the dead will be raised incorruptible. At the resurrection, death will cease to exist (1 Cor. 15:55). After this, there will be no need for another resurrection, as no one will die after the last trumpet. According to 1 Corinthians 15:26, death will be the *last enemy* to be destroyed.

There can be no doubt that in 1 Thessalonians 4:13-18 a resurrection takes place. This makes these two passages, 1 Thess. 4:13-18 and 1 Cor. 15:51-55, the same event, as the Bible does not speak of the living believers being changed in a moment in the twinkling of an eye at two different occasions.

First Corinthians 15:54-55 states that at the resurrection, death will come to an end, for it will be swallowed up by victory. After this, no one will die. Yet dispensationalists have people dying during both the tribulation and the millennium. Who is right, the Bible or dispensationalism?

Revelation 11:15-19 is the sounding of the seventh and last trumpet, which corresponds to 1 Corinthians 15:51-55, when believers at the last trumpet are changed in a moment in the twinkling of an eye. Revelation 11:15 states that at that time, Christ will come to reign eternally, not just for a thousand years. Revelation 11:18 also states that at the same time, the dead shall be judged and the saints of God rewarded. These references, then, have to be one and the same event. According to Revelation 10:5-7, the consummation of all things will come to pass at the sounding of the seventh and last trumpet, as time will be no longer. This is in harmony with 1 Corinthians 15:51-55.

SYNONYMOUS THINGS THAT TAKE PLACE AT CHRIST'S PAROUSIA	
Clouds	Matt. 24:30; Matt. 26:64; Mark 13:26; Mark 14:62; Acts 1:9; 1 Thess. 4:17; Rev. 1:7; Rev. 14:14
Trumpet	Matt. 24:31; 1 Cor.15:52; Rev. 11:15; 1 Thess. 4:16
Angels	Matt. 13:39, 41, 49; Matt. 16:27; Matt. 24:31; Mark 8:38; Mark 13:27; Luke 9:26; 1 Thess. 4:16; 2 Thess.1:7
Loud Noise	Matt. 24:31; 1 Thess. 4:16; 2 Pet. 3:10
Thief	1 Thess. 5:2, 4; Matt 24:43; Luke 12:39; 2 Pet. 3:10; Rev. 3:3; Rev. 16:15
Day of the Lord	Amos 5:18; Isa. 2:12; 1 Thess. 5:2; 2 Pet. 3:10–13
Resurrection	1 Thess. 4:16; John 6:39, 40, 44, 54; 11:24; Matt. 24:31; 1 Cor. 15:51, 52, 54, 55; Isa. 25:8; Job 14:12, 14; 19:25–27; Hos. 13:14

All these events take place at the second coming of Christ, not at a secret rapture seven years before the second coming. It must be stated that I believe we will be caught up, but that it will occur when Jesus comes back during the second advent.

THE BIBLE AND DANIEL'S SEVENTIETH WEEK, THE TRIBULATION PERIOD

Dispensationalists tell us Daniel's seventieth week has been postponed and will become the tribulation period. Where in Scripture is this specifically stated or even implied? It is not found in the Bible. If the Bible teaches that Daniel's seventieth week is already fulfilled, then the dispensational position cannot be held as biblically tenable. Yet dispensational *futurism* is built around the postponement of Daniel's seventieth week.

If Daniel's seventieth week were postponed, it would mean that the Messiah has not yet been cut off. But Daniel says that the Messiah was to be cut off after the seven weeks and the sixty-two-week period of time, which together make up sixty-nine weeks. It is after this time that the Messiah was to be cut off (Dan. 9:26). This would mean that the Messiah had to be cut off during the seventieth week. Since this does not fit the dispensational scheme, they postponed the seventieth week without biblical warrant until after the Church Age. This is to become the tribulation period.

In his book *God's Plan of the Ages,* Talbot says that the crucifixion was at the end of the sixty-ninth week (Talbot 1946, 155), whereas Daniel 9:26 states that the Messiah would be cut off *after* the sixty-nine weeks, which would be in the seventieth week. This, is a direct violation of what Daniel 9:26 says. It seems dispensationalists do not care how they handle or violate God's Word to make their system work.

Dispensationalists also tell us that because the week has been postponed, Daniel 9:24 is still unfulfilled, but that it will be fulfilled by Christ in the millennium. This is dangerous, because it takes away what Christ the Messiah has already accomplished by His death on the cross. "Seventy weeks are determined for your people and for your holy city to finish the transgression, to make an end of sins, to make reconciliation for iniquity, to bring in everlasting righteousness, to seal up vision and prophecy, and to anoint the Most Holy" (Dan. 9:24). This Christ did!

The fulfillment of Daniel 9:24 by Christ is seen in the following references:

- Isaiah 53:5, 8; Hebrews 9:15: Christ has already taken care of transgression.
- Hebrews 9:26: Christ has already made an end of sins.
- Hebrews 10:18: Christ's sacrifice was sufficient, and there will never be another sacrifice for sin.
- 2 Corinthians 5:19: Christ already has made reconciliation for iniquity.
- 2 Corinthians 5:21: Christ already has brought in everlasting righteousness.
- 1 Corinthians 1:30; Jeremiah 23:5-6: Christ is our righteousness. There is no greater righteousness to come than the righteousness of God given us in Christ.

Based on these scriptures, Daniel 9:24 cannot be in the future. This prophecy has been fulfilled.

Harold J. Ockenga has this to say on Daniel 9:24: "Daniel is definite concerning the work of Christ in His first coming by saying, 'to finish transgression, and to make an end of sins, and to make reconciliation for iniquity, and to bring in everlasting righteousness, and to seal up the vision and prophecy, and to anoint the most Holy.' This is what Christ did when He came the first time" (Ockenga 1956, 174-175).

CONCERNING THE WRATH OF GOD

It has been stated that the Church, God's people, must be taken out to escape the wrath of God during the tribulation. But where in the Bible does it state that wrath from God will be poured out on His people? This theory is a fabrication that is not found in Scripture. The text that dispensationalists have used to support this claim has been taken out of context and puts fear into God's people. A text taken out of context is a pre-text.

We are told that this wrath is the wrath of God that is poured out in Revelation 6–19 under the seals, trumpets, and vials. This period of time is also supposed to be Daniel's seventieth week, which dispensationalists have postponed and made to be the tribulation period after the Church has been raptured. However, as we have seen, Daniel's seventieth week was fulfilled in chronological sequence relative to that of the sixty-nine weeks.

The text that dispensationalists use for this wrath is 1 Thessalonians 5:9. Read in context with verses 9-11, this passage states, "For God did not appoint us to wrath, but to obtain *salvation* through our Lord Jesus Christ, who *died* for us, that whether we wake or sleep, we should live together with Him. Therefore comfort each other and edify one another, just as you also are doing" (emphasis mine).

Does this not tell us that the wrath we are delivered from is the wrath that rests on sin and the unrepentant? This wrath has been removed by salvation through Christ's death on the cross and therefore has nothing to do with tribulation wrath. The Thessalonians were to comfort one another personally with these words. Since the text was applicable to the Thessalonians during their time, how can it be said to apply to a tribulation wrath that would occur thousands of years later?

The Bible teaches that the gospel includes the wrath of God. John the Baptist, in his message to repent, warned of the wrath to come (Matt. 3:7). The Pharisees and Sadducees who came to him were asked, "Who warned you to flee from the wrath to come?" Because the "wrath" applied to them at that time due to their lack of repentance, it could not be tribulation wrath.

In Romans 1:16-18, Paul affirms that the gospel includes the wrath of God. Paul states that the gospel of which he is not ashamed includes salvation, the righteousness of God, and the wrath of God. Verse 18 states: "For the wrath of God is revealed from heaven against all ungodliness and unrighteousness of men, who suppress the truth in unrighteousness." Romans 5:9 likewise states the same truth: "Much more then, having now been justified by His blood, we shall be saved from wrath through Him."

The blood of Christ has released the believer from the wrath of God upon sin. John 3 also confirms this position. In verses 3-5, Jesus was talking to Nicodemus about being born again. In verses 14-18, Christ is depicted as being lifted up on the cross, bearing the sins of mankind and giving eternal life to those who believe on Him. Verses 19-20 state that those who do not come to Christ, who is the light, are still under the condemnation and wrath of sin. John 3:36 succinctly verifies the preceding: "He who believes in the Son has everlasting life; and he who does not believe the Son shall not see life, but the *wrath* of God abides on him" (emphasis mine).

In conclusion, the wrath depicted in 1 Thessalonians 5:9 is not tribulation wrath but God's judgment of wrath on the unrepentant during the Day of Judgment. Therefore, dispensationalists take the text out of context. There is no compilation of Scripture that can prove their point in question.

The Bible teaches that Daniel's seventieth week began with the ministry of Christ and John the Baptist. John in his baptizing revealed Christ as the Messiah to Israel (John 1:31). Jesus said the law and the prophets were until John (Matt. 11:12-13; Luke 16:16). What does this tell us? It certainly states that the Old Covenant ended with John the Baptist's ministry.

CHRIST IS THE COVENANT MAKER OF DANIEL 9

Daniel 9:27 states, "Then he shall confirm a covenant with many for one week." Isaiah 42:6 states that Christ was given as a covenant to the people (Isaiah 49:6-8 says the same thing). Matthew 4:15-16 confirms that Isaiah 49:6 has been fulfilled. Likewise, Isaiah 49:8 is confirmed as being fulfilled in 2 Corinthians 6:2, where it is applied to New Covenant ministry. Jesus said He inaugurated the New Covenant (Luke 22:14-20).

Malachi 3:1 states that at that time Christ's forerunner would be sent, "The Lord whom you seek, will suddenly come to His temple even the Messenger of the covenant." This Jesus did. There is not one verse in the Bible stating that the antichrist will make a covenant.

Luke 3:23 states that Christ was thirty years old when He began His public ministry. This is an affirmation of Numbers 4:3. By all accounts, Christ's ministry lasted for a period of three and half years. He was then crucified. This brings us to the middle of the seventieth week, which is prophetically confirmed by Zechariah 11:4-14:

- The Messiah was to come as a shepherd (Zech. 11:4-9). This Christ did. He was the Good Shepherd of John 10 and the fulfillment of Genesis 49:24.
- Zechariah 11:7 says the Good Shepherd will come with two staffs, one called "beauty" (grace) and the other "bonds" (unity), in order to unite the broken unity between Judah and Israel. John 1:17 states, "For the law was given through Moses, but grace and truth came through Jesus Christ."

- The Good Shepherd was not accepted by His own people. In Zechariah 11:8 we read, "My soul loathed them, and their soul also abhorred me." John 1:11 says, "He came to His own and His own received Him not."

CHRIST IS THE COVENANT BREAKER

Zechariah 11:10 states that when the Messiah was rejected, He broke the shepherds' staff "that I might break the covenant which I had made with all the peoples." It is right here that dispensationalists tell us the antichrist makes and breaks the covenant. There is no place in the Scripture that even hints at the antichrist making and breaking a covenant. It is all added to make up a good story. It is Christ who made the covenant, and the Scripture states that He broke the covenant.

When was this covenant broken? It was broken when Christ was crucified. Zechariah 11:12 reads, "Then I said to them, 'If it is agreeable to you, give me my wages; and if not refrain.' So they weighed out for my wages thirty pieces of silver." Matthew 26:15; 27:3 affirms that this was fulfilled in Jesus Christ at the crucifixion, whereas Talbot said Christ was crucified at the end of the sixty-ninth week (Talbot 1946, 156). Who is telling us the truth?

The covenant was broken in the middle of the week, three and a half years after Christ began His public ministry. This is the fulfillment of Daniel 9:27, which states that a covenant was confirmed for one week and in the middle of the week the prophecy also states that He would cause sacrifice and offering to cease. Since Calvary, the sacrifice of His Son, God refused all Old Testament sacrifices and offerings. He caused them to cease in His sight. Antichrist could never do this. How unscriptural can a doctrine get? Dispensational eschatology hinges on the idea that the antichrist will do something Christ the Messiah has already done and alone could only do. This is not a supposition; it is solely based on Old Testament prophecy and New Testament fulfillment.

CONCLUSION AND ANALYSIS OF THE DANIEL'S SEVENTIETH WEEK

Because the Bible affirms these truths, there is no room for an antichrist or a tribulation to come after the *parousia* of Christ. The dramatic composition of an antichrist to come and fulfill Daniel's seventieth week is an improbable plot. It has turned into a moneymaking scheme on behalf of those who are supposedly "left behind" to go through the great tribulation. I recently read an article from the *Los Angeles Times* by Neal Gabler with the headline, "Why Let Truth Get in the Way of a Good Story?" Dispensationalism has a good story, but the Bible has the truth.

The Bible teaches that the first half of Daniel's seventieth week was fulfilled at the middle of the week at the time of the cross. This proves that Christ is both the covenant maker and the covenant breaker, which destroys the theory that the antichrist will ever make or break a covenant with the Jews. This also eliminates the theory of a secret rapture at the beginning of that week, because the week has already been fulfilled. What is going to happen to all the charts that have been made on the subject? It is peculiar that the adherents of this system seem to speak with an air of authority as if by divine inspiration, though there is no biblical truth in it

But someone may ask the question, "How about the last half of Daniel's seventieth week?" Is it not reasonable to believe that if the first half of the seventieth week followed the sixty-ninth week, the last half would also follow the first half? To say otherwise is to go beyond what is written (1 Cor. 4:6). Daniel 9:24 states that seventy weeks are determined upon "your people." Daniel's people were the Jews. The crucifixion of Christ on the cross was the fulfillment of the first half of the week. After this, there was something yet to take place among Daniel's people that would forever close out the nation of Israel from being God's chosen people and sole heirs of the covenant that they broke.

Chronologically, history tells us that it was about three and a half years after Calvary that Stephen's message in Acts 7 and Saul's persecution and conversion in Acts 9 took place. The Jews rejected Stephen's message because they were stiff-necked and uncircumcised in heart and ears. They resisted the Holy Spirit speaking through him concerning their own history (Acts 7:51-60). What is the impetus here? The Jews killed God's messenger who told them the truth.

After his conversion, Paul, who was present and heard Stephen's message, put this same truth in similar terms. He picks up his message in Acts 13 from Stephen's message in Acts 7. Paul, preaching to the Jews of his day, gave them their history as was written in the Old Testament. The prophetic Messiah had come and fulfilled the covenant of David that was promised to Israel (Acts 13:32, 37). However, Israel did not recognize Christ to be their Messiah (vv. 27-41), so they had Pilate put Him on the cross and kill Him. But God raised Him from the dead to grant the forgiveness of sins.

Verses 45-46 tells us the Jews judged themselves unworthy of eternal life, so now the message was to go to the Gentiles. In 1 Thessalonians 2:14-16, Paul, writing of the Jews, said, "Forbidding us to speak to the Gentiles that they may be saved, so as always to fill up the measure of their sins; but wrath has come upon them to the uttermost." Jesus had already said to the Jews in Matthew 23:32, "Fill up then the measure of your fathers' guilt."

Thus ends the seventieth week, with the official rejection of the gospel of Christ by the Jews. God had opened the door so the Gentiles could now also become His people. The Church was now God's holy nation, a kingly priesthood, and 1 Peter 2:9 and Matthew 21:43 were now affirmed. The kingdom was taken from Israel and given to the Church (1 Pet. 2:4-10). The Church would now be the Israel of God (Gal. 6:15-16). The Bible is simple on this point. Why make it complex?

The rapture, or the catching up of God's people to be with Christ in the air, does not happen seven years *before* the second coming, but takes place *at* the second coming. This is because Daniel's seventieth week has been fulfilled and is now in the past. Because of this, there is no such thing as a secret rapture that will occur seven years before the second coming. This also means that the *parousia* and the apocalypse of Christ are one and the same event and are not divided by a seven-year period of time.

The resurrection will also take place at this time. When did Jesus say the dead believers would be resurrected (John 6:39-40, 44, 54)? Why four times in one chapter did Jesus say, "I will raise them up in the last day"? In John 11:24, who taught Martha and where did she learn to say her brother would be resurrected on "the last day," not seven years before the last day?

The Bible then eliminates the possibility that a resurrection occurs seven years before Christ comes in glory. It also eliminates the seven-year tribulation period as being the seventieth week of Daniel because it has already been fulfilled. Needless to say, the Church will go through tribulation until Jesus comes.

An article that appeared in the *Christian Beacon* gives us some insight into the problems of the doctrine of a pre-tribulation rapture. It is entitled "Prepare for the Rapture?"

> The two-thousand-member First Assembly of God congregation in North Hollywood, Calif., believing that the Rapture of the saints into heaven may be very soon, have changed the church's by-laws to provide continued leadership if its officers are suddenly taken to heaven. This was reported by the Rev. D. Leroy Sanders, the congregation's pastor.
>
> Mr. Sanders noted: "The blessed hope…clearly speaks of an instantaneous and general translation of the Assembly members. All pastors, deacons, elders, and other…church leaders and officers are expected to be caught up alive in a moment of time, thus depriving the church of duly constituted legal representation. In such an event the remaining members…shall meet in an emergency church council the following Sunday morning at eleven o'clock and elect…a temporary chairman." Mr. Sanders said the chairman was empowered to call for a new church council to oversee operations of the $1.5 million property.
>
> This post-rapture church, run by infidels who remain on earth, can only do the bidding of the forces of evil. The Hollywood church must fervently work today to get its own members converted to Christ and prepare them for the Rapture.

WHO IS LEFT BEHIND AND WHO IS TAKEN?

How about the "left behind" theory that dispensationalists claim based on Matthew 24:40-41? The one who is left behind is supposed to go through the tribulation. Doesn't that prove that there is a tribulation? The question is, where in the Bible is such a seven-year tribulation explicitly taught? It simply is not found in the Word of God. It is a man-made theory based on an assumption.

The next question is, who will be taken and who will be left behind? Does the text in Matthew 24:40-41 tell us who will be taken and who will be left behind? If it does not, who are we to add to the Scripture to make up our own answer? Why not let the Scripture speak for itself?

In Luke 17:34-37, Jesus was talking about the same event as spoken of in Matthew:

I tell you, in that night there will be two men in one bed: the one will be taken and the other left. Two women will be grinding together: the one will be taken and the other left. Two men will be in the field: the one will be taken and the other left. And they answered and said to Him, "Where, Lord?" So He said to them, "Wherever the body is, there the eagles will be gathered together."

Note in verse 37 that the disciples are in a quandary as to where the one taken will be taken to. Jesus gives the answer: "Where the body is there the eagles will be gathered together." What is this a picture of? It certainly is not a picture of heaven. It is that of a battlefield where the dead bodies are left for the vultures to eat. Does this sound like the one taken is taken to heaven? Other scriptural references that speak to the point include Jeremiah 7:33, which says, "The corpses of this people will be food for the birds of the heaven and for the beasts of the earth. And no one will frighten then away" (cf. Ezek. 39:17-20; Rev. 19:17-18). This gives a vivid description of the place where the ones taken are taken to. Therefore, the one taken is the unsaved and is taken to judgment.

JESUS AFFIRMS THAT THE TARES (THE WICKED) ARE TAKEN FIRST

In Matthew 13:36-43, Jesus gives us the sequence of events of His second coming and affirms that it is the wicked who will be taken out first:

- Verse 39: The harvest is the end of the age. The reapers are the angels.
- Verse 40: The tares [wicked] are gathered out first and burned in the fire. So this will occur at the end of this age.
- Verse 41: The Son of Man will send forth His angels to gather out all things that offend.
- Verse 49: The angels will come forth and separate the wicked from among the just.
- Verse 42: They will be cast into a furnace of fire.
- Verse 43: The righteous will then shine forth in the kingdom of the Father.

In 2 Thessalonians 1:6-10, Paul also affirms this position. He writes:

> Since it is a righteous thing with God to repay with tribulation those who trouble you, and to give you who are troubled rest with us when the Lord Jesus is revealed from heaven with His mighty angels, in flaming fire taking vengeance on those who do not know God, and on those who do not obey the gospel of our Lord Jesus Christ, "These shall be punished with everlasting destruction from the presence of the Lord and from the glory of His power, when He comes, in that Day, to be glorified in His saints and to be admired among all those who believe, because our testimony among you was believed."

When Jesus is revealed in flaming fire from heaven, He will first take vengeance on those who do not know God or obey the gospel (vv. 7-9). They are to be punished with an everlasting destruction from the presence of the Lord and from the glory of His power. It is after this that Christ is glorified in His saints (v. 10). Therefore, the scriptures agree that when Jesus comes, the unsaved will be dealt with first.

Furthermore, Jesus declares that everyone, both believer and unbeliever, will be rewarded and judged for their works at the same time, not seven years apart. It is to be when He comes in the glory of His Father with the angels. Matthew 16:26-27 states, "For what profit is it to a man if he gains the whole world, and loses his own soul? Or what will a man give in exchange for his soul? For the Son of Man will come in the glory of His Father with His angels, and then He will reward each according to his works" (cf. 2 Thess. 1:7).

None of these references state that God will judge and reward the righteous and the wicked at two different times. Revelation 11:15-18 states that both will be judged and rewarded at the last trumpet, when Jesus comes to reign eternally. Let Jesus end the argument in Revelation 22:12 when He speaks of the same truth: "And behold, I am coming quickly, and My reward is with Me, to give to every one according to his work."

It is amazing that from one Scripture to another, the Bible never contradicts itself but always affirms the harmony of truth.

WHAT DOES 2 THESSALONIANS 2:1-14 *REALLY* SAY?

Harold J. Ockenga states the following regarding the events of 2 Thessalonians 2: "These things will precede the revelation of the wicked one...whom the Lord shall consume with the spirit of his mouth, and shall destroy with the brightness of his coming...No believers will be caught in this outpouring of divine wrath" (Ockenga 1956, 250).

According to dispensationalism, the content of 2 Thessalonians 2:1-8 is supposed to happen during a seven-year period of time after the so-called rapture of the church. To dispensationalists, the rapture is the coming (*parousia*) of Christ, that is, Christ's coming *for* His saints; an event that precedes the seven-year tribulation.

However, Paul is saying just the opposite in this passage: "Concerning the coming [*parousia* or rapture] of the Lord Jesus, and *our* [believers] gathering together to Him" (2 Thess. 2:1). By using the word *our*, Paul includes himself in the same group as the Thessalonians when they are gathered together with Christ at His *parousia*. If this chapter applies after the tribulation, then Paul did not make it into the rapture. This would be devastating to the dispensational theory!

In 2 Thessalonians 2:2, a false report had been circulating as to what Paul taught on the subject: "That the day of Christ [literally, "Lord"] had come [the same day as in verse 1, where Paul calls this coming the *parousia*]." In verse 3, Paul says, "That Day will not come [*parousia*, or day of the Lord] until the falling away." The "man of sin," the son of perdition, must be revealed first.

Verses 4-10 describe the workings of this man of sin. Verse 8 states that at Christ's rapture (*parousia*) He will destroy the man of sin "with the brightness [epiphany] of His coming (*parousia*)." This makes the parousia and the epiphany the same event.

This passage makes it plain that believers will not be gathered out before all these events happen. This was not new to them, for in verse 5, Paul states that he had told them this same truth beforehand.

As to the "day" in 2 Thessalonians 2:2, the time referred to is called "the day of Christ," or literally, "the day of the Lord." To dispensationalists, "the day of the Lord" means the seven-year tribulation. In 1 Thessalonians 5:2, Paul already had told them that the day of the Lord would come "as a thief in the night."

However, the Bible states in 2 Peter 3:10-13 that the day of the Lord will occur when Christ comes as a thief in the night, at which time the present heavens and earth will be burnt up and the new heaven and earth will appear. Is it possible then that there can be a seven-year tribulation and a thousand-year millennium on earth after this event? Was Peter inspired? Is the Bible the inspired truth or not?

Second Thessalonians 2:3 discusses the events that will happen before the *parousia* takes place. Paul says "that day" (*parousia*) cannot come until the "falling away" comes first and "the man of lawlessness [is] revealed," who is the son of perdition. On the other hand, dispensationalists teach that there are no signs or prophecies that are to take place before the rapture (*parousia*) happens. They say it is a sign-less and timeless event. But the text says just the opposite.

Furthermore, in 2 Thessalonians 2:1-14, Paul is talking about the rapture (*parousia*) of the Church and is actually telling us there are prophesied events that the Church can see, know, and be looking for relative to the "man of sin" and "the apostasy." Therefore, those who teach a "sign-less" coming of Christ in His *parousia* are teaching an unscriptural doctrine. It makes the Bible contradict itself.

RELATIONAL EVENTS OF THE MAN OF SIN IN 2 THESSALONIANS 2:4-7

In 2 Thessalonians 2:4, the man of sin exalts himself above God. He sits in the temple of God as God. What is the temple of God in the New Testament (John 2:18-21; Eph. 2:19-22)? Scofield says the man of sin is the beast mentioned in Revelation 13:1.

In verse 5, Paul says, "I told you these things." In verse 6, he says something restrains—and that they know what it is—so he might be revealed in his own time. In verse 7, he states, "The mystery of lawlessness [the working of the man of sin] is already at work; only He who now restrains will do so until He is taken out of the way." Dispensationalists say it is the Holy Spirit that is taken out of the way, but they give no biblical evidence for their statement. Does the text really say this?

In verse 8, Paul then says the wicked one will be revealed, whom the Lord will consume with the spirit of His mouth and destroy with the brightness (epiphany) of His coming (*parousia*). If the *parousia* is the pre-tribulation rapture and the man of sin is destroyed at that time, the dispensational position is unscriptural and cannot be tenable.

In verse 9, Paul says the man of sin comes (his coming is also called the *parousia*) with all the working of Satan—with all power, signs, and lying wonders (Rev. 13:13-14; 16:14). In verse 10, the man of sin comes with all deceivableness of unrighteousness in them that perish.

What is the fate of those who follow the man of sin? In verse 10, Paul says these are the ones who perish—those who did not believe the truth of salvation (Heb. 2:3). In verse 11, God will therefore send them strong delusion to believe a lie that they (v. 12) might be damned who did not believe the truth of being saved. Finally, in verses 13-14, Paul thanks God for the salvation of the Thessalonians via the gospel, because God from the beginning chose them to be saved.

PETER AND THE SECOND COMING OF CHRIST IN HIS *PAROUSIA*

Second Peter 3:10-13 states:

> But the day of the Lord will come as a thief in the night, in which the heavens will pass away with a great noise, and the elements will melt with fervent heat; both the earth and the works that are in it will be burned up. Therefore, since all these things will be dissolved, what manner of persons ought you to be in holy conduct and godliness, looking for and hastening the coming of the day of God, because of which the heavens will be dissolved, being on fire, and the elements will melt with fervent heat? Nevertheless we, according to His promise, look for new heavens and a new earth in which righteousness dwells.

In these verses, Peter plainly states that the day of the Lord will come as a thief in the night in which the present heavens and the earth are to pass away. The believer will then enter the new heavens and the new earth. In 2 Peter 3:4, Peter calls this coming of the Lord the rapture (*parousia*). Therefore, Peter does not teach a pre-tribulation rapture or a millennium!

Since the Bible mentions all these events to be one and the same, how can the *parousia* (pre-tribulation rapture) be sign-less and timeless when the believer is told to watch for these events to come to pass before the Lord comes in the *parousia*? Paul in 2 Thessalonians 2:1-14 calls these prophesied events that precede this coming of Christ the *parousia,* or rapture. This coming of Christ, then, cannot be imminent or without signs.

Dispensationalists use the word *parousia* to mean the rapture, which they say is to be seven years before the revelation or the second coming of

Christ. The second coming, they say, will have signs of its approach, but not the rapture. They say 2 Thessalonians 2:1-8 is supposed to be the signs that precede the revelation or the second coming of Christ. However, it should be noted that as Paul introduces this passage of Scripture, he uses the word *parousia* to describe this coming of Christ, that the signs given will precede the *parousia*, and that this *parousia* cannot take place until these signs have come to pass (v. 3). In verse 5, Paul reminds the Thessalonians that he already had told them these things; therefore, it was not a new theory to them. They had been deluded by false eschatological teachers (vv. 2-3). (See Chapter 14, "The Doctrine of Imminence.")

THE QUESTION OF THE RAPTURE AND THE CHURCH IN REVELATION 4:1

Revelation 4:1 states, "After these things I looked, and behold, a door standing open in heaven. And the first voice which I heard was like a trumpet speaking with me, saying, 'Come up here, and I will show you things which must take place after this.'"

Dr. Sale Harrison says the following on this passage: "Though not mentioned, the rapture of the church is viewed as having taken place; (i.e. between the third and fourth chapters of Revelation)" (McGavern 1943, 31). Scofield makes the following comment on this verse: "This call seems clearly to indicate the fulfillment of 1 Thess. 4:14-17" (Scofield 1945, 1334). Keith L. Brooks affirms the same position.

According to dispensationalists, "come up here" in Revelation 4:1 is supposed to mean that the Church is caught up in the rapture. This makes the person of John a type of the Church. By using the same rationale, can we then take "come up here" in Revelation 11:12 to mean a second rapture? By what biblical reasoning can such a doctrine be accepted?

Needless to say, I do not agree with this type of dispensational hermeneutics in interpreting the Word of God. A simple hermeneutic is that you cannot read something into a text that is not there or take away from what the text says. Neither can we use the silence of Scripture to inject a doctrinal position.

Dispensationalists say because the Church is not mentioned after Revelation 4:1, it is no longer on earth, for it went in the rapture. It would be just as fallacious to say the Gospels of Mark, Luke and John are not for the Church because the Church is not mentioned in them. Can we say by the same reasoning that because the word *gospel* is not in what we call the Gospel of John, it is not therefore a gospel, and we must look elsewhere for the gospel?

Revelation 6–19 is supposed to be for the Jew and the unsaved that did not go in the rapture. Therefore, only unsaved people will be on earth during this period of time (called the great tribulation). If this is true, how is anyone ever to get saved during this time? There will be no one to preach the saving message of the gospel unless the unsaved get the unsaved saved. That would be ridiculous.

In Revelation 22:6-17, Jesus was talking about His coming. He said when He does come again, it will be too late for anyone to repent from their sins and turn to righteousness (v. 11). By the time we come to verse 17, the Holy Spirit is still calling those who hear. Under the trumpets and vials, God is still calling men to repent (9:20-21; 16:9). Therefore, the Holy Spirit must still be operative in the earth at this time. Consider the following:

- If Christians are not on earth after Revelation 6–19, who are the redeemed ones mentioned in Revelation 5:9, and how did they get redeemed?
- Who are the kings and priests mentioned in Revelation 5:10? Are they the same as those in Revelation 1:6, before Revelation 4:1 took place?
- Who are the "sealed" and the servants of God in Revelation 7:1-4? How and why are they sealed?
- In Revelation 7:9-14, who is the great multitude that no man could number before the throne that were crying, "salvation to our God," and how did they get there? They had been washed in the blood of the Lamb.
- Who in Revelation 12:11 overcame by the blood of the Lamb?
- In Revelation 12:17, who are the offspring of the woman whom Satan wars against?
- Who are the saints under the first beast in Revelation 13:7?
- Who is harvested in Revelation 14:14-20? Why two aspects of reaping or harvesting?
- Who is the Lamb's wife in Revelation 19:7-8? Is she not the bride of Revelation 21:9? Is this bride different than the one in

Matthew 25? Does Christ have two brides? That would be absurd, but when absurdity reigns, confusion makes it look good.

- If the Church is not present after Revelation 4:1, who are the hosts in Revelation 15:2-3 that did not take the mark of the beast?
- Who is being talked about in Revelation 16:15 as keeping their garments clean?

If the rapture occurred in Revelation 4:1 when Christ was to come as a thief, why under the sixth plague in Revelation 16:15 does Christ say He still has not yet come as a thief? This is supposed to be two-thirds of the way through the tribulation. Is Christ coming twice as a thief? If so, where in Scripture can it be validated?

THE FOLLY OF EVANGELISM AFTER THE RAPTURE

In *Prophecy Today*, Dwight Pentecost makes it clear that "at the moment of the rapture, there will not be left one single believer on earth" (*Prophecy Today*, p. 145). Yet, dispensationalists preach and teach that after the rapture, the greatest evangelism ever will take place during the time of the tribulation. Thousands upon thousands of Jews are supposed to get saved (144,000) plus a number so great that no man could number them. All of this is what we are called to believe happens without the Holy Spirit, the Church, or even one single believer on earth. What a preposterous imagination!

If this is true, knowing the biblical principles of the preaching of the gospel to the unsaved, why has God suddenly changed His mind regarding using the preaching of the gospel by saved sinners as the means of salvation to the lost (Mark 16:15-16; Matt. 28:18-20)? Christ on His ascension could have sent the angels of heaven to evangelize the world, but He did not break His Word that He had already given. He chose saved sinners whom He commissioned to carry out His world plan of evangelism.

Furthermore, at the heart of the saving message is the preaching of the gospel. "How can they call on Him in whom they have not believed? And how shall they believe in Him whom they have not heard? And how shall they hear without a preacher?" (Rom. 10:14). God's method of salvation is by faith (Eph. 2:8-9), which is a gift of God given through the preaching of the gospel, and that faith comes by hearing and hearing by the Word of God (Rom.10:8, 17). How is salvation to be received apart from this?

The gospel, with these truths, was to be effectually preached until Jesus returned (Matt. 24:14). There is no other message of salvation found in the Bible outside of Christ that is preached (Acts 4:11-12). Where in the Bible does it state that God has changed His mind about what these verses state? No place!

Does not saving faith come by hearing and hearing by the Word of God (Rom. 10:17)? Since not one single believer would be left to preach the gospel on earth, how could evangelism take place? Furthermore, without the Holy Spirit present to convict of sin (John 16:8), no one can be drawn to the Savior for forgiveness.

Second Peter 3:10 states that when Jesus comes as a thief in the night, the present heavens and earth will be burnt up. How can evangelism take place after that event? Would it not be better to let the Scripture speak for itself than to controvert it with man-made suppositions? In no biblical passage does it make room for evangelism or salvation from sin after Jesus comes as a thief in the night. Truly evangelism after the rapture is folly!

Nor can one be saved after death, as some cults teach. Hebrews 9:27 states, "And it is appointed for men to die once, but after this the judgment." In Matthew 12:32, Jesus says, "Whoever speaks against the Holy Spirit, it will not be forgiven him, either in this age or in the age to come." In Luke 16:19-31, Jesus speaks about the rich man and Lazarus. After his death, the rich man found that it was too late to repent.

Christianity must cease to give the world a false hope of a second chance salvation after Jesus returns. The Bible does not teach a back door entrance into the kingdom of God: "But {whoever} climbs up some other way, the same is a thief and a robber" (John 10:1). Second-chance theory is built on a system of interpretation without any explicit statement from the Word of God. Therefore, it is a false doctrine.

CONCLUSION OF THE PROBLEM

According to dispensationalists, the rapture requires a resurrection of the saints (1 Thess. 4:16). If this is the case, how is it that Paul in 1 Corinthians 15 can state that the resurrection of the believers will be at the "last trumpet" (1 Cor. 15:51-52), that the living believer will then be changed in the twinkling of an eye, and that death will be destroyed (the last trumpet being in Revelation 11:15-19)? Is this not the Lord's second coming and the end of human existence on earth as we know it?

Revelation 11:15-19 states that the seventh and last trumpet will be the time of Christ's second coming when He comes to reign eternally. At this time, both the righteous and the wicked will be rewarded and judged at the same time. Note that this is an eternal reign, not just for a thousand years. Therefore, the seventh trumpet must indicate the end of this world as we know it. This also proves that the book of Revelation cannot have been written in chronological order.

Was Job wrong when he stated that man does not rise until the heavens be no more (Job 14:12-14)? Do not all these references agree with 2 Peter 3:9-13, in which Peter says the day of the Lord will come as a thief in the night and the heavens and earth as we know them will be dissolved? The believer is exhorted to look for a new heaven and a new earth in which dwells righteousness, not for a Jewish millennium.

What biblical proof do the dispensationalists have in saying the Church will be gone before Revelation 6–19? If this is true, it means these chapters in Revelation do not apply to the Church today. So what business do we have in studying them or even reading them? What kind of hermeneutical scissors are being used to cut those chapters out of the Bible? Jesus knew better. In Revelation 1:3, He pronounced a blessing on those who read and keep the sayings of the book. Was Jesus not talking to the Church (1:4, 11; 22:16)?

Samuel J. Andrews, author of *Christianity and Anti-Christianity*, in speaking of the first beast of Revelation 13 says, "The teachings of The Revelation directly concern only the Christian Church" (Andrews 1898, 61). At this point, there are several different aspects that are brought into question:

- The question of a pre-tribulation rapture.
- When this rapture is supposed to happen.
- The biblical source for the seven years of tribulation. Is it man-made?
- The question of the chronology of the book of Revelation.
- The question of whether there will be a literal physical reign of Christ on earth in Jerusalem for a thousand years.

Dispensationalism deduces a reign of Christ for a literal thousand years in literal Jerusalem from Revelation 20:1-7. But this contradicts

Revelation 11:15, which states that when Jesus comes, He will come to reign eternally. Because of this, Revelation 20 must be interpreted in the light of Revelation 11:15-19, or the Bible contradicts itself.

Furthermore, according to 1 Thessalonians 4:13-18, when does it say that the dead in Christ are to be resurrected and the living saints transformed and meet Christ in the air (vv. 16-17)? Paul is the best interpreter of Paul. In 1 Corinthians 15:51-52, he specifically states that it will be at the "last trumpet" (the resurrection) when the living believers are transformed in the twinkling of an eye.

Second Thessalonians 2:1-4 is also used by premillennialists to prove that the rapture occurs prior to the tribulation. However, in fact, these verses prove the very opposite: "Now, brethren, concerning the coming [*parousia*, the word for rapture] of our Lord Jesus Christ and our gathering together to Him." This text certainly speaks of the time when believers are gathered together at the *parousia* of Christ, and Paul includes himself in this gathering when he says "our" gathering together.

In the latter part of verse 2, Paul states that the coming of Christ (*parousia*) and the day of Christ [the Lord] are one and the same day, and that before that day could come, there had to first be a falling away and the man of sin revealed. All of this dispensationalists put into the tribulation period after the rapture, whereas Paul says it is to happen before the rapture or the coming of the Lord (*parousia*) takes place (2 Thess. 2:1).

Also in 1 Thessalonians 3:13, Paul says the living believers will still be here on earth when the Lord Jesus Christ comes *with* all His saints. The coming (*parousia*) of Jesus *with* His saints, according to dispensationalists, is not supposed to happen until after the tribulation. However, 1 Thessalonians 4:13-18 states that the *parousia* (rapture) is Christ coming *for* His saints as well as *with* His saints (at the same time). If Paul contradicted himself in any of these references, it would do violence to the divine inspiration of Scripture. This would be a very serious charge as to the credibility of God's Word.

The Bible has put the second coming of Christ in as simple of terms as possible. Second Peter 3:1-13 is a good example. The question is, "Where is the promise of His coming?" Peter calls this coming, the *parousia* of Christ (vv. 4, 12). Dispensationalists put the *parousia* before the tribulation and the millennium, whereas Peter says it occurs at the day of the Lord, when Christ comes as a thief in the night and in which both the heavens and the earth will be renovated and renewed. If this is the *parousia*, there can be no such thing as a tribulation or a millennium afterward. Was Peter divinely inspired when he wrote? This agrees with Jesus' teaching on the wheat and the tares. It also agrees with Paul in 2 Thessalonians 1:6-10.

The scriptures speak loud and clear. The conclusion should be obvious. There cannot be a tribulation or a millennium after this coming of the Lord. (See Appendix E for scripture references related to Christ's coming.)

SECOND CHANCE SALVATION?

Dispensationalism teaches a *second chance salvation,* in that there will be people saved after Jesus returns the second time. Finis Jennings Dake states the following:

> There is only one company saved and raptured between the rapture of the church at the beginning of Daniel's seventieth week and the rapture of the tribulation saints at the end of this week. That company is symbolized by the manchild and clearly revealed to be 144,000 Jews (7:1-8; 9:4; 12:5; 14:1-5). If they are not the same, then there are two translations in the middle of the week–one revealed and the other not; the history of one given after reaching heaven and the other not, the identity of one clearly stated and the other not. Thus, mystery after mystery appears if there are two companies instead of one.
>
> (Dake undated, note #10 on Revelation)

Such teaching is a man-made mystery and unscriptural.

Tim Lahaye and Jerry B. Jenkins state the following on behalf of those left behind: "On the one hand, I don't want to give you the spirit of fear, but we all know we're still here because we neglected salvation before the Rapture. I know we're all grateful for the second chance, but we cannot expect to escape the trials that are coming" (Lahaye and Jenkins 1995, 310-311).

Scofield says, "The great tribulation will be, however, a period of salvation. An election of Israel…and, with an innumerable multitude of Gentiles" (Scofield 1945, 1337).

THE BIBLE DOES NOT TEACH A SECOND CHANCE SALVATION

Does the Bible teach such a doctrine of second chance salvation? It is the compound testimony of Scripture that it does not. There is only one coming of Christ in glory with His holy angels, after which time the door of salvation will be closed forever. The following are thirteen scriptural reasons why there will be no salvation after Christ's coming. Let the scriptures speak for themselves.

1. In Matthew 25:10-12, Jesus Himself states that when the Bridegroom comes for the Bride (the Church), the door of salvation will be forever closed. "And while they went to buy, the bridegroom came, and those who were ready went in with him to the wedding; and the door was shut. Afterward the other virgins came also, saying, 'Lord, Lord, open to us' But he answered and said, 'Assuredly, I say to you, I do not know you.'" After this the five foolish virgins (the unsaved) could not gain entrance.
2. Luke 13:25 affirms the same position: "When once the master of the house has risen up and shut the door, and you begin to stand outside and knock at the door, saying, 'Lord, Lord, open for us,' and he will answer and say to you, 'I do not know you, where you are from.'" Verse 28 stipulates that at this time, "There will be weeping and gnashing of teeth, when you see Abraham and Isaac and Jacob and all the prophets in the kingdom of God and yourselves thrust out." Weeping and gnashing of teeth occur when Jesus returns at the final judgment (Matt. 22:13; 24:51; 25:30). Therefore, there is no salvation obtainable after this event.
3. Revelation 22:11-12 affirms that at Christ's second coming, it will be too late for the unsaved to obtain salvation. "He who is unjust, let him be unjust still; and he who is righteous let him be righteous still; he who is holy, let him be holy still. And behold, I am coming quickly, and My reward is with Me, to give every one according to his work."

4. In Matthew 24:14, Jesus states that the gospel was only to be preached until the *end*, not after the *end*. "And this gospel of the kingdom will be preached in all the world as a witness to all nations, and then the *end* will come."

5. In Matthew 28:19-20, Jesus tells His followers to make disciples *until* the end of the age, not *after* the end of the age.

6. In Matthew 13:39-40, Jesus states that the harvest will occur at the *end* of the age, at which time all the tares (the wicked) will be gathered and burned in the fire. He gives no indication of a time of salvation after this happens, as all the wicked have been burnt up.

7. Matthew 25:31, 41 states that when Jesus comes in His glory with His holy angels, the goats (the unsaved) will be sent into everlasting fire. When will the wicked be judged? Jesus said, "He who rejects Me, and does not receive My words, has that which judges him—the word that I have spoken will judge him in *the last day*" (John 12:48, emphasis mine). There is no time for salvation after the last day, as there can be no other days.

8. First Thessalonians 4:13-18 affirms that when Jesus comes with His angels, the righteous will be resurrected and go to be with Him. There is no indication in the text as to when this event will happen. However, in the Gospel of John, Jesus clearly teaches that the righteous will be resurrected in the *last day* (John 6:39-40, 44, 54; 11:24). Since the righteous will be resurrected in *the last day,* there can be no days after the *last day,* or words would be meaningless. To be resurrected at the last day also destroys the "any moment" theory. We must wait until the last day.

9. First Corinthians 15:51-57 states that when the *last trumpet* sounds, the dead will be resurrected, the living saints will be changed in the twinkling of an eye, and death (which is the last enemy, v. 26) will be destroyed and swallowed up in victory. When death is thus destroyed, there will never be another resurrection, as there will be no more death.

10. Revelation 11:15-19 concurs that at the seventh and *last trumpet,* Christ will at that time come to reign *eternally,* not for just a thousand years. When this happens, both the righteous and the wicked will be rewarded and judged at the same time, not seven

years apart (Acts 10:42; 2 Tim. 4:1; 1 Pet. 4:5). Matthew 25:31-46 affirms this position. The finality of things on the earth as we know it will have reached its end.

11. Second Thessalonians 1:7-10 concurs with Matthew 25:31-32, 46, which states that when Jesus is revealed from heaven with His mighty angels, the wicked will be first gathered out and punished with everlasting destruction from the presence of the Lord and the glory of His power. After this, Christ will be glorified in His saints. Since the wicked are punished with everlasting destruction when Jesus comes with His mighty angels, there will be no wicked left to get saved!

12. Second Peter 3:1-13 affirms that when Jesus comes as a thief in the night, the present system of things will be burnt up and we will enter the new heavens and the new earth, not a millennium. Did Jesus not say there will be no forgiveness in the age to come (Matt. 12:32)?

13. Second Corinthians 6:2 states that *now* is the day of salvation. Salvation is limited to the period of time called "today" (Heb. 3:13-15). *Today* is the time preceding the coming of Christ.

Based on these scriptures, it is apparent that the Bible does not teach there will be a second chance for people to be saved after Christ's return. The Bible never speaks of the grace or salvation extending beyond the resurrection or the second coming of Christ.

Dispensationalists, then, do teach a *second chance salvation*. They tell us that during the tribulation after the rapture—as well as during the millennium—people will be getting saved. Getting saved after the rapture is an unscriptural doctrine. It is also dangerous in that it gives a false hope to unbelievers in delaying their salvation.

Chapter 14

THE DOCTRINE OF
IMMINENCE

Imminence is the doctrine of an "any moment" second coming of Christ or of the rapture, as dispensationalism teaches. Imminence means "impending" or "ready to take place at any moment". It is taken to mean that no prophesied event must take place before the rapture of the Church.

Walvoord says, "By common consent imminence means that so far as we know no predicted event will *necessarily* precede the coming of Christ" (Walvoord 1976, 70). Is such a doctrine of Christ's coming scriptural? It is not! The word *imminence* has no scriptural warrant or support outside of an assumption. Where in the Bible is it stated that no prophesied event has to happen before Christ's return? It is a statement unfounded by Scripture.

First, let it be said that it is not being spiritual to quote clichés that are unbiblical. To repeat the phrase "Jesus could come at any moment" does not make it true. To say the Bible teaches this is true is to fabricate that which the Bible does not say or teach. For centuries, the blessed hope of the Church has been Christ's second coming coupled with the end of the world as we know it. Of late, especially since 1830, the "hope of Christ's return" has been stolen from that context and its venue moved to a "secret rapture" that could occur at any moment as the hope of the Church.

J. Dwight Pentecost, quoting Henry C. Thiessen on the subject of imminency, states, "The Lord had taught them (His disciples) to expect his return at any moment, and so they looked for him to come in their day. Not only so, but they also taught His personal return as being immediately" (Pentecost 1978, 203). Where in Scripture did Jesus teach His disciples to look for Him to return in their day? Where in Scripture did His disciples teach that Christ's return would happen immediately? If they did so, they have missed it by two thousand years. What would this do to the veracity of Christ and to the truth of the divine inspiration of Scripture? Since divine inspiration cannot err, it is to falsify God's Word to say that it teaches the doctrine of imminence. Is not adding to Scripture putting oneself on equal par with God Himself?

As Christians, we are called to believe that biblical truth backed up by the preponderance of Scripture must prove the truth of every doctrine we espouse. What does the Bible teach about the subject of imminence as to Christ's second coming? The Scripture alone must be our guide without supposition. The Bible does not teach that the Early Church—that is, Christ or His apostles—wrote about, believed, or taught imminence or an immediate return of Christ in their day.

JESUS NEVER TAUGHT IMMINENCE

In Matthew 28:18-20, Jesus taught that before He could or would return, the gospel (and obedience to it) was to be preached and taught "to the end of the age." It is now some two thousand years since that time, yet still not all the world of every tribe and tongue and people and nation (Rev. 5:9) have heard the saving message of Christ's gospel. Therefore, it would not be true to say that Jesus taught the doctrine of imminence.

In Acts 1:8, Jesus told His disciples, "You shall be witnesses to Me in Jerusalem, and in all Judea and Samaria, and to the end of the earth." After His resurrection, Jesus told His disciples that they were to evangelize the world to the ends of the earth. Why has this truth been twisted to meet the fancy of some? When Jesus was teaching about end time events and the destruction of the temple and Jerusalem, why did He say, "These things must come to pass, but the end is not yet" (Matt. 24:6)?

In Matthew 25:14-29, the Parable of the Talents, why did Jesus talk about a man (Himself) going into a far country and then not returning until "after a long time"? What was a "long time" in the mind of Jesus? If the doctrine of imminence was in the mind of Jesus, He would have personally come back after the destruction of the city of Jerusalem in

A.D. 70 and not after a "long time." Furthermore, in John 21:18-23, Jesus did not teach that an immediate return from heaven would occur, because He told Peter he would die first.

T. Myron Webb states, "It is quite evident from the study of Scriptures that the early church was impressed by the possibility of our Lord's return at any moment" (Webb 1932, 8). However, Webb does not give one scripture to support his position. Concerning Matthew 24:14, which states, "And this gospel of the kingdom will be preached in all the world as a witness to all the nations, and then the end will come," Webb says, "This task of world evangelism was never possible until the last few decades" (Ibid., 25). Since this last statement is true, how can both of his statements be reconciled? It is impossible, and so is his teaching.

Acts 15:18 declares that "known to God from eternity are all of His works." If Jesus is omniscient, why since the time of the Early Church did He change His mind as to an imminent return? What can we say about the millions of souls who have been born since the time of the Early Church? Were they not in the mind of God because He knew all His works from the foundation of the world?

After receiving Christ's teachings, why would His disciples twist His words to mean an imminent return? It would be preposterous to make such a claim. Therefore, we must conclude that neither Jesus nor His inspired writers ever taught the doctrine of imminence. All such interpretation must be brought to light by the direct teachings of Christ, or we have a Bible that is self-contradictory. In the world in which we live, we all wish for the Lord's quick return. That does not mean that God is going to change His mind according to our wishes. In fact, by the time the book of Acts was written, the day had already been set: "He has appointed a day in which He will judge the world" (Acts 17:31). Is there anything man can do that will change that day? Our test of any Bible doctrine is not how we may feel about it, but what the Scripture says on the subject.

THE APOSTLES DID NOT TEACH IMMINENCE

Jesus told Peter he would die before the end would come. Therefore, Peter could not have (nor did he) teach an immediate coming of Christ (John 21:18-19; 2 Pet. 1:13-14). In John 16:2, Jesus told the apostles they would be killed before the end would come. How could they have taught that the Lord would come during their lifetime?

In Acts 3:19-21, Peter, anointed by the Holy Spirit, said that Jesus could not come back but would have to remain in heaven until all things were restored. "Whom heaven must receive until the times of restoration of all things, which God has spoken by the mouth of all His holy prophets since the world began" (v. 21).

Paul taught in 2 Thessalonians 2:1-8 that the coming of Christ (the *parousia,* or rapture), which is the believers gathering together to Him, could not take place until all the events mentioned in verses 3-4 had taken place. Paul included himself in this gathering. He further states that at the time of this coming, Christ would destroy the lawless one with the breath of His mouth. Paul thus never taught a two-stage coming of Christ that included a secret rapture prior to a tribulation. The Church will be here until all these events have taken place! Paul also knew he would die before the Lord returned (2 Tim. 4:6-8).

The concept of imminency is also certainly not taught in James 5:8. In this passage, James was talking about the judgment of God to come upon those who had lived luxuriously at the expense of those who had labored for them. He is basically saying God is presently watching and is ready to judge us: "Behold He stands at the door." He is that close to us. The phrase, "the coming of the Lord is at hand" in the Greek is η παρουσια του κυριου νγγικεν, of which a direct translation is "the presence of the Lord is near." The word *parousia* literally means "presence." Other scriptures in which *parousia* is used in the same manner include:

- Philippians 2:12: Paul uses *parousia* to describe his own presence among the members of the Philippian church.
- First Corinthians 16:17: *parousia* is used of the presence of Stephanas.
- Second Corinthians 7:6-7: *parousia* is used of the presence of Titus.

All the other references to *parousia* in Scripture are those that encourage the believer to be ready at all times because Jesus' coming is a surety. One day He is coming, and we must all in that day stand before the judgment seat of Christ (Rom. 14:7-13; 2 Cor. 5:10).

Some say Christ did teach imminence in the book of Revelation. Oh? If He did, He must have changed His mind since the time of the gospels.

Is it possible that happened? If so, we have a Bible that is self-contradictory and a Savior that taught two opposite opinions on the same subject. The scripture that is used to support this position is Revelation 22:20: "Surely I am coming quickly."

According to *The Englishman's Greek Concordance of the New Testament,* the Greek word used in this verse is ταχοσ (*taxos*) with its cognates, which in all the following references means "swiftly, quickly, with speed." Luke 18:8 may be used as the lead in for all the rest, which says, "I tell you that he will avenge them speedily [*taxos*]." Thayer adds "speedily without delay."

The rest of the references in which *taxos* is used include Acts 12:7; 22:18; 25:4; Rom. 16:20; Matt. 5:25; 28:7-8; Mark 9:39; 16:8; John 11:29; Rev. 2:16; 3:11; 11:14; Rev. 22:6-7, 12, 20; Jas. 1:19. As to these references, the implication is that when these things do happen, they will happen quickly, with speed, and without delay. In other words, Christ's coming will be as sudden as lightning: "As the lightning that flashes out of one part under heaven, so also the Son of Man will be in His day" (Luke 17:24). It also could be said it will be "in a moment in the twinkling of an eye"—that fast! In no way could the word be taken to mean His coming was imminent.

After these scriptural injunctions, for one to continue to believe in the doctrine of imminence, he or she would have to refute the truths of the scriptures presented and then prove that they mean just the opposite of the way in which they are here used. Imminence therefore is an unscriptural doctrine and biblically unwarranted, because it makes for a faulty Bible and destroys the divine inspiration of the scriptures. The Bible cannot teach two views that are the opposite of each other and both be held as scripturally tenable.

Chapter 15

THE BODILY RESURRECTION FROM THE DEAD

There is a great need to clarify this subject today, for it deals with the issue of whether there is life after death or whether death is the end of existence. All humanity feels that they were made for more than this life. Solomon said, "He has put eternity in their heart" (Eccl. 3:11).

The teachings of false cults have invaded the world with an old false doctrine that was already prevalent in Jesus' day. Namely, that of "the Sadducees who say there is no resurrection" (Matt. 22:23-33; Mark 12:18-26; Luke 20:27-36; Acts 23:6-8). To prove the resurrection to the Sadducees, God probably had people come out of their graves in Matthew 27:53. The Pharisees did believe in the resurrection.

Others said that the resurrection was already past, which had overthrown the faith of some (2 Tim. 2:18). Some of the Corinthians also denied the resurrection (1 Cor. 15:29). Celsus was an early opponent of Christianity, and he made jokes about the resurrection. In Acts 17:32, Paul on Mars Hill was mocked because he preached the resurrection. Gnostics believed that matter was evil, and therefore they rejected a bodily resurrection. A final reason as to why this subject is necessary today is there has arisen in theology a doctrine that teaches there will yet be two or maybe three bodily resurrections from the dead.

The Bible speaks of only one bodily resurrection to come. It will be at the second coming of Christ, which will occur at "the last day" or "the end of the age." However, dispensationalists teach there will be two comings of Christ and, therefore, two resurrections. In reality, they teach three resurrections: one at the rapture before the tribulation, another at the end of the tribulation, and yet another after the millennium.

Take note that the word *resurrection* in the Bible is never found in the plural. The chart on page 160, titled "The Dispensational Position," depicts the position of dispensationalists. Listed below are scriptures that prove their position, as depicted in that chart, to be contradictory to the Bible.

EVENTS THAT HAPPEN AT THE RAPTURE

The Bible says that the following events will happen at the rapture:

1. There will be a resurrection of dead believers in Christ (1 Thess. 4:16).
2. The rapture (*parousia*) will catch up into the clouds all the believers (1 Thess. 4:17).
3. The Bridegroom will come for the Bride (Matt. 25:1-13).
4. Jesus will come as a thief in the night (Matt. 24:42-43).
5. Believers will be changed in a moment in the twinkling of an eye (1 Cor. 15:51-52).

What does the Bible say will happen when Jesus comes as a thief in the night?

1. Matthew 24:42-43: It will be unexpected and unannounced.
2. First Thessalonians 5:2: It is called "the Day of the Lord."
3. Second Thessalonians 2:1-2: It is called both the *parousia* (rapture) and "the Day of the Lord."
4. Second Peter 3:10: Christ's coming as a thief is called "the Day of the Lord." Peter says all these things will take place when Christ comes as a thief in the night:
   - Verse 4: This same coming is called the *parousia*.
   - Verse 7: It is called the day of judgment; the perdition of ungodly men.
   - Verse 10: It is also when the earth is burnt up.
   - Verse 12: It is called the coming day of God.
   - Verse 13: It will occur when we look for a new heaven and new earth.

- Verse 14: The believer is exhorted to be without spot at that time.
5. Revelation 16:15: During the sixth seal, Jesus has not come as a thief, yet the scripture says, "I am coming as a thief."

The previous ten points are therefore one and the same event. Because the Bible is the inspired Word of God and cannot be broken (John 10:35), then either the Bible or the dispensationalists are wrong. Which is it?

Certainly both these views cannot be exegetically substantiated by Scripture or the Bible would contradict itself. Historically, all the great confessions of the Church are agreed as to one resurrection called the general resurrection. The resurrection is an eschatological event that takes place at Christ's second coming, which is the hope of the Church. Dispensationalists teach that the rapture is the hope of the Church, but the Bible says the second coming of Christ is the hope of the Church (Titus 2:11-13). Paul says, "If in this life only we have hope in Christ, we are of all men most pitiable" (1 Cor. 15:19).

It should be known from the outset that in this chapter, we will not depend on quoting many authors (good as they may be). The Scripture—and the Scripture alone—qualifies to answer the subject. The Bible is the inspired and infallible truth on which we all deem to build our lives. The Bible is replete with the fact that there will be a resurrection from the dead. All four Gospels record Christ's resurrection. Additionally, the resurrection is mentioned in Acts 1:3, 1 Corinthians 15:1-8 and Revelation 20:12-13, as well as in other places.

Jesus was resurrected from the dead to give us a living hope. "Blessed be the God and Father of our Lord Jesus Christ, who according to His abundant mercy has begotten us again to a living hope through the resurrection of Jesus Christ from the dead" (1 Pet.1:3). Paul concurs with this when he says Christ "was delivered up for our offenses, and was raised [resurrected] because of our justification" (Rom. 4:25).

But what is the resurrection about? Why is there going to be one in the future? First of all, it is necessary because Jesus took on a human body and was resurrected. Therefore, in the resurrection, Christ's followers will have a body like His (Phil. 3:21). The resurrection is also necessary to determine the final destiny of man—whether unto eternal life or to eternal damnation (John 5:27-29). One resurrection, two destinies.

The Early Church continually preached Christ as risen from the dead. "Now as they spoke to the people the priests, the captain of the temple, and the Sadducees came upon them, being greatly disturbed that they taught the people and preached in Jesus the resurrection from the dead" (Acts 4:1-2). Paul is very explicit on this subject. In 1 Corinthians 15:13 he says, "But if there is no resurrection of the dead, then Christ is not risen. And if Christ is not risen, your faith is futile; you are still in your sins" (v. 17)!

Standing before Felix, Paul said, "I have hope in God, which they themselves also accept, that there will be *a resurrection* of the dead, both of the just and the unjust" (Acts 24:15, emphasis mine; see also Acts 17:18; 1 Cor. 15:21; Heb. 6:2). Just because the Bible talks about the resurrection in more than one place does not mean there is going to be more than one resurrection. It is speaking about various aspects of but one and the same resurrection.

It was Adam's sin that brought death to the human race, which necessitates the resurrection if man is to live eternally. Adam was told not to eat of the tree of knowledge of good and evil: "But of the tree of the knowledge of good and evil you shall not eat, for in the day that you eat of it you shall surely die" (Gen. 2:17). In Genesis 3:6, Adam and Eve disobeyed and ate of the tree. God in His mercy (v. 15) through the Messiah, paid the penalty: "For since by man came death, by Man also came the resurrection of the dead. For as in Adam all die, even so in Christ all shall be made alive" (1 Cor. 15:21-22). It is Christ's resurrection that gives us the divine assurance that He has put away sin and death by the sacrifice of Himself (Rom. 3:23-25; 4:23-25; 6:23; Heb. 9:26; 10:12).

WHY IS THE BODY DESTINED TO BE RESURRECTED?

The body is destined to be resurrected because Jesus, being God, took upon Himself a physical body in which He died for our sins, was raised from the dead, and will come back in that resurrected body (Acts 1:11). The body of a Christian has become the temple of the Holy Spirit (1 Cor. 6:19). Our physical body (as well as our soul) has been bought by the price of Christ's sacrifice (1 Cor. 6:20). Christ's resurrection is divine proof of the resurrection of the elect to eternal life (Rom. 6:3-5; 1 Cor. 6:14; Phil. 3:21; Heb. 11:35; 1 John 3:2).

So, what is the resurrection? The resurrection is the resuscitation of our physically dead body that once had life but died and will be raised to a state of eternal life. Therefore, the resurrection for the believer is a coming back from the dead in an entirely new and immortal body.

A biblical definition of death is needed. Death is a separation of life, whether physical or spiritual. The Bible speaks to the fact that man's soul and spirit may be dead to God while he is still alive physically:

- Ezekiel 18:4: "The soul that sins it shall die."
- Genesis 2:17: "For in the day that you eat of it you shall surely die."
- Romans 6:23: "The wages of sin is death"
- Ephesians 2:1: "You who were dead in trespasses and sin."
- Ephesians 2:5: "Even when we were dead in trespasses, made us alive together with Christ."
- 1 Timothy 5:6: "But she who lives in pleasure is dead while she lives."

How are we to take the word *dead* in these passages? These verses speak of a living dead person. It is not physical death, but as sinners, they are spiritually dead in trespasses and sins. These passages teach us that there is such a thing as *spiritual death*, which is our human spirit cut off from the life of God. "But of the tree of the knowledge of good and evil you shall not eat, for in the day that you eat of it you shall surely die" (Gen. 2:17). Adam did not die physically within twenty-four hours.

A spiritual death requires a spiritual resurrection (Eph. 2:1). This resurrection is obtained by being born again (John 3:3-5). The spiritually dead hear the voice of the Son of God and live (John 5:24-25). Physical death is when the body itself dies (James 2:26).

THE EARLY CHURCH'S TEACHING
ON THE RESURRECTION

Note that the Early Church's teaching on the resurrection was based on the Old Testament. Jesus Himself said the resurrection was an Old Testament truth (Matt. 12:40; 22:31-32; Luke 20:35-38). Genesis 22:1-4 along with Hebrews 11:17-19 imply a resurrection. Jesus spoke of the resurrection relative to the burning bush (Mark 12:26; Ex. 3:6; Matt. 22:29-33). Consider the following other scriptural evidence:

- Job 14:12: "So man lies down and does not rise, till the heavens be no more." This concurs with 2 Peter 3:10-13.
- Job 19:25-27: "For I know that my Redeemer lives, and He shall stand on the earth; and after my skin is destroyed this I know, that in my flesh I shall see God, Whom I shall see for myself, and my eyes shall behold and not another. How my heart yearns within me!"
- Psalm 17:15: "As for me, I will see Your face in righteousness; I shall be satisfied when I awake in Your likeness" (cf. 1 John 3:2).
- Daniel 12:2: "And many of those who sleep in the dust of the earth shall awake, some to everlasting life, some to shame and everlasting contempt." There will be one resurrection, two destinies.
- Hosea 13:14: "I will ransom them from the power of the grave; I will redeem them from death. O death, I will be your plagues! O Grave, I will be your destruction" (cf. 1 Cor. 15:54-55).
- Isaiah 25:8: "He will swallow up death forever, and the Lord God will wipe away tears from all faces." Paul cites this verse in 1 Corinthians 15:54. In Revelation 21:4, John speaks of tears being wiped away at the time we enter the new heavens and the new earth.
- Isaiah 26:19: "Your dead shall live; together with my dead body they shall arise, wake and sing, you who dwell in dust; for your dew is like the dew of herbs, and the earth shall cast out the dead."

WHERE DO PEOPLE GO AT DEATH?

The Bible says at death, the believer in Christ goes to be with Christ (2 Cor. 5:1-8; Phil. 1:21-23). The person without Christ at death goes into hell and eternal punishment (Luke 16:19-31; Matt. 25:41; John 5:29; Heb. 9:27; Rev. 20:11-15; Dan. 12:2).

Will everybody be raised from the dead to the same end? No! Each person will be judged by his or her own deeds as to rewards or punishment:

- The believer will be rewarded (Luke 19:17, 19; Heb. 9:27; 2 Cor. 5:10; 1 Cor. 3:11-15; 1 Cor. 15:39-44, 58).

- The unbeliever will be condemned (Matt. 25:41; John 5:29; Heb. 9:27; Dan. 12:2; Rev. 14:9-12; 20:6, 11-15; 21:8; 22:11).
- Both the believer and the unbeliever are mentioned as being rewarded and judged *at the same time*. In Matt. 13:36-43, Jesus taught that there would be a separation of the wheat and the tares at the end of the age—not seven or a thousand years before the end. Paul taught the same in 2 Thessalonians 1:6-10, and the same truth is taught in John 5:28-29, Acts 24:15, and Revelation 11:15-19 and 20:11-15. To say otherwise is to distort the Word of God and make it self-contradictory.
- Some of the wicked will receive a greater punishment than others (Luke 12:47; Matt. 10:15).
- The day of judgment has already been set by God (Acts 17:31), and Christ will be the judge (John 5:22).

JESUS TAUGHT A GENERAL RESURRECTION

Matthew 12:40 and 25:31-32 and John 5:28-29 speak of the resurrection of the righteous to life and of the wicked to damnation. *Both* are resurrected and rewarded at the same time: one resurrection, two different directions.

Jesus demonstrated and proved that there would be a resurrection from the dead. In John 11:25, He said He was the resurrection and the life. In John 11:43-45, He raised Lazarus from the dead, thus demonstrating that He was the resurrection and the life. Matthew 27:51-53 states that many rose from the dead at the time of Christ to prove the resurrection. This agrees with Jesus' teaching in Matthew 25:31-36:

- All nations are to be gathered before Him (v. 32).
- Jesus, seated on the throne of His glory, will come with the holy angels (v. 31).
- He will separate the people as sheep from goats (v. 32), with the sheep on His right hand and goats on the left (v. 33).
- He is the king (v. 34).
- The sheep inherit the eternal kingdom (v. 34).
- The goats on the left depart into eternal fire (vv. 41-46).

Dispensationalists state that at the time when all nations are judged, the righteous will rule over the unrighteous, constituting the millennial rule. If this is true, according to these verses, the millennium will be spent in the lake of fire.

When did Jesus say the resurrection of the righteous would occur? Jesus taught that the resurrection of the righteous and day of judgment would be at the *last day* (John 6:39-40, 44, 54). John 11:21-24 states, "Martha said to Him, 'I know that he will rise again in the resurrection *at the last day.*'" Who taught this to Martha? John 12:47-48 states that judgment will happen at the last day.

Why is Jesus so insistent in using this phrase? If the resurrection of the righteous is on the last day, then 1 Thessalonians 4:16 has to be the last day, because there the righteous are resurrected! Believers will be resurrected and changed in a moment in the twinkling of an eye at the last trumpet (1 Cor. 15:51-52). Revelation 11:15-19 mentions the last trumpet; therefore, this has to be the "last day."

The Bible itself states seven times that Christ will resurrect and judge both the living and the dead at His coming:

1. First Peter 4:5: Christ is ready to judge the living and the dead.
2. Acts 10:42: Christ is ordained to be judge of the living and the dead.
3. Romans 14:9: Christ is Lord both of the living and the dead.
4. 2 Timothy 4:1: Christ is to judge the living and the dead at His appearing and His kingdom.
5. Revelation 11:18: gives the time of the dead, that they should be judged.
6. Revelation 20:11-15: states that at the time of the Great White Throne, the books will be opened, the sea will give up the dead, and the dead will be judged by the things written in the books.
7. Revelation 22:12: "And behold I am coming quickly, and My reward is with Me, to give every one according to his work."

This all agrees with Daniel 12:1-2, in which everyone found written in the book is delivered and those who sleep in the dust of the ground will awake either to everlasting life or disgrace and everlasting contempt. This is what Jesus taught in John 5:28-29. The Bible, then, teaches a general resurrection from the dead.

There can be no days after the "last day." The Bible teaches only one bodily resurrection from the dead that is yet to come, thus it is only rational to believe that the last day and the "hour" (John 5:28) when the graves are opened are one and the same day.

In his *Bible Handbook,* Joseph Angus says passages "in 1 and 2 Thessalonians and in 1 Corinthians that speak of the resurrection of the dead, are referred to the *one* resurrection" (Angus 1857, 301). Bengel says Revelation 11:15-18, Matthew 24:31, and 1 Thessalonians 4:16 are the same trumpet (Reese 1934, 74). Bickerseth, a premillennialist, says, "The last trumpet of 1 Cor. 15 and Rev. 11:15 are the same" (Bickerseth 1845, 159).

In Matthew 13:36-43, Jesus taught there would be a separation of the tares from the wheat "at the consummation of the age," not seven or 1007 years before the end of the age. If these references are not as so stated, the Bible is full of contradictions.

THE ANSWER TO 1 THESSALONIANS 4:13-18
CONCERNING THE *PAROUSIA* OF CHRIST

According to the dispensationalists, the *parousia* is the rapture. In 1 Thessalonians 3:13, Paul talks about the believers' "hearts being blameless in holiness at the coming [*parousia*] of our Lord Jesus Christ with all His saints." Therefore, the *parousia* is Christ coming with His saints, not just for them. The question is, when will the resurrection of the believer take place?

In 1 Thessalonians 4:13-18, Paul restates Christ's coming. This portion of Scripture is talking about the resurrection of the righteous believer, answering the question of whether the living believer would have an advantage over the believer that had died before the return of the Lord. Much has been read into this text that is not there by stating that Christ coming *for* His saints and His coming *with* His saints are two separate comings, one before the tribulation and the other after the tribulation.

This is the dispensational position and has resulted in the formulation of a new doctrine and speculation as to the time of the resurrection. This doctrine also teaches that there will be more than one bodily resurrection in the future. However, if you read the text carefully you will see that Christ coming for and with His saints happens at the same time, which the text calls the *parousia* or rapture. First Thessalonians 3:13 has already stated that believers will be here until Christ's coming *parousia* with all His saints.

There is nothing in 1 Thessalonians 4:13-18 that implies when this resurrection will take place, except that it will be when the Lord Jesus returns the second time. At that time, Jesus will descend with a shout, with the voice of an archangel and the trumpet of God. Then the dead in Christ will arise. The living believer, together with the resurrected believer, will be caught up in the clouds to meet the Lord in the air, and so shall we ever be with the Lord. This is the same trumpet that Paul calls the "last trumpet" in 1 Corinthians 15:51-52, and it is when the believer is changed in a moment in the twinkling of an eye. This is what is to happen to the living believer at Christ's coming in 1 Thessalonians 4:13-18. Therefore, 1 Corinthians 15:51-52 and 1 Thessalonians 4:13-18 describe the same event.

John speaks of the last trumpet in Revelation 11:15-19. In this passage, it is stated that when this happens:

- The kingdoms of the world will become the kingdoms of our Lord and of His Christ.
- Christ will come to reign eternally, not just for a thousand years.
- It is the time when all the dead are to be judged.
- It is the time when God's servants, the prophets and the saints are rewarded.

There are not two comings of Christ in this event. To read into the text a pre-tribulation rapture is preposterous, arbitrary, and absurd. It is doing that which 1 Corinthians 4:6 forbids: to go beyond what is written.

John Cumming writes, "The Bible…is a revelation that comes down from heaven in all its beauty and in all its completeness, so much so that he that attempts to add to it takes the place of God and 'shows himself as if he were God,' professing to mend what is already perfect, and to add to that which God has pronounced complete" (Cumming 1854, 2).

We make Bible truths void when we manufacture doctrines and then add them to God's Word (see appendix A, "You Shall Not Add to the Word of God"). We decry false cults for doing this, yet evangelical Christians turn right around and do the very same thing, as if they have the right to do so. Second Corinthians 4:2 strictly forbids us from "handling the word of God deceitfully."

First Corinthians 15:51-52 verifies the above text and the conclusions reached: "Behold I tell you a mystery: We shall not all sleep, but we shall be changed in a moment, in the twinkling of an eye, at the last trumpet. For the trumpet will sound and the dead will be raised incorruptible, and we shall be changed." Furthermore, Revelation 10:6-7 verifies the events of the last trumpet as being the time when the mystery of God is finished and *kronos* (time), not delay, will be no longer. Time runs out when the seventh trumpet sounds and eternity begins, not the millennium.

Therefore, a pre-tribulation rapture is purely a human conjecture. To set a date for the rapture as being an event prior to the last day is to add to the text something that is not there, as well as to pre-date the second coming of Christ. Jesus declared in Matt. 24:30-31 that He is coming in the clouds of heaven with power and great glory at the sound of a great trumpet. Then He will gather His elect together from one end of heaven to another. This has to be the same event as in 1 Thessalonians 4:13-18.

WHAT ABOUT 1 CORINTHIANS 15:20-26, 42?

First Corinthians 15 provides proof of the resurrection of the dead and the events that accompany it. Christ is the "first fruits" of the resurrection (v. 23). The first fruits guarantee the full harvest. Jesus said, "The harvest is the end of the age" (Matt. 13:39-40).

Verse 24 states, "Then comes the end." What end? Is this end different than that told of in Matthew 13:40? Is it different than the last day as taught by Jesus in John 6? Dispensationalists take the word *then* (*eita*) in 1 Corinthians 15:24, "then comes the end," to mean another day other than that of verse 23. At this point, they build a thousand years into the word *then*. However, biblical usage of a word is more important than guess work to fit a man-made theology. In Mark 4:17, *eita* is used with *euthus* to say and mean "immediately."

In 1 Corinthians 15:51-52, 54, Paul's teaching is that the living believer will be changed in a moment in the twinkling of an eye at the last trumpet. Therefore, the believer is here during the time of the trumpets. Paul also states that death will be destroyed at the same time that the living believer is transformed in the twinkling of an eye. After this event, there is no more death!

So, when is the last trumpet? According to Revelation 8:2, there are to be seven trumpets. Revelation 11:15-19 tells us when the last trumpet is: When Christ takes over the kingdoms of this world and comes to reign eternally. This will be the consummation of the age as we know it to be. Revelation 10:7 states that in the days of the seventh angel, the mystery of God is finished. Revelation 10:6 states that time will have run out. This proves that the book of Revelation is not written in chronological order.

First Corinthians 15:23 states that the resurrection will be at Christ's coming. The Greek word used in this verse is *parousia,* His bodily presence. The same word is used in 1 Thessalonians 4:13-18. Therefore, these two references have to be talking about the same event.

Job 14:12 affirms that the resurrection will be at the time when the heavens are no more: "So man lies down and does not rise, till the heavens be no more." This agrees with 2 Peter 3:9-13 and confirms that there will be new heavens and a new earth at that time. According to 2 Peter 3:4, this takes place at the time of Christ's *parousia.*

In Hosea 13:14, the prophet spoke of a time when man would be redeemed from the power of the grave. Paul uses this verse as his background in 1 Corinthians 15:54 as death being swallowed up in victory.

In Isaiah 25:8, Isaiah prophesied that God would swallow up death forever. At the same time, God would wipe away tears from all faces. Revelation 21:1-4 states that this will happen when we enter the new heavens and the new earth.

A LOOK AT REVELATION 20:4-6 AND WHAT IS THE "FIRST RESURRECTION"

Does Revelation 20:4-6 annul the foregoing, or is there a biblical answer? The Bible teaches that there is an answer:

> I saw thrones, and they sat on them, and judgment was committed to them. Then I saw the souls of those who had been beheaded for their witness to Jesus and for the word of God, who had not worshipped the beast or his image, and had not received his mark on their foreheads or on their hands, and they lived and reigned with Christ for a thousand years. But the rest of the dead did not live again until the thousand years were finished. This is the first resurrection. Blessed and holy is he who has part in the first resurrection. Over such the second death has no power, but they shall be priests of God and of Christ, and shall reign with Him a thousand years.

This is the only place in the Bible in which the phrase "first resurrection" is used, and it speaks of those who were martyred during the tribulation. The question is, what is the first resurrection spoken of here, and why is it called the first resurrection? To fully understand these verses, seven aspects need to be analyzed:

1. John saw the *souls* (not bodies) of those beheaded for Jesus and His word.
2. These had not worshipped the beast.
3. They had not worshipped its image.
4. They did not receive his mark or their hands or forehead.
5. These *souls* lived and reigned with Christ a thousand years.
6. They are priests of God and of Christ.
7. They are called "the first resurrection."

Dispensationalists teach that the beast and his image do not appear until after the seven-year tribulation begins. During this time, those who refuse the mark of the beast are martyred. Revelation 20:4-6 calls these martyrs "the first resurrection." Does this not make it certain that the first resurrection comes after the tribulation when the beast and his image have already taken place? However, dispensationalists state that believers were already resurrected at the rapture before the seven-year tribulation began. Yet would not this have been the first resurrection?

Can you have two resurrections seven years apart and have the second one called the first resurrection? Where in the Bible can this be substantiated? Does this not catch dispensationalists in the snare and configuration of their multiple resurrections? Or was John not acquainted with the idea of more than one bodily resurrection from the dead? Note the following:

- Revelation 20:4-6: These martyrs are "priests of God and of Christ" and shall reign with him a thousand years.
- Revelation 1:6: God calls those who compose the seven churches "kings and priests to God."
- Revelation 5:6-10: Those around the throne in heaven sing a new song: "And have redeemed us to God by Your blood out of every tribe and tongue and people and nation, and have made us *kings and priests* to our God and we shall reign on the earth (vv. 9-10, emphasis mine). This group would have had to have been

martyred before the seals and the tribulation began, as the seals do not begin until Chapter 6. Do we have three different groups of martyrs in the book of Revelation called "kings and priests to God," or do they all compose one group of martyrs? If so, then those who reign with Christ compose more than just the seven-year tribulation martyrs.

- Does not Revelation 18:24 group the martyrs of all ages together in one? "And in her [Babylon] was found the blood of prophets and saints, and of all who were slain on the earth." Who then are the martyrs that compose Revelation 20:4-6, and who is the beast as such?

Charles R. Erdman, in talking about the martyrs and the timing of the mark of the beast, states the following about Revelation 20:1-6: "One thing is absolutely certain; this passage makes it impossible for anyone to believe in a 'secret rapture' of the church, or that the return of Christ may be 'at any moment'. This false theory (he says) has been very prominent in the teachings of many modern exponents of Premillennial views" (Erdman 1922, 70).

Was John not acquainted with the modern idea of more then one bodily resurrection from the dead, or did Jesus forget to tell him? What would that do to biblical inspiration and inerrancy? Contrary to some people's belief, in Revelation 20:4-6, there is no resurrection of the body. It is a spiritual resurrection. John saw souls of the martyrs, not their bodies, and he called them the first resurrection.

In Matthew 22:23-32, Jesus, when talking to the Sadducees who did not believe in a resurrection, told them that they were mistaken, deceived, and not knowing the scriptures or the power of God. He specifically spells out a spiritual resurrection in Matthew 22:31 when He says, "But concerning the resurrection of the dead, have you not read what was spoken to you by God, saying, 'I am the God of Abraham, the God of Isaac, and the God of Jacob.' God is not the God of the dead, but of the living."

Jesus saw Abraham, Isaac, and Jacob as alive to God and called it a resurrection (v. 31). This was while their bodies were still in the grave. Therefore, we have here a resurrection that does not entail the body but is that of their soul and spirit being alive to God in heaven. This is the same relationship that we see in Revelation 20:4-5. John saw the souls of the martyrs living and reigning with God in heaven, which is what he calls the first resurrection. This aspect is further accentuated in Revelation 6:9-11, where John sees "souls" under the altar in heaven, crying, "How long, O Lord." These martyrs were alive to God.

This is comparable with 2 Corinthians 5:6-8, in which Paul says, "To be absent from the body is to be present with the Lord?" The question may be asked, how can you see souls which are supposed to be invisible? Second Corinthians 5:2 provides the answer: "For we know that if our earthly house, this tent, is destroyed, we have a building from God, a house not made with hands, eternal in the heavens."

What is meant in Philippians 1:21-23 when Paul says, "To die is gain and to depart and be with Christ is far better?" Is this not being alive with Christ at death, apart from the body? Therefore, there is such a thing as a spiritual resurrection. Is this not what Jesus was talking about in John 5:24-25 when He said, "Most assuredly, I say to you, the hour is coming and *now is*, when the dead [spiritually dead] will hear the voice of the Son of God; and those who hear will live." In this verse, Jesus was not talking about the resurrection of the body but of the soul and spirit that were dead before God (Eph. 2:1). In John 5:28-29 Jesus was talking about the physical resurrection of the body. There He does not say "now is," but "is coming."

Therefore the first resurrection is of the spirit and soul. It is of those who are saved and have come to spiritual life with God.

ANNIHILATION?

This is a subject in which much wrangling over God's Word has taken place over the course of time. False cults have never believed in the ultimate truth of God's Word. It is peculiar that in Christendom, that which for many centuries was called heresy can later become orthodox. All of this is produced by the mind of man as he changes God's Word to fit his personal belief. Hermeneutics certainly should be called into place as to the substituting of one word for another or the adding of a word to a text. Personal feelings should have no part in the interpretation of God's Word.

The question of annihilation is important today because a renowned theologian in evangelical circles has approved the doctrine of ultimate annihilation, namely Dr. John Stott. In modern opinion, it is repugnant and out of date to believe in eternal punishment. The slogan "time changes things" has never gone out of style and more than once has cast its spell on the Word of God. But let us be simpleminded enough to believe what Jesus said: "Till heaven and earth pass away, one jot or one title will by no means pass from the law till all is fulfilled" (Matt. 5:18).

As far as the scriptures go, there is no question as to the difference of the fate of the godly and the ungodly. So is the issue that of eternal damnation? Is death instant destruction, annihilation, and non-existence? What do the scriptures mean by stating such a thing as eternal torment?

First of all, we should remember when talking about this subject that we are dealing with the biblical doctrine of sin, and that in the light of the nature and character of a righteous and holy God. We are also dealing with the fact that man was made in God's divine image, endowed with a righteous and moral conscience and without any moral blemishes. This image in man was to produce a behavior pattern compatible with that nature. Sin is the enemy of God, not just an act of man. Sin relates one to the author of sin (John 8:44). We must therefore deal with the subject of sin in the light of a holy God.

This being the case, we must look at the source of man's fall. Satan the tempter was created perfect and endowed with a righteous constitution, but he willfully chose not to abide in his original state (Ezek. 28:1-19; Isa. 14:4-15; Jude 6). In the Old Testament, Satan is depicted as the personification of two kings. Satan was created as a cherub, but wanted to take the place of God Himself. The creator is always greater than the thing created. Therefore, as a created moral being, Satan was obliged to be subject to his Creator.

It must be held in mind that God did not create Satan as Satan. He created an angel that fell and became Satan. The text states that he was created perfect until iniquity was found in him and he willingly chose not to abide in that state. He therefore put himself under God's judgment and, as a spirit being, was pronounced to be cast into the lake of fire (Rev. 20:10,12-15; 19:20; 21:8).

Jesus said hell was prepared for the devil and his angels and it consisted of eternal fire (Matt. 25:41). Is there anyone who would question the duration of Satan's judgment? Would anyone question whether or not Jesus was telling the truth? It is safe therefore to say that those who follow Satan must be judged with him and also go to his place. First Timothy 3:6 warns of falling into the same condemnation as the devil. Sin is no small thing with God!

Revelation 14:9-11 states the eternal condition of the lost. Never once is there an indication given as to an immediate end of their suffering and torment. Some take fire in the natural sense and believe that as a piece of paper set on fire is soon consumed, so it must be with man in hell. However, these verses as given by God reveal that the condemned are tormented with fire (Rev. 14:10-11) and have no rest day or night. This certainly does not indicate extinction! This is the decree as written in God's Word. Who has the power to alter or change it?

In 1854, the Rev. John Cumming said, "He that attempts to add to [God's Word] takes the place of God, and 'shows himself as if he were God'" (Cumming 1854, 2). This is strong language. However, it is the truth of God as set forth in His Holy Word and with a warning not to add or take away from what is written (see appendix A). Nevertheless, together with the warnings, through the gospel God gives us the privilege of turning from the way of destruction. Look at the awesome cost God Himself paid to redeem man from that destruction: His own Son! Because of sin, Christ was put to death by a cruel and ignominious death at the hands of wicked men.

Jesus Himself in Luke 16:19-31 speaks of the final state of an unrepentant sinner as being in Hades and tormented in flames. This certainly does not lend to annihilation. The sinner is locked into that position and cannot get out (v. 26). He then asks another man named Lazarus, who is in a state of comfort, to go tell his five brothers to repent so they do not come to that place (vv. 27-28). How long has the sinner been there in that state of suffering? The man knew he got there because he did not repent (v. 30). A person's eternal destiny is based on his relationship to the Word of God (v. 31). Thank God for grace given to heed the gospel message and to allow the Holy Spirit to convict of sin and draw us to the Savior.

As to fire, man always looks at things from the natural point of view, but God looks at it from His point of view. For example, when Nicodemus was told he must be "born again," he thought about natural birth and the entering into his mother's womb. When Jesus talked to the woman at the well about "living water," she immediately thought of natural means—something by which to draw water. So it is with fire in man's sense of the word. However, in Exodus 3:2, Moses saw a bush on fire, yet it was not consumed. Who says we can compare God's fire with man's fire? The Bible warns us not to compare natural things with the spiritual, but to compare spiritual things with spiritual things (1 Cor. 2:13-14).

Man has been told. He has been warned. The choice is his to turn from the path of destruction on which Satan has put him. Jesus warned that the end of the broad road leads to destruction (Matt. 7:13-14). Condemnation and destruction are part of the preaching of the gospel. In Mark 16:15-16, Jesus states, "But he that does not believe will be condemned." To choose to go one's own way is to pay the awful price in the end.

THE BIBLE AND THE WORD ETERNAL

Let us take the word *eternal* as found in the Bible and see if the same word means one thing in one place and another in another place. The Greek word for eternal is αιωνιον. It is sometimes translated "everlasting" or "forever and ever," but it always means "eternal." The following references are in relation to the Godhood of God:

- 1 Timothy 1:17: "Now unto the King eternal." Can we change the word *eternal* to mean "temporary in time" or "not forever and ever"?
- Romans 16:26: "The commandment of the everlasting [eternal] God."
- Revelation 4:9: John writes of Christ on the throne "who lives forever and ever [eternally]."
- Revelation 11:15: John, speaking of Christ, says, "He shall reign forever and ever [eternally]."
- Revelation 10:6: "Swore by Him who lives forever and ever [eternally]."
- Hebrews 9:14: "The eternal Spirit."

No one can justify changing the word *eternal* in these references to mean "temporary in time," thus saying that God, Christ, or the Holy Spirit are not eternal or that they have an end. God in His holy Word uses the same word in the following references to refer to the eternal punishment of the wicked:

- Revelation 14:11: "And the smoke of their torment ascends forever and ever [eternally]; and they have no rest day or night." Are we now allowed to take the word *eternal* and make it mean "temporary"? It is not just the smoke that is eternal, but "they [that] have no rest day or night." This speaks of continued existence, not extinction or annihilation.

- Revelation 20:10: "The devil, who deceived them, was cast into the lake of fire and brimstone where the beast and the false prophet are. And they will be tormented day and night forever and ever [eternally]."
- Revelation 20:15: "And anyone not found written in the Book of Life was cast into the lake of fire."
- Matthew 25:41: "Depart from Me you cursed, into the everlasting [eternal] fire prepared for the devil and his angels."

If annihilation were true, what would be the purpose of the fire being eternal?

The Bible teaches that all whose names are not found written in the Book of Life will be cast into the same place as the devil and that they will be tormented day and night forever and ever. Frightful, yes! But who are we to change God's Word? It is better to change one's behavior and avoid this awful time of eternal punishment. If we change Jesus' teachings, are we not then preaching another gospel? Are we not then also made subject to the plagues written in the book (Rev. 22:18-19)?

Upon what are you going to make your decision?

SUMMATION ON RESURRECTION

1. What is the resurrection?
   - It is the physical resuscitation of our dead body.
   - It is the physical resurrection of our dead body to a state of eternal life in a new body.
2. What kind of life will the resurrection body have?
   - It will not be as the life we now possess, which is mortal and subject to death.
   - It will have eternal life (Phil. 3:21).
3. What was Jesus' body like after the resurrection?
   - It was a glorious body (Phil. 3:21).
   - He could appear inside of a locked room (John 20:19, 26).
   - It was not a body of flesh and blood (Luke 24:39).
   - It was not subject to death again (Rom. 6:9).
4. What will our body be like in the resurrection?

- It will be like that of Christ (Phil. 3:21; 1 John 3:2).
- It will not be subject to death (Rom. 6:9).
- It will be a spiritual body, not a spirit body (1 Cor. 15:44).

5. How many bodily resurrections are yet to come?
   - The Bible teaches only one at the last trumpet (1 Cor. 15:51, 53).
   - Some say three or even as high as seven.
   - If there is a resurrection at the rapture before the tribulation and another after the tribulation, which one is the first resurrection (Rev. 20:5)?

6. Did Paul and Peter teach more than one resurrection?
   - Paul taught a resurrection (singular) of both the just and the unjust at the same time (Acts 24:14-5; Acts 10:42; 2 Tim. 4:1).
   - Peter taught the same as Paul (1 Pet. 4:5).
   - Paul said the day of judgment is already set (Acts 17:31).

7. How many resurrections did Jesus teach?
   - Jesus taught only one bodily resurrection from the dead (John 5:28-29).
   - He taught that it would be one at "the last day" (John 6:39-40, 44, 54).
   - Jesus taught the same to Martha (John 11:24). Could it be possible that Jesus was wrong?

8. What did Jesus teach in Matthew 13:36-43?
   - The harvest is the end of the age (v. 39).
   - The tares are taken first to be judged (v. 40).
   - After that the righteous will shine forth in the kingdom (v. 43).

9. What did Jesus teach in Matthew 25:31-46?
   - He taught that when He comes in glory with His holy angels, He will gather all nations before Him and divide them as sheep and goats.
   - The sheep will be on His right hand and the goats on the left.
   - The sheep will inherit the kingdom (v. 34) while the goats will go to everlasting fire (v. 41). Each occurs at the same time.

10. Paul taught the same sequence as Jesus!

- Jesus comes with His mighty angels in flaming fire. First the wicked are punished with an everlasting destruction from the presence of the Lord (2 Thess. 1:7-9).
- "Then" (after that) Christ is glorified in His saints (v. 10).

11. When did Paul teach that the righteous would be changed in a moment?
    - At the last trumpet (1 Cor. 15:51, 52).
    - This must happen to the living believer when the events in 1 Thessalonians 4:13-18 take place. These references are descriptions of the same event.

12. John tells us when the last trumpet will be!
    - The seventh trumpet is the last of the trumpets (Rev. 11:15-19).
    - Christ then comes to reign eternally (v. 15).
    - The dead, both righteous and unrighteous, are rewarded or judged (v. 18). No two separate judgments.
    - This is the same as the great white throne judgment. All the dead are there (Rev. 20:11-14).

WHEN DOES THE RESURRECTION HAPPEN?		
The Last Day	**The Last Trumpet**	**When To Take Place?**
John 6:39	Rev. 11:15–19	Dan. 12:1–2
John 6:40	Matt. 24:31	Job 14:12
John 6:44	1 Cor. 15:51–52	Job 14:14
John 6:54	1 Thess. 4:16	Job 19:25–27
John 11:24	Rev. 10:6–7	Hos. 13:14
John 12:48	Isa. 27:13	Isa. 25:8
Rev. 11:15–19	1 Cor. 15:54	

WHAT DOES THE BIBLE TEACH?

1. Does the Bible teach that there will be a resurrection prior to a tribulation? If so, where is it specifically stated?
2. Does it teach there will be a resurrection after the thousand-year period? If so, where? Does it teach a resurrection apart from the columns in the illustration above?
3. If so, where? Did Jesus teach a resurrection of the righteous and the unrighteous at the same time (John 5:28-29)?

If 1 Thessalonians 4:13-17 is speaking of the rapture and at that time the believer will changed in a moment in the twinkling of an eye (1 Cor. 15:51-52), then both of these references have to be the same event and take place at the *last trumpet*!

How Many Times Will Christ Come "as a Thief in the Night"?

1. Matthew 24:43: Christ spoke of His coming as a thief.
2. First Thessalonians 5:2: The day of the Lord comes as a thief in night.
3. Second Peter 3:10: The day of the Lord comes as a thief in the night in which the heavens and earth pass away.
4. Revelation 16:15: Christ is yet to come as a thief under the sixth vial.

Are these one and the same event, or is Jesus coming as a thief four times?

Does "the Day of the Lord," "the Day of God," and "the Day of Christ" Refer to the Same Day?

1. Peter 3:10-13: The day of the Lord comes as a thief in the night, and heavens and earth pass away.
2. 1 Thessalonians 5:2: The day of the Lord will come as a thief in the night.
3. 2 Thessalonians 2:1-12: The *parousia* is the day of Christ (the Greek word is *Lord*) and is the same day.
4. Matthew 13:36-43: The harvest is at the end of the age.
5. 1 Thessalonians 3:13: The *parousia* is Christ coming *with* all His saints.
6. Revelation 16:14-15: The great day of God almighty is like as a thief in the night.

IS GOD GOING TO JUDGE ALL HUMANITY AT THE SAME TIME?

1. According to Matthew 13:36-43, the harvest is at the end of the age. The tares and wheat are taken care of at same the time, which indicates a general judgment.
2. 2 Thessalonians 1:3-10 states the same truth as Matthew 13:36-43.
3. In Acts 10:40-43, the living and the dead will be judged at the same time (cf. Rom. 14:9; 2 Tim. 4:1; 1 Pet. 4:5).
4. In Revelation 11:15-19, the wicked and the righteous are judged at the last trumpet.

THE BIBLE TEACHES ONE BODILY RESURRECTION TO COME

The Bible teaches one bodily resurrection to come when the righteous and the wicked are both judged and rewarded at the same time. (Matt. 25:31-46; 2 Thess. 1:6-10; 2:1-10; 1 Cor. 15:51-55; Rev. 11:15-19; 20:11-15; Dan. 12:1-2; John 5:28-29; 6:38-40,44-45,54; Acts 24:15.)

QUESTIONS TO REVIEW REGARDING THE RESURRECTION OF THE BODY

1. What is the biblical position on the resurrection?
2. What is the resurrection?
3. When is the resurrection?
4. Why does the Bible teach a resurrection of the body?
5. Is the resurrection a part of God's eschatological plan?
6. Will the resurrection culminate life on earth as we know it?
7. How many bodily resurrections does the Bible teach are yet to come?
8. Is there a resurrection in John 5:24-25?
9. Is there a bodily resurrection in Revelation 20:4?
10. Is there a bodily resurrection in John 5:28-29?
11. Is there a bodily resurrection found in 1 Corinthians 15?
12. Is there a bodily resurrection in Revelation 20:11-14?
13. Is there a bodily resurrection in Revelation 11:15-19?

14. Is Revelation 11:18 a final judgment?
15. Will Christ judge all humanity at the same time, or will He judge the unbeliever at a different time than He rewards the believer (Rev. 11:18)?
16. Do all the various places in the Bible that speak of a bodily resurrection mean that there will be that many resurrections?
17. Does the Bible teach a bodily resurrection before the thousand years? If so, where?
18. Does the Bible teach a resurrection of believers before that of the wicked? If so, where?
19. Does the Bible teach a general resurrection from the dead?
20. Does the Bible use the word *resurrection* in the plural?
21. When does the Bible say that all the dead, small and great, stand before God?
22. Is there such a thing as a spiritual resurrection?
23. When does the Old Testament say man will rise or be resurrected?
24. Does the Bible teach a resurrection at a rapture before the second coming of Christ?
25. Does the Bible teach another resurrection after the tribulation, making it the second resurrection from the dead, but calling it the first?
26. Does the Bible teach a resurrection after the thousand years, making it the third resurrection?
27. What other events are associated with the resurrection?
28. Does the Bible teach more than one resurrection of believers? If so, where?
29. Will all mankind, believer and unbeliever, be resurrected at the same time?
30. How many times is Christ to come as a thief in the night?
31. Is 1 Thessalonians 4:13-18 and 1 Corinthians 15:51-52 the same event?

THE BINDING OF SATAN IN REVELATION 20

What is the binding of Satan, and when did it (or does it) take place? What is included in the binding of Satan? And what does the "thousand years" in Revelation 20:1-8 signify?

J. Dwight Pentecost wrote, "Immediately following the second advent Satan is bound for a thousand years" (Pentecost 1978, 77). This subject has been an ongoing debate because of different beliefs in various denominations. Much of the time, the binding of Satan is discussed on an emotional or presuppositional basis and not on exegesis of the Scripture. The theological presupposition in one's mind can take precedence and become the basis for one's position.

We have all heard the song, "Satan will be bound a thousand years; we'll have no tempter then." What is this phrase implying? First of all, it implants in one's mind that it is biblical. Then it suggests a *future* date in time when Satan will be bound. It also implies that when this takes place, no one will be tempted. It is peculiar how these positions hold such a strong place in our minds without a thread of scriptural evidence for them.

Revelation 20 is the only passage in the Bible that mentions the binding of Satan for a thousand years. But this text does not imply *when* it will take place or that there will be no temptation when it happens. To say otherwise is to read into the text, which is against all proper hermeneutics (1 Cor. 4:6).

The book of Revelation is written in apocalyptic language, which means that it is highly symbolical. This fact is stated in the book itself (Rev. 1:1). The message of the book was sent and *signified* to John by Christ's angel. The word *signified* means God gave the book to John through the use of signs. A sign indicates and points to something outside of itself as the real meaning of the message.

An illustration here may help to explain. Suppose a person wants to catch a bus, so he goes down the street, where he sees a sign indicating a bus stop. Does that person ride the sign or wait for the bus? We have too many who are riding signs today. Another example in the book itself: in Revelation 1:12-13, John saw the glorified Christ in the midst of seven golden lamp stands. The lamp stands are a sign pointing to something outside of themselves. What do the lamp stands indicate? The context reveals the answer. In Revelation 1:20, we are told the candlesticks represent the churches to which John is to address his message. All such symbolism in the book of Revelation is answerable in the book itself or verified by symbols from Old Testament usage. Another such example is found in Revelation 17:1, where someone is sitting on "many waters." What do the many waters symbolize? Revelation 17:15 plainly states that the "waters" symbolize "peoples, multitudes and nations and tongues." Therefore, it cannot be literal waters.

As we have just seen in Revelation 1:20 and 17:1, 15, figurative language adds dimension to truth that cannot be expressed in any other manner. For example, in Revelation 5–6 and John 1:29, Jesus is figuratively called the "Lamb." Would that make Him a literal lamb? No, it is symbolical language.

Biblical interpreters must stay within certain parameters to correctly interpret signs, symbols, and/or figurative language. It is certain that one cannot interpret figurative or symbolic language literally. The Bible states in 1 Corinthians 2:13-14 that the Bible is to be spiritually discerned and that we are to compare spiritual things with spiritual things, not with carnal or natural things.

True, there are places in the book of Revelation that can be taken literally. However, as to Revelation 13:8, no one can say that Jesus was literally slain at the time of the laying of the foundation of the earth. Revelation 11:8 also uses symbolical language to describe the literal city of Jerusalem by *spiritually* calling it "Sodom and Egypt." At the same time, we must be careful not to jump from literal to figurative, or vise versa. Albert Barnes,

George Ladd, Charles Hodge and many more say that obscure passages should be interpreted in the light of clear passages.

Let us take Revelation 20:1-10, which encompasses the events described in "the binding of Satan," and look at eight phrases in the text. In each instance, we must ask ourselves whether the text is to be taken literally or figuratively. We must also be consistent in our interpretation.

1. An angel from heaven
2. The key
3. The bottomless pit
4. A great chain
5. The dragon
6. Satan bound
7. The thousand years and the reign of Christ
8. Deception of nations

Biblical usage by itself answers and puts significance to each of these words or phrases. Let's treat each of these symbols individually.

AN ANGEL FROM HEAVEN

Who is this angel? Is it a literal angel or is it symbolic? In biblical use, the first meaning of the word *angel* in the Greek is that of a messenger, not a literal angel. In Revelation 1, we learn that John wrote to the "angels" of the seven churches. No one believes John wrote to seven literal angels. They are interpreted to be the leaders of each local church.

- In Jude 9, we learn that even Michael, the archangel, did not dare bring a railing accusation against Satan, but said, "The Lord rebuke you." This tells us even archangels do not have the power in themselves to come against Satan. This may also mean Satan could have been the highest-ranking angel God created before the Fall. Satan was called "Lucifer," the son of the morning, and he was in charge of Eden, the garden of God (Isa. 14; Ezek. 28).
- In Luke 7:27, the word *messenger* is the Greek word for angel, yet it refers to John the Baptist as being the forerunner of Christ.
- In 2 Corinthians 12:7, Paul says a "messenger" of Satan was sent to buffet him. The original word is angel.

- Revelation 10:1-2 speaks of another angel (messenger) coming down from heaven whose description is that of Jesus as found in Chapters 4 and 5 of Revelation.

In conclusion, this angel-messenger has to be someone with more authority and power than that of a literal angel. The angel-messenger is the means or medium God chose to communicate His message to mankind. This angel-messenger had to be none other than Christ Himself.

THE KEY

Is the key literal, or is it to be interpreted figuratively? Biblical usage and context must determine the answer.

- In Revelation 1:18, Jesus has the keys of death and of hell! Is this literal or figurative? If literal, what kind of keys would they be?
- In Revelation 3:7, Jesus has the key of David! Was this a literal key or figurative?
- Revelation 9:1 mentions a "key of the bottomless pit." What kind of a key would that be?
- In Luke 11:52, Jesus spoke about the "key of knowledge." What kind of literal key would this have to be? Would Matthew 23:13 be the answer?
- Isaiah 22:20-25 speaks about a key of the house of David that Jesus has (Rev. 3:7). Is this a literal key?
- In Matthew 16:19, Jesus says He had the "keys of the kingdom of heaven" and gave them to Peter. What kind of a key did Jesus pull out of His pocket to give to Peter? How did Peter use the keys? (See Acts 2:38; 3:19). Peter used them by preaching the gospel to let people into the kingdom of God.

It would be the height of absurdity to interpret any of these references in the literal sense of the word. From this, we see that biblical usage determines the function of the word. Therefore, the conclusion is that biblically, the word *key* is not literal.

THE BOTTOMLESS PIT

Is this pit literal or figurative?

- Revelation 9:1, 11:7, and 17:8 each use the same Greek word for "abyss." If this is a literal bottomless pit, there would have to be a hole in the earth from here to China. Preposterous? Yes!
- Luke 8:31 uses the same word for "abyss" as to where Jesus commanded the demons to depart.
- In Revelation 20:7 this pit is called a "prison" where Satan was bound.

Therefore, we must conclude that the bottomless pit is not a literal pit.

A GREAT CHAIN

Is the chain literal? Can evil spirits who are incorporeal (do not possess material substance) be bound with a literal chain?

- Mark 5:1-4 informs us that even a demon-possessed person could not be bound by a literal chain.
- Jude 6 tells us the fallen angels are reserved in everlasting chains until the judgment of the last day. Is this literal or figurative?
- 2 Peter 2:4 speaks of "chains of darkness." Are these literal chains? A chain speaks of limitations or restraint.
- In Matthew 12:25, 29, Jesus bound Satan. Satan is limited under the New Covenant so he cannot do the things he did under the Old Covenant. In pristine Eden, Satan was there to tempt man (Gen. 3). In the book of Job, Satan was allowed to enter heaven and accuse Job in God's presence (Job 1). In the book of Zechariah, he was also allowed to appear in God's presence to oppose Joshua the High Priest (Zech. 3).
- Second Peter 2:4 and Jude 6 declare that demons have been put in everlasting chains. By the arrival of King Jesus on earth, demons knew their time was limited (Matt. 8:29).
- Revelation 12:1-9 says upon the ascension of Christ into heaven, Satan was cast out of the very presence of God in heaven and is not

allowed there any more. Christ and the gospel have put a noose around Satan's neck!

We must therefore arrive at the conclusion that the chain is not a literal chain.

THE DRAGON

Does Revelation 20:2 refer to a literal dragon? This verse is self-interpretive: The dragon is called "the Old Serpent," who is the devil and Satan. It should not be too hard to identify who this is. No literal construction will work. It is important to note that each time in Revelation the word *dragon* is mentioned, it cannot be taken literally. (For further references, see Rev. 12:3, 7-9; he is the same serpent as that of Gen. 3:1.) Also, in 2 Corinthians 11:3, Paul calls him the serpent that deceived Eve.

Thus far, not one of the aspects mentioned in Revelation 20:1-10 can be taken literally without doing violence to the text.

SATAN BOUND

This is probably the area in which most of the problems arise concerning the text. The question is *when* the binding is to take place. Premillennialists claim this will occur at the second coming of Christ when He comes to set up His kingdom on the earth. In other words, at the millennium. But does the text say this?

In Matthew 12:28-29 and Luke 11:22, while Jesus was on earth, He went into the strongman's [Satan's] house and bound him. This He did in the context of casting out demons. Scripture tells us Jesus is the One who is stronger than the strongman, Satan. In Jude 9, we learn Satan may have been stronger than Michael, the archangel, who did not dare to bring an accusation against him, but he is not stronger than Christ. According to Matthew 12, it cannot be denied that Jesus did bind Satan! We must now come to grips with this fact.

In John 12:31-33, Jesus states that by His death and resurrection, "Now the ruler of this world would be cast out." Does not the word *now* put a restraint on Satan at that time? In Matthew 12:28, Jesus declared that by the act of casting out demons, the kingdom of God had come on the people. Therefore, the binding of Satan has something to do with the inauguration of the kingdom of God. The same word for "cast" is used in Revelation 20:3 to describe Satan being cast into the bottomless pit. These references could harmonize as to the same event.

Paul says in Colossians 2:15 Jesus disarmed principalities and powers and He "made a public spectacle of them, triumphing over them in it." These principalities and powers are thus not free to do as they will.

In John 16:11, Jesus states that due to the coming of the Holy Spirit, "the ruler of this world is judged [past tense]." This is clearly a judgmental restraint put on Satan at that time. After His resurrection, Jesus declared all power and authority in heaven and on earth was now His (Matt. 28:18-20). Where is Satan's power now, then? Jesus said, "The ruler of this world is coming and has nothing in Me" (John 14:30). Yes, Jesus has already bound Satan in the manner of Revelation 20:2!

In what sense was this binding, and what effect did it produce? Revelation 12:1-9 says that upon His ascension into heaven, Jesus cast Satan out of heaven with his angels and *no place* was found for them in heaven any longer. The effect of Jesus' arrival into heaven is stated in Revelation 12:10: "Now salvation, and strength, and the kingdom of our God, and the power of His Christ have come." Through this act of Christ, the kingdom of God became fully realized. Therefore, the Kingdom of God being established on earth had something to do with Satan's binding. Those who are born again are in the Kingdom and can overcome Satan by the blood of the Lamb and the word of their testimony.

Furthermore, the binding of Satan relates directly to the "deception of nations" in Revelation 20:3, 8. This is true because when Satan was released from his prison, he went out to deceive the nations.

When Jesus began to preach the gospel in Mark 1:14-15, He stated the time was fulfilled and the kingdom of God was at hand. From 606 B.C., the kingdom of God in Israel was dominated by four heathen kingdoms: Babylon, Medo-Persia, Greece, and Rome. These nations ruled the known world until Christ came, and they effectually denied God's kingdom. These four kingdoms were dominated by Satanic powers (Dan. 10:13, 20).

When Christ came, He bound Satan and reestablished the kingdom of God on earth, as stated in Mark 1:14-15 and John 3:3-5. This is the kingdom that John the Revelator said he was in and for which he was suffering (Rev. 1:9). When Christ met Satan in Matthew 4:8-9 Satan claimed all the kingdoms of the world were his. This Jesus did not deny. Since then, Jesus has invaded Satan's territory and taken many captive for Christ's kingdom through the preaching of the gospel of the kingdom.

When writing to a Gentile church, Paul said God had delivered them from the domain of darkness and transferred them into the kingdom of His beloved Son (Col. 1:13). Jesus told Nicodemus that through the new birth, he would enter the kingdom of God (John 3:3-5). On the basis of being born again, every soul enters God's kingdom—a kingdom Paul in Colossians calls "the kingdom of His Son." The dispensationalists say the kingdom of the Son is the millennium. In these texts, however, neither Paul nor Jesus agrees with that position.

Isaiah 53:12 prophetically states that through His death, the Messiah (Jesus) would divide the spoil with the strong. First John 3:8 says Jesus came to destroy the works of the devil. Is this not what is included in the Messianic prediction made in the Garden of Eden (Gen. 3:15)? Luke 10:17-19 states that Jesus gave His disciples the power to tread on serpents, and they came back rejoicing because demons were subject to them. Jesus then said, "I saw Satan as lightning fall from heaven [past tense]." In Acts 26:18, Jesus said it is the gospel that turns people "from darkness to light, and from the power of Satan to God."

These scriptures tell us Satan's power has been taken from him and now people from all nations can enter the kingdom of God. God has made both Jew and Gentile one in Christ's kingdom (Eph. 2:11-22). Jesus Christ has already bound the strong man (Satan), thus preventing him from deceiving people about the kingdom of God. Since Calvary, no one nation has dominated the known world as they did prior the cross.

THE THOUSAND YEARS

Are the thousand years literal, or are they figurative? Since the other subjects discussed thus far were figurative, then by parity of reasoning and the laws of hermeneutics so must be the thousand years. In true hermeneutics, one cannot take one phrase out of all that are figurative and make it literal.

- Psalm 50:10, Deuteronomy 1:10-11, 2 Peter 3:8, Matthew 18:21-22, and Revelation 5:11 all use numbers as an indefinite period of time, and therefore must be viewed figuratively. If the thousand years of Revelation 20 is figurative, where are we to place it, or how are we to account for it?

- Ephesians 1:10 speaks of "the fullness of times"; the era when God will gather together all things under the headship of Christ. Galatians 4:4 states that the fullness of time began with Christ being born of a woman. We live in the era of the fullness of times.
- Scofield, commenting on Ephesians 1:10, says this verse belongs to the millennium. However, Galatians 4:4 proves that theory wrong. The millennium has become a glove box for dispensationalists in which they attempt to stash that which does not fit their scheme. Postponing biblical truth always leaves room for a private interpretation.

The thousand years must fit into the fullness of time or it has to happen outside of time. Which is it? If it is in time, it has to be between the first and the second coming of Christ. Therefore, it is the kingdom of God now in its present form.

THE REIGN OF CHRIST

What about the reign of Christ? Who is it that reigns with Christ, and when do they reign? Revelation 20:4 states that the martyrs who witnessed for Christ and the Word of God will reign with him for thousand years. This could refer to the martyrs of Revelation 6:9-11, as well as others.

Ephesians 1:10 does not belong to the millennium but to the period of time between the first and second coming of Christ, however long that period of time might be. It will run until the fullness of time is over and eternity begins. This is affirmed by Revelation 10:6-7, which states that when the mystery of God is finished at the sounding of the seventh trumpet, "time" (*kronos*), not delay, will be no longer. When time ceases on earth, we enter into eternity, not a millennium.

Peter states this succinctly in 2 Peter 3:10-13. This in turn is affirmed in Revelation 11:15-19: At the sounding of the seventh and last trumpet, the kingdoms of this world will become the kingdoms of our Lord and of His Christ. He will then reign eternally, not just for a thousand years. This leaves no room for a seven-year tribulation or thousand-year millennium after Jesus comes to reign forever and ever. Since the Bible does not contradict itself, the thousand years of Revelation 20 has to line up with the timing of Revelation 11:15, or these two verses contradict each other. Biblically, this would be impossible.

Hebrews 9:1-9 agrees in type with these references as to the thousand years of Revelation 20. The author of Hebrews tells us the two compartments of the tabernacle represented the Old and New Testaments. Hebrews 8:5 states that the tabernacle on earth was a type of the tabernacle in heaven. It prefigured both the Old Testament and the New Testament periods of time. This is why it was important for Moses to make the tabernacle according to the pattern shown to him on the mount (Ex. 25:40; Acts 7:44; Heb. 8:5). Moses had no right to change any part of it. Nor have we the right to change any part of God's Word.

Hebrews 9:2, 6 states that the tabernacle was divided into two compartments that were separated by a veil. The first tabernacle was where the priests ministered. The second tabernacle, or the Holy of Holies, was where the high priest ministered but once a year (Heb. 9:3, 5, 7). Hebrews 9:8-9 states, "The Holy Spirit indicating this, that the way into the Holiest of All was not yet made manifest while the first tabernacle was still standing. It was symbolical for the present time [Old Testament] in which both gifts and sacrifices are offered which cannot make him who performed the service perfect in regard to the conscience." Note the following:

- In order to get into the Holy of Holies, the high priest had to go behind the veil that separated the two compartments.
- The author of Hebrews states that the veil represented Christ's flesh (Heb. 10:20).
- The Holy of Holies is the place where Christ entered to obtain eternal redemption for us (Heb. 9:12).
- When Christ entered the Holiest of All, the veil was rent from top to bottom (Matt. 27:51).
- Because Christ entered into the Holy of Holies in heaven, this had to represent the beginning of the New Covenant, the time between His first and second comings. The Holy of Holies was a cube that measured $10 \times 10 \times 10 = $ thousand. This, in type, answers to the thousand years of Revelation 20.
- Since Christ has now entered the Holy of Holies, every believer can enter the Holy of Holies based on the shed blood of Christ (Heb. 10:19).

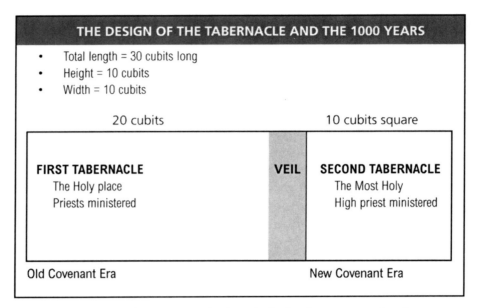

Because the veil represented Christ's flesh, the Most Holy place must represent the New Covenant, just as the first tabernacle represented the Old Covenant (Heb. 9:9).

Note that the Most Holy place was a cube measuring 10 x 10 x 10 = thousand. This, then, must represent the New Covenant era. Because numbers in the book of Revelation are symbolic, they must answer to the one thousand years in Revelation 20:2. This number is used to express the period of time in which Christ reigns with His martyrs and in which Satan is bound so as not to deceive the nations relative to the kingdom of God.

The pattern of the tabernacle relates to the fact that there is nothing after the Most Holy place that is symbolic of the New Covenant. God's work on earth has been finished (John 17:4). Hebrews 9 fits no other pattern.

The Most Holy place represents the "fullness of times" in Ephesians 1:10 and is verified by Galatians 4:4 as the time when Christ came into this world. It is the time when God is gathering together all things under the headship of Christ. There can be no time after the fullness of time, or words would be meaningless. Ephesians 1:10 does not belong to the millennium as Scofield says, but is the period of time between the first and second comings of Christ. This is again affirmed by Revelation 10:6-7, which states that when the mystery of God is finished at the sounding of the seventh trumpet, "time" (*kronos*), not delay, will be no longer. When time ceases on earth, we will enter into eternity, not a millennium. Peter states this succinctly in 2 Peter 3:10-13. Revelation 11:15-19 also affirms that at the sounding of the seventh and last trumpet, the kingdoms of this world will become the kingdoms of our Lord and of His Christ. He will then reign eternally, not just for a thousand years. This leaves no room for a seven-year tribulation or thousand-year millennium after Jesus comes to reign forever and ever. Since the Bible does not contradict itself, the timing of the one thousand years of Revelation 20 has to coincide with the timing of Revelation 11:15, or there would be a contradiction in the Bible.

The New Testament certainly pictures the time of Ephesians 1:10 as being when all things are placed under Christ's control and headship. Jesus' own statement in Matthew 28:18 verifies this, as do many other scriptures that state that Christ ascended far above principalities and power and has them under His feet (e.g, Eph. 1:19-23; Phil. 2:9-11). This we do not yet see, but we see Jesus (Heb. 2:8-9). We live in the gospel age, which Hebrews 9 aligns with that part of the tabernacle called the "Most Holy."

In Revelation 20:4 there can be no question but that the martyrs, who witnessed for Christ and the word of God, reign with Christ in heaven for a thousand years. Disembodied souls do not reign on earth.

There is a spiritual side of Christ's reign in the Church while on earth. Did Jesus not say upon His ascension that all power and authority were His both in heaven and on earth (Matt. 28:18)? Jesus also promised that the gates of hell would not prevail against the Church (Matt. 16:18). Do you think Jesus is not doing what these verses say?

Around 740 B.C., Isaiah prophesied that Christ's reign would be in the realm of salvation. "How beautiful upon the mountains are the feet of him who brings good news, who proclaims peace, who brings glad tidings of good things, who proclaims salvation, who says to Zion, 'Your God reigns!'" (Isa. 52:7). In Romans 10:15, Paul used this verse in the context of the salvation that Christ brought in the New Covenant.

To prove that Christ was reigning, Paul says in Romans 5:17, "Those who receive the abundance of grace and the gift of righteousness will reign in life through One, Jesus Christ." To accentuate this, in verse 21, Paul says, "So that as sin reigned in death even so grace might reign through righteousness to eternal life through Jesus Christ our Lord." Furthermore, in 1 Corinthians 15:25-26, Paul states, "For He must reign till He has put all enemies under His feet. The last enemy that will be destroyed is death."

If Christ must reign until the resurrection, when all things literally are put under His feet, He must therefore be reigning now. Romans 15:12 states that Christ is the fulfillment of Isaiah 11:10 and that He arose from the dead to "reign over the Gentiles." Nothing could be any more plain than the fact that this constitutes a part of Christ's present reign.

WHAT IS THE DECEPTION OF NATIONS?

Ever since the time of Exodus 19:6, when God pronounced Israel to be a "kingdom of priests," the kingdom of God as a nation among men was established on earth. Israel was to be the head nation and not the tail (Deut. 28:13). They were given a covenant of law as to how to live on earth under God. The nation was a theocracy. However, Israel failed by not living up to its theocratic calling. They wanted to become like other nations that had an earthly visible king to rule over them instead of God who ruled them through His law and prophets. It was not long until Israel failed in God's kingdom and adopted heathen gods and rituals.

For Israel's punishment, the nation was split in two after the death of Solomon. Israel became the northern kingdom and Judah the southern kingdom. From Amos's time and onward, God sent prophets to warn Israel and Judah about their backsliding and to tell the people that sanctions would be put in place according to Leviticus 26 and Deuteronomy 28. Neither Judah nor Israel heeded the prophetic warnings, and both were sold into the captivity of heathen nations. Israel was taken over by the Assyrians, and many were deported out of their country in 722 B.C. Judah followed in Israel's footsteps and was sold into Babylonian captivity in 606 B.C., 597 B.C., and 586 B.C. From this time on, the age of the Gentiles began. They overtook and subjugated God's people and ruled the known world until the time of Christ.

Nebuchadnezzar thought he had gained control of the various nations of the day through his own genius and power. However, God showed him differently. He was overcome by the Medes and Persians. Later, Greece took control of the then entire known world. After that time, Rome came into power and ruled the entire known world until the time of Christ and His gospel. Those heathen nations were ruled by Satan and his hosts (Dan. 10:13, 20). This period of time began with an "image of a man" (Dan. 2:31-45), indicating that man, not God, was in control of the world. When Rome was in power, Christ the king was born, and He reestablished the kingdom of God on earth.

The deception of nations was that these kingdoms thought they could rule the world of man and leave God and His kingdom out of the picture. However, the kingdom of God arrived with the King. Christ was born king (Matt. 2), and He reestablished the kingdom of God on earth (Mark 1:14-15). He issued the same message as His forerunner, John the Baptist (Matt. 3:1-12). In John 3:3-5, Jesus said only a person who was born again would enter the kingdom of God. Gentiles no longer would have to convert to Judaism, be circumcised, or become a proselyte to enter God's kingdom. They now could repent, be converted, and thereby enter God's kingdom.

Christ set up His kingdom. His kingdom invaded, took over the Roman Empire, and then spread to all the kingdoms of the world. Since Calvary and Christianity came, there has never been any one nation that has ruled the entire known world as the previous nations had done. All power and authority both in heaven and on the earth has been put into the hands of Christ, who sits on the throne at the right hand of God and rules the world from above. Jesus said the gospel of His kingdom should be preached in the whole world as a witness to all nations. Then the end will come (Matt. 24:14).

The deception of nations was that man thought he could govern the world without God and His kingdom. Christ showed them differently:

- Being born king, Christ had a kingdom (John 18:36).
- Christ died as a king and rose triumphant over death, hell and the grave. He is now king on the throne in heaven, ruling the world from above (Rev. 3:21; 4–5).
- John said he was in the kingdom and patience of Jesus Christ.
- Jesus told Nicodemus that by being born again, he would be in the kingdom of God.
- Paul told the Colossian Gentiles they had been taken out of the kingdom of darkness (Satan's kingdom) and transferred into the kingdom of His dear Son (Col. 1:13).

God spoiled Satan's deceptive plan through His Son via the cross. At the seventh trumpet (Rev. 11:15-19) when Christ returns, all the kingdoms of the world will become the kingdom of Christ. He will reign forever and ever, not just for a thousand years. Because the Bible does not contradict itself, the reign of Christ in Revelation 20 has to synchronize with Revelation 11:15, in which Christ is said to come and reign eternally. The seventh trumpet only can mean time has run out and eternity has begun. The Bible leaves no place for a tribulation or millennium after Jesus comes to reign eternally. Is this not what Peter says in 2 Peter 3:10-14, that we enter into eternity, not a tribulation period or a millennium? The Bible teaches that the "fullness of times" is the period between the first and second coming of Christ. Revelation 20 cannot be put into a calculated period of time yet to come. It also follows that it cannot be used as the basis of a premillennial advent of Christ.

The following provides further evidence that Revelation 20 does not lend itself to a literal interpretation. Nor can it be used to support a millennium on earth. This data has been culled from various sources through the years (some is from the writings of John Bray).

Revelation 20 does not say *anything* about:

1. Christ's second coming
2. A bodily resurrection
3. Live people on earth
4. Thrones on earth
5. Reigning on earth
6. A literal throne of David
7. Christ reigning on the earth
8. The city of Jerusalem
9. Israel or Palestine
10. Christ on the earth
11. A Jewish kingdom
12. Righteousness on earth
13. Peace and prosperity
14. Re-gathered Israel
15. A temple in Palestine
16. Restored sacrifices
17. The Jews being saved
18. A converted world
19. A fertile Palestine
20. One thousand years of peace on earth

Chapter 17

THE GREAT TRIBULATION

The so-called "great tribulation" is postulated on a man-made pre-suppositional postponement of Daniel's seventieth week. Take away the unscriptural postponement and you have no seven-year tribulation period. (Please refer to the chart on page 160 to review The Dispensational Position on Daniel's 70th week). Those who believe in the tribulation as such do so based on the assumption that the week was postponed. They accept it without question and then proceed on the assumption that it is true. Biblical proof for such a postponement is needed.

Nevertheless, it is necessary to expand on the biblical meaning of the word *tribulation* and how it is used. Do some theologies misuse and/or go beyond scriptural bounds (1 Cor. 4:6) in their use of the word *tribulation*? Consider the following:

- The Greek word for "tribulation" is *thlipsis*, which is translated "affliction or tribulation." Paul called all the pressure and persecution he endured by the Judaizers "*thlipsis*," tribulation or persecution.
- In 1 Thessalonians 3:3-7, Paul uses this word three times to describe the persecution that the Thessalonians were experiencing at that time.
- In Matthew 24:21 and Revelation 7:14, we read of the "great tribulation," the same word used in both references. Therefore, the

word cannot lend itself only to the time that the dispensationalists say it does or to what they say it is.

The remarkable assumption dispensationalists make is they can postulate that all these events take place during the postponed seventieth week of Daniel without scriptural evidence as to the same. Time-wise, it is a hiding place for a lot of biblical truth.

Dispensationalists say the tribulation is a time when God's wrath will be poured out of heaven on the earth after the Church has been taken up in the rapture (Rev. 6–19). This is an endeavor to frighten people by the use of the word so they will believe in a pre-tribulation rapture. Their endeavor is to make Revelation 6–19 the period of time they call the "great tribulation," from which believers are supposed to be raptured. In other words, they are saying Revelation 6–19 has no application to the Church today but is solely in the future after the rapture.

If this were the case, why are we told in the book of Revelation itself that those who read and obey the contents of the book are blessed (Rev. 1:3)? We must ask the question, how can the Christian keep something today that does not apply until after the Church is taken away? Does this not make null and void this portion of the Word of God for the believer in this age? Jesus Himself said these things were to be testified to the churches (Rev. 22:16). The events of Revelation 6–19 will work themselves out in history, but not always according to newspaper headlines.

Dispensationalists also say it is the time of Jacob's trouble. "Alas! For the day is great, so that none is like it; and it is the time of Jacob's trouble, but he shall be saved out of it" (Jer. 30:7). However, the context reveals that this verse was applied to Israel's captivity while in Babylon. Jeremiah 30:8 says they will be delivered out of it, then verse 9 states that upon being delivered out of it, "They shall serve the Lord their God, and David their king, whom I will raise up for them." Who is this "David their king" that is to be resurrected for them? This can be none other than the Messiah, the seed of David that God already resurrected to sit on David's throne as Israel's prince and king, as recorded in Acts 2:30-33. Therefore Jeremiah 30:7 has already been fulfilled and cannot apply to the future.

Furthermore, dispensationalists postpone Daniel's seventieth week for over two thousand years until after the rapture, calling it the great tribulation. Ryrie, in his book *Dispensationalism Today,* states: "It would be a very unusual thing to reinstate a dispensation after the lapse of two thousand years or more" (Ryrie 1964, 50). However, he finds no problem in postponing Daniel's seventieth week for over two thousand years. There is no biblical warrant for postponing Daniel's seventieth week. It is a man-made assumption that cannot be verified by Scripture. Therefore, it cannot be held as tenable.

J. Dwight Pentecost, believing that the Church would be raptured before the tribulation, states that the testing time of Revelation 3:10 that applies to the Philadelphia church is the testing of the tribulation of Daniel's seventieth week. He says, "The nature of the testing in *the seventieth week*, as stated in *Revelation 3:10* is not to bring the individual to cleansing, but to reveal the *degradation* and need of the *unregenerate heart*" (Pentecost 1978, 20, emphasis mine).

Pentecost has just said the testing of the Philadelphia church of Revelation 3:10 is the testing of the seventieth week. Yet his claim is that the Church is raptured and not in the tribulation of the seventieth week. How then can the testing of this Church belong in the seventieth week? On the same page, Pentecost also says, "Inasmuch as the church has been perfected and delivered from all judgment (Rom. 8:1; John 5:24; 1 John 4:17), if she is subjected to judgment again the promises of God would be of none effect and the death of Christ would be ineffectual" (Ibid.). Since the church is already perfected, how can a degradation and an unregenerate heart exist in her, as he says?

As a literalist, how can Pentecost say that this Church literally will be in the tribulation known as Daniel's seventieth week when that Church literally no longer exists? If she did exist, she would have been raptured, because according to his theory the Church is not supposed to go through the tribulation. This is double-talk and profoundly confusing for a literalist to say because it is denying that which he actually believes. The Bible teaches that the seventieth week of Daniel is already fulfilled. (See Chapter 12, "The Rapture and the Second Coming of Christ.")

WHAT DOES THE BOOK OF REVELATION SAY ABOUT SUFFERING?

What are the dispensationalists afraid of in the book of Revelation? Why do they assume Revelation 6–19 is not for us today, but is to take place after Jesus comes back the second time? The entire book of Revelation declares it was written to the Church and it applies to the Church until the end of time (see Rev. 1:3; 22:7, 12, 16-17). The Bible never says the Church will be removed before the events of Revelation 6–19 take place.

Does Jesus in the book of Revelation concur with the dispensational position? He does not. In fact, when declaring to the seven churches, Jesus told them to "be faithful unto death" (Rev. 2:10) and "they loved not their lives unto the death" (Rev. 12:11). Where and when did Jesus ever say His followers would escape tribulation? Rather, He informed them in the Gospels that "in the world they would have tribulation, but not to fear because I have overcome the world" (John 16:33). And in John 17:15, Jesus said, "I do not pray that You will take them out of the world, but that You should keep them from the evil one."

In Revelation 7:14, we are told the ones in heaven dressed in white robes are the ones who have come out of great tribulation and have washed their robes and made them white in the blood of the Lamb. If these are those who have already come out of great tribulation when John saw them in the seventh chapter, how could it apply only to the last seven years at the end of time? This passage refers to those who have come out of *great tribulation*. Chronologically, this verse is stated before the trumpets and the vials take place, which to dispensationalists is "the great tribulation." According to this view, then, these have come out of tribulation before the tribulation begins. How could this be?

Why are dispensationalists afraid to suffer for the faith when the Bible tells us if we suffer with Him we shall also reign with Him (2 Tim. 2:11-12)? Christ's followers are those who follow Him wherever He goes (Rev. 14:4). Why are dispensationalists afraid to suffer for Christ when He says His followers were not to "fear any of those things which you are about to suffer. Indeed, the devil is about to throw some of you into prison, that you may be tested, and you will have tribulation ten days. Be faithful until death, and I will give you the crown of life" (Rev. 2:10). Is Jesus not telling the truth? How can we say the opposite without twisting the scriptures? Does Paul not warn us about handling the Word of God deceitfully (2 Cor. 4:2)?

In all their struggles against the devil, God's people overcame him by the blood of the Lamb and the word of their testimony (Rev. 12:11). This is certainly the opposite of dispensational writings.

THE GREAT TRIBULATION   239

Why are dispensationalists afraid of dying for Christ? The Bible says the followers of Christ "loved not their lives unto the death" (Rev. 12:11). Why should Christ's followers be afraid of suffering even unto death when the Bible promises "blessed are the dead, who die in the Lord from now on…that they may rest from their labors, and their works do follow them" (Rev. 14:13)?

Why are dispensationalists afraid to suffer and die for Christ when the promise of martyrdom is to reign with Him (Rev. 20:4-6)? Does Christ ever promise His people that they shall never suffer death (see Rev. 6:9-11)? In the light of the foregoing scriptures, how can dispensationalists teach their doctrine of escapism from this world by an unbiblical doctrine of a pre-tribulation rapture?

What Does the Rest of the Bible Say as to Tribulation or Afflictions of God's People?

Paul, who was called to suffer (Acts 9:16), has much to say about tribulation and affliction relative to the gospel and to God's people:

- Paul tells his converts in Lystra, Iconium, and Antioch that they must through much tribulation enter the kingdom of God (Acts 14:22).
- In 1 Thessalonians 1:6, he tells the Thessalonians they had received the Word of God in much affliction (tribulation), and in 1 Thessalonians 3:3-7 he says they would be suffering tribulation for the faith.
- In 2 Thessalonians 1:4-5, Paul writes to encourage them in the "persecutions and tribulations" they were suffering for the kingdom of God.
- In 2 Timothy 2:3-4 he states Timothy was to endure hardness as a good soldier of Jesus Christ. It seems to Paul that there would be no lack of suffering, tribulation, or distress for the believers.
- Paul even goes so far as to say suffering is a part of the call of every Christian (Phil. 1:29). None were promised a flowery bed of ease or an escape mechanism from tribulation or affliction.

I can hear the dispensationalist say this is not the kind of tribulation about which they are talking—they mean the tribulation in Revelation 6–19. However, since the Bible uses the same word for tribulation and affliction, how are we to discern the difference? Basically, there is none! Any judgment or wrath of God in the book of Revelation is never said to be directed at God's people, only at the ungodly and unrepentant.

WHAT DOES PETER HAVE TO SAY ON
THE SUBJECT OF TRIBULATION?

Did Peter say Christians would be immune from afflictions or tribulations? In fact, Peter says Christ suffered and left us an example we should follow (1 Pet. 2:21). In 1 Peter 4:12-16, he tells believers that to suffer for Christ's sake should not be counted as a strange thing, but that they are to glorify God in their sufferings because the Spirit of glory and of God would rest on them during those times. In 1 Peter 5:8-10, he says it would be for their perfection that they go through these afflictions.

We are reminded in 1 Corinthians 4:9 and Hebrews 10:33 that the believer is a spectacle to the world, angels, and men. The word *spectacle* comes from the Greek word for "theater." The theater was the place where dramas were acted out on the stage. The world is the stage; the theater is where God has His children acting out His program.

Let us give Jesus the final word on the matter and of the phase "great tribulation." In Matthew 24, Jesus spoke of a time of "great tribulation." He said these words in connection with the destruction of the temple and the city of Jerusalem (Matt. 24:1-21), which took place in A.D. 70. Jesus said, "For then there will be great tribulation, such as has not been since the beginning of the world until this time, no, nor ever shall be."

Therefore, we must conclude that the great tribulation that was revealed to John, the Revelator, has to be the same one of which Jesus spoke in Matthew 24, which took place when the Roman army under Titus captured Jerusalem in A.D. 70. Jesus said this event of that great tribulation would never be superseded. Is the great tribulation of Revelation 7:14 something yet to come, or has it been fulfilled in the destruction of Jerusalem? I am sure Jesus would not contradict Himself from the Gospels to the book of Revelation. If you have not read Josephus's account of the destruction of Jerusalem, you should!

DISPENSATIONALISM AND THE GREAT TRIBULATION

Scofield said, "The great tribulation will be, however, a period of salvation" (Scofield 1945, 1337). J. Dwight Pentecost wrote:

> During the Tribulation, according to Revelation 7, God will raise up a host of witnesses to his grace. They will be born again sovereignly, as the Apostle Paul was brought out of darkness into light by the sovereign act of God…. So God will lay hold of 144,000 Jews, will bring them out of darkness into light, and will send them over the face of the earth to announce salvation through the blood of Christ (Revelation 7:14)…. The majority of those who accept Jesus Christ as Saviour during the Tribulation will pay with their lives for their faith in Christ for Satan will seek to exterminate every believer on the face of the earth through the reign of the Beast and the False Prophet.
>
> (Pentecost 1964, 40-41)

As to people getting saved during the time of the tribulation and after Jesus comes, the Bible in no way teaches that multitudes or individuals are to be saved during this time. Here are some of the biblical reasons why:

- Second Thessalonians 2:1-3 teaches a falling away, not a revival.
- Revelation 9:20-21 and 16:9, 11 relate that people during this period of time repented not of their evil deeds (16:11); they blasphemed God instead.
- Matthew 24:37 states, "But as the days of Noah were, so also will the coming of the Son of man be." How many were saved after the door of the ark was closed?
- Revelation 22:11 states what happens when Christ actually comes: "He who is unjust, let him be unjust still: he who is filthy, let him be filthy still; he who is righteous, let him be righteous still; he who is holy, let him be holy still." This does not sound like anyone gets saved after Jesus returns.
- In Matthew 25:1-13, Jesus taught that no one gets saved after the Bridegroom comes for the Bride, which is the rapture. The door of salvation was shut and the five virgins who came back knocking could not get in. Luke 13:25 makes the same point. Does the Bible teach contradictions?

WRATH AND THE BIBLICAL USE OF
1 THESSALONIANS 5:9-10

First Thessalonians 5:9-10, says, "For God did not appoint us to wrath, but to obtain salvation through our Lord Jesus Christ, who died for us." Dispensationalists use these verses to speak of the wrath of God in the tribulation. They are robbing it from its own context by making it mean a short period of time at the end of the age whereas the immediate context, verses 5-11, is that of the personal salvation of the Thessalonians in bringing them into the light of God's salvation. Their personal salvation removed them from the wrath of God. They were delivered from the wrath of eternal damnation.

In Romans 1:18, Paul states that the gospel reveals the wrath of God: "For the wrath of God is revealed from heaven against all ungodliness and unrighteousness of men, who suppress the truth in unrighteousness." John 3, the great chapter on God's salvation of the sinner, states that the principle of the wrath of God is on all who do not believe in the Son of God: "He who believes in the Son has everlasting life; and he who does not believe the Son shall not see life, but the wrath of God abides on him" (John 3:36).

First Thessalonians 1:9-10 states the same principle: personal salvation delivers us from wrath to come; this wrath rests on the unsaved. This is the biblical answer to 1 Thessalonians 5:9-10. It is the wrath of God upon sin, not a momentary wrath of God for a short time at the end the age. Because Paul applied this wrath to the Thessalonians themselves, how can it be said that it applies to a tribulation wrath over two thousand years later? This truth is also verified by what John the Baptist inquired of the Pharisees: "Who has warned you to flee from the wrath to come?" (Matt. 3:7). It was a wrath that those Pharisees would experience due to their unrepentance, not a tribulation wrath that would occur thousands of years later. Paul further accentuates this principle in Romans 5:9: "Much more then, having now been justified by His blood, we shall be saved from wrath through Him."

Therefore this is the wrath of God upon sin from which we are delivered by being saved and becoming children of God. It is not something yet to come in a so-called tribulation in which an antichrist is supposed to reign.

THE TIMING OF THE TRIBULATION

For the last sixty years, I have heard and read many a so-called prophetic statement about the tribulation being this or that. At the time of Napoleon, many were saying it was the tribulation period. During the Second World War, many authors were saying Hitler was the antichrist; then Mussolini was the antichrist. We heard the rapture was to happen in 1988. When that did not happen, another charismatic leader prophesied it would take place in 1992. Well, so much for magazine articles and prognostications of false prophecies. Certainly, current events have taken over the headlines in prophecy today!

Our Lord Himself gave warning that no one knows the day or the hour of his return. Yet many claimed they were spiritual enough to know the times and seasons and to set dates. I have a list of over forty-five people who have set dates from A.D 365 to 1992. This does not include some cults. Why has man not learned from the folly of such foolishness?

We are now told that if the Bible is partially "decodified," that the tribulation can be known in amazingly concrete terms. In *Progressive Dispensationalism*, we read:

> Classical and revised dispensationalists have shared with historicist premillennialism a belief that apocalyptic visions and descriptions in the Old and New Testaments offer a detailed blueprint of interconnecting events, partially codified, which specifically describe the setting of Christ's return. Once decodified, that portion of history, the Tribulation, can be known in amazingly concrete terms. Dispensationalists and historicists differed with each other only on the point of whether Tribulation events were presently transpiring. The doctrine of a pretribulational Rapture allowed dispensationalists to keep the Tribulation entirely in the future and thus eliminate the embarrassment of repeated failure in the attempt to relate current events to prophecy…While one could not read the times as the actual transpiring of Tribulation history, one could observe *the formation* of features of Tribulation history prior to that history's actual commencement.
>
> (Blaising and Bock 1993, 292-293)

So the Bible has to be "decodified" so that we may know in concrete terms the time of the tribulation? Is this not Gnosticism? Since when has orthodoxy believed that any part of the Bible was written in mystery form and needed to be decodified? In 700 B.C., the prophet Isaiah, speaking about the ways of God, said even "a fool, shall not go astray" (Isa. 35:8). Isaiah even went further than that when he said, "To the law and to the testimony! If they do not speak according to this word, it is because there is no light in them" (Isa. 8:20). We must say as Joel said in his prophecy, "Blow the trumpet in Zion, and sound an alarm in My holy mountain" (Joel 2:1). Yes, it is time true orthodoxy did just that instead of fiddling around with half-truths.

Hopefully, it is now clear that the great tribulation, according to Christ in Matthew (which parallels that of Revelation 7:14), took place at the time of the destruction of Jerusalem in A.D. 70. Therefore, it cannot be a future event.

WHAT DOES HISTORY RECORD ON THE SUBJECT OF TRIBULATION?

At this point, I would be amiss not to include more on Revelation 3:10, as dispensationalists claim that this verse is a reference to the great tribulation of the end time. In this passage, Jesus says to the Philadelphia church, "Because you have kept My command to persevere, I also will keep you from the hour of trial which shall come upon the whole world, to test those who dwell on the earth."

In *Prophecy for Today*, J. Dwight Pentecost says, "The Lord is addressing a letter to the church in Philadelphia, the true church of the last days. He says to these true believers, 'Because thou hast kept the word of my patience, I also will keep thee from the hour of temptation, which shall come upon all the world, to try them that dwell upon the earth.' The phrase, 'hour of temptation,' can be translated hour of testing, and is certainly a reference to the Tribulation" (p. 48).

Why is it that dispensationalists who claim to interpret the Bible literally spiritualize this verse? This was a literal promise given to the Philadelphia church, and thus its primary application must be to them. This church went out of existence long ago.

Many authorities believe the book of Revelation was written around A.D. 95-100. Trajan, who became Roman emperor in A.D. 98, issued a policy against Christians that was pursued by every emperor for a hundred years afterward. Trajan's persecution lasted for a period of ten years against the Christians. Other emperors later increased the severity of the persecution.

Does Revelation 3:10 have a direct reference to Trajan's ten years of persecution against the Christians? If this promise in Revelation 3:10 was to be applied universally to the entire Church, why was it not mentioned to every church, as are some of the other statements? And why did they not escape? Is it not because Revelation 3:10 was a specific promise only to the church at Philadelphia?

In his book *Apocalyptic Sketches*, Dr. John Cumming says the following on this passage in Revelation:

> The hour of temptation thus alluded to, is the ten years of almost un-precedented persecution to which the Christians were subjected under the reign of Trajan; and that the promise here given, has a prior specific reference to the Church of Philadelphia, to which it is addressed in the first instance, and this the promise of our Lord primarily is, that he will keep the Church of Philadelphia unscathed, its ministers unmartyred, its people undestroyed, in the midst of those the years of fiery persecution, which were to fall upon the whole—"oikoumene"—the inhabited world, or Roman empire. This promise was literally and verbatim fulfilled. Philadelphia was the only church in the seven which escaped unscathed from the persecutions of Trajan; and the reason which philosophers assigned and historians have stated is, that Philadelphia was subject to earthquakes; and the Roman emperor, with all his sanguinary cruelty, was afraid to go there himself, or to trust his generals and his armies in a place so dangerous. No doubt this was the secondary cause, which many modern philosophers worship; but the secret of Philadelphia's safety was the first great and glorious reason that Christians trust in—that Jesus had recorded it as his truth. "I will keep thee from the hour of temptation, that shall come upon all the world." "I may do it by terrifying Caesar by earthquakes to which your are subjected, I may do it by a hundred secondary causes; but all these are but instruments, and it is my hand that wields them."
>
> (Cumming 1858, 1:436-437)

For those who think the earth's locality at that time was too small to be the fulfillment, the word used in Revelation 3:10 for "the whole world" is *oikoumene,* which means "the inhabited world." Colossians 1:23 provides a similar illustration.

In his book *Interpreting Revelation,* Merrill C. Tenney says, "The Greek word *keep* is *tereo ek* and is used elsewhere only in (John 17:15) and means to preserve from the attack of evil rather than to remove from it by physical separation." Leon Morris, commenting on the same passage, agrees (*Tyndale New Testament Commentaries*, 80).

As to tribulation in the future, we have yet to mention 2 Thessalonians 2:1-12. The events depicted in these verses seem to be taking place in the last days just prior to the second coming (*parousia*) of Christ (v. 1). There will be great deception and apostasy from the faith. Are we not now seeing an apostasy already? Many churches that once presented the saving gospel of Christ have swerved from the faith and have lost the saving message of the gospel. Modernism and secular humanism have replaced the truth as it is in Jesus. Second Thessalonians 2:10 specifically states that they did not love the truth that they might be saved. The working of the man of sin is called the mystery of lawlessness, which was already at work in Paul's day (v. 7). This principle is alive today and has risen to the point that even governments cannot control the carnage of the day. It only will get worse and worse.

A final word: Jesus taught that the church would always suffer persecution and tribulation: "These things I have spoken to you, that in Me you may have peace. In the world you will have tribulation; but be of good cheer, I have overcome the world" (John 16:33). It would have been hard to tell the Christians in Russia under Stalin and Lenin or the many believers in China slaughtered for their faith that they were not going through tribulation. All other speculation and prognostications are not worth refuting.

Chapter 18

THE HISTORY AND ORIGIN OF THE MILLENNIUM

The history of the origin of any doctrine is important. Thus, the origin and history of the millennium cannot be left out of any thesis on eschatology.

Scofield says the following regarding Ephesians 1:10: "The Dispensation of the fullness of Times is the seventh and last of the ordered ages and is identical with the Davidic Kingdom (2 Sam. 7:8-17; Zech. 12:8; Luke 1:31-33; 1 Cor. 15:24)" (Scofield 1945, 1250). By this, Scofield means Ephesians 1:10 belongs to the millennium.

However, the Bible says differently. It declares "the fullness of the times" (Eph.1:10) began with the first coming of Christ. Paul, writing to the Galatians, confirms this: "But when the fullness of time had come, God sent forth His Son, born of a woman born under the law" (Gal. 4:4). Therefore, Scofield and his followers have utterly and mistakenly misinterpreted the timeframe of Ephesians 1:10.

The Davidic kingdom is identical to the kingdom Christ set up when He came during the first advent. The angel Gabriel promised this to Mary in Luke 1:30-33. Peter declared the fulfillment of this in Acts 2:30-36, when he declared Christ was the son of David and was resurrected from the dead to sit on David's throne. For this reason, the Davidic kingdom cannot be something Christ will set up when He comes back the second time. He is already on David's throne.

Millennialism—from *chiliasm,* the Greek word for one thousand—has become a doctrine stating that Christ will set up a literal kingdom and reign on earth in Jerusalem with the Jews as His chosen people for a thousand years under the economy of the Mosaic law. Ultimately, this makes salvation by race and not by grace. The text proponents of this doctrine use is taken from a literal view of Revelation 20:1-6. The problem of literally interpreting a book so highly symbolic and apocalyptic is questionable, as the book itself is given by signs and symbols, and therefore much of it should be interpreted figuratively. (See Chapter 16, "The Binding of Satan in Revelation 20.)

In *Church History,* Gregory and Ruter say the following about Cerinthus's millennium: "It will be spent in the highest sensual indulgencies" (Gregory and Ruter 1934, p. 30). During the first half of the second century, Eusebius states that "Papias' doctrine of the Millennium was received by him from unwritten tradition" (Eusebius, bk, III, chp. 39, 115).

K. R. Hagenbach says, "There is no trace of a Millennium in: Clement of Rome (died in 101), in Ignatius of Antioch (died in 115), in Polycarp of Smyrna (died 155). Iranaeus says that Polycarp taught the things which 'he had learned from the Apostles and which the church handed down'" (Hagenbach 1861, 1:52).

Nepos, bishop in Egypt in A.D. 255, states the following under the heading of "Nepos and His Schism": "He taught that the promises should be understood more as the Jews understood them. The Millennium would be of a sensual luxury on this earth."

As to Papias, Herbert M. Riggle says, "Historians generally tell us that Papias was a very zealous advocate of this imaginary reign of Christ on earth" (Riggle 1899, 29). Riggle then quotes from *Wadington's History:*

> The first distinguished opponent of this doctrine was Origen, who attacked it with great earnestness and ingenuity, and seems, in spite of some opposition to have thrown it into general discredit…This obscure doctrine was probably known to but very few except the Fathers of the church, and is very sparingly mentioned by them during the first two centuries; and there is reason to believe that it scarcely attained much notoriety, even among the learned Christians, until it was made a matter of controversy by Origen, and then rejected by the great majority. In fact we find Origen himself asserting that it was confined to *those of the simpler sort.*
>
> (Ibid., 56)

Dr. Schaff wrote, "Nowhere in the discourses of Jesus is there a hint of a limited duration of the Messianic Kingdom. The apostolic epistles are equally free from any trace of Chiliasm" (*Encyclopedia Brittannica* 1964, 299). In his book *Millennialism,* Lawence J. Chesnut, B.Th., D.D. states:

> Though some eminent fathers held millenarianism, it was never generally accepted. Montanism, which gave much prominence to millenarianism was condemned by different groups of Asia Minor as heresy about A.D. 160. Dr. C. A. Briggs says of Chiliasm (the doctrine that Christ will return to earth to reign one thousand years), "The mass of writers as well as churches, speaking through their local assemblies, bishops and patriarchs either show a different conception of eschatology (last and final things) or else, as in the great churches of Rome, Alexandria, and Asia Minor they condemned the heresy so that before the first Ecumenical Council of Nice, Chiliasm (doctrine of millennium) had been suppressed in all parts of the Christian Church. That it was not generally accepted from an early date is evident from the fact that the four greatest early Church symbols—The Apostles creed, The Nicene, the Constantinopolitan and the Athanasian—all exclude it by affirming a single resurrection of the dead, including both the righteous and the wicked. Origen rejected millenarianism and Augustine in identifying the kingdom of God with the Church excluded it. From his time it ceased to be held almost entirely for many centuries."
>
> (Chestnut 1973, 12-13)

Herbert M. Riggle, D.D., in his book *Christ's Kingdom and Reign,* gives a brief history of the millennial theory: "The idea of a millennial reign proceeded from Judaism, for 'among the Jews the representation was growing, that the Messiah would reign a thousand years upon earth. Such products of Jewish imagination passed over into Christianity.'" This Riggle quotes from Neander's *History of Christian Dogmas,* vol. 1, p. 248. Continuing to quote from Riggle, "The Jews generally believed that the Messiah would establish a literal or earthly kingdom. And even some of them believed that Messiah's reign would last a thousand years. Before the death of all the first apostles, this Jewish notion was revived in the teaching of an ungodly heretic by the name of Cerinthus."

In *Eusebius' Ecclesiastical History* is preserved a fragment of the writings of Caius, who lived during the close of the second century. This excerpt gives us the following account of Cerinthus' heresy: "But Cerinthus, by means of revelations which he pretended were written by a great apostle, also falsely pretended to wonderful things, as if they were shown him by angels, asserting, that after the resurrection there would be an earthly kingdom of Christ, and that the flesh, i.e., men, again inhabiting Jerusalem would be subject to desires and pleasures" (Eusebius, bk. III, chp. 28). Eusebius says of Cerinthus, "Being also an enemy to the scriptures, with a view to deceive men, he said, 'that there would be a space of a thousand years for celebrating nuptial festivities. One of the doctrines that he taught was that Christ would have an earthly kingdom'" (Ibid.).

Irenaeus, who was born circa A.D. 120 and who was acquainted with Polycarp, the disciple of John, states that while John was at Ephesus, he entered a bath to wash, but when he found Cerinthus was there he refused to bathe there, left the building, and exhorted those with him to do the same, saying, "Let us flee lest the bath fall in, as long as Cerinthus, the enemy of truth is within" (Ibid., bk. V, chp. 24). Riggle states, "Let this be a rebuke to modern millennial advocates. They claim their doctrine is well founded in the revelation of John. But John called the founder of their theory, 'that enemy of truth'" (Riggle 1899, p. 26).

John Calvin (1509-1564) wrote, "Not long after [the days of Paul] arose the Millennarians, who limited the reign of Christ to a thousand years. Their fiction is too puerile [childish] to require or deserve refutation" (Landis 1946, 26). Mother Ann Lee (1770), founder of a "Millennial Church," the Shakers, claimed she was the female Jesus Christ returned to inaugurate the millennium. She neither could read nor write. She had a biographer (Morris 1914, 364).

James Hastings wrote, "The doctrine of the millennium is not found in the Old Testament" (Hastings 1908, III:370). Hastings says non-millennialists of the Early Church included Hermas and the second Epistle of Clement, Ignatius, Polycarp, Epistle to Diognetus, Didache, Jerome, and Augustine (Ibid., 372).

Hastings says millennialists included Papias (who presented a millennium in a gross form), Cerinthus, Irenaeus, Tertullian, and Hippolytus (Ibid.). He goes on to say, *"The prevalence of* the millennium was due to Jewish apocalypses" (Ibid).

John Warwick Montgomery, a millennialist, states, "Although these prophecies are compatible with a time of millennial bliss they do not expressly require it" (Armerding 1977, 175).

According to Montgomery, the scriptural passages generally used for a millennium include: "Isa. 9:6; 11:1-12; 40:9-11; 52:7-12; Jer. 33:1-22; Ezek. 37:25; Hos. 3:4-5; Joel 3:20; Amos 9:14-15; Zech. 9:9-10" (Ibid.). However, most of these references are fulfilled in the New Testament Church and thus cannot be applied to a millennium. Montgomery also notes that there are no time limits ever stated with any of these passages; that is, as to when they apply or how long they last. To insert a time limit on these passages certainly is to add to God's Word something that is not there. Montgomery states that the doctrine of the millennium has to rest squarely on the exegesis of Revelation 20.

Montgomery continues, "In spite of attempts such as those presented in *The Millennium Bible* by W. E. Biederwolf, to find the doctrine of the millennium clearly set forth in the Old Testament, it is impossible to locate its biblical foundation there" (Ibid., 176).

Speaking about Chiliasm (millennialism), Geerhardus Vos says the following: "The question is of course, a question of evidence, to be considered and settled on the basis of scriptural testimony and of calm, sober, dogmatically-unprejudiced exegesis" (*The Pauline Eschatology*, p. 226). Vos continues, "The substance of the matter is that Chiliasm divides the eschatological future following upon the parousia into two distinct stages, the one a temporary provisional, the other an eternal, absolute character. The old traditional view of orthodox theology, and the current interpretation of Paul know of no such dualism in eschatological prospect; they make the eternal state, strictly so called, begin with the return of the Lord" (p. 228).

It is evident from these authors that this dualism finds its origin outside of the Bible. It therefore comes from Jewish apocalyptic writers. To millennialists, this dualism carries more weight than the truths found in the scriptures themselves. They divide the second coming of Christ into two separate stages with a thousand years in between. However, the Bible does not teach two future comings of Christ. Classical premillennialists before 1830 did not believe in two comings of Christ. Peter sums up the eschatological coming of Christ in his second epistle. As an apostle of Christ, we can safely say Peter was stating that which Christ (and then that which the Holy Spirit) revealed to him. Peter specifically stated that when Christ returned in His *parousia,* the next state is that of the new heavens and the new earth (2 Pet. 3:4-13).

NO MILLENNIUM IN THE ANCIENT
CREEDS OF THE CHURCH

Ira D. Landis, in *The Faith of Our Fathers on Eschatology*, finds no millennium in the following fifteen creeds of the Church:

1. The Apostles' Creed (second century).
2. The Nicaeno-Constantinopolitan Creed (A.D. 381).
3. The Athanasian Creed (fourth century).
4. The English (Episcopalian) Confession of Edward VI, (A.D. 1553). Article XLI states, "Those who endeavor to recall the fable of the Millenarians, oppose the sacred Scriptures and precipitate themselves into Jewish insanities."
5. The Belgic (Dutch Reformed) Confession (A.D. 1561).
6. The Anabaptist Confession (A.D.1600).
7. The First Dutch Mennonite Confession (A.D.1627).
8. The Second Dutch Mennonite Confession (A.D.1630).
9. The Memorable Mennonite Confession (A.D.1632).
10. The Augsburg (Lutheran) Confession (A.D. 1530).
11. The Westminster (Presbyterian) Confession (A.D. 1647).
12. The Westminster (Presbyterian) Larger Catechism (A.D. 1647).
13. The Westminster (Presbyterian) Shorter Catechism (A.D. 1647).
14. The New Hampshire Baptist Confession (A.D. 1833).
15. The Free Will Baptist (A.D. 1834 and 1868).

(Landis 1946, 4-29).

For nineteen centuries, neither millennialism nor premillennial dispensationalism was ever found to be recorded in the historical creeds of the Church.

MODERN HISTORY OF MILLENNIUM DOCTRINE

In his book *The History of Christian Doctrines,* Louis Berkhof says of the Early Church:

Some of them dwelt very fondly on these millennial hopes and pictured the enjoyments of the future age in a crassly materialistic manner. This is true especially of Papias and Irenaeus. Others such as Barnabas, Hermas,

Justin, and Tertullian, while teaching the doctrine, avoided its extrava-
gances. The Millennial doctrine also found favour with Cerinthus, the
Ebionites, and the Montanists. But it is not correct to say, as Premillenarians do, that it was generally accepted in the first three centuries. The
truth of the matter is that the adherents of this doctrine were a rather
limited number. There is no trace of it in Clement of Rome, Ignatius,
Polycarp, Tatian, Athnenagoaras, Theophilus, Clement of Alexandria,
Origen, Dionysius, and other important Church Fathers.

(Berkhof 1978, 262)

Berkhof adds: "During the Middle Ages Millenarianism was generally regarded as heretical" (Ibid., 263). Furthermore, "At the time of the
Reformation the doctrine of the millennium was rejected by the Protestant
Churches, but revived in some sects, as such as that of the more fanati-
cal Anabaptists, and that of the Fifth Monarchy Men. Luther scornfully
rejected 'the dream' that there would be an earthly kingdom of Christ
preceding the day of judgment. The Augsburg Confession condemns
those 'who now scatter Jewish opinions, that before the resurrection of
the dead, the godly shall occupy the kingdom of the world, the wicked
being everywhere suppressed'" (Ibid.).

Harris F. Rall says that around 1850 and on, premillennialists became
aggressive. This is seen by their literature published on the subject. The
Plymouth Brethren and the Seventh Day Adventists headed the aggressive-
ness, and Dowies Zionism and the Jehovah's Witnesses followed. The main
stance that the premillennialists took was based on a literal interpretation
of the Scripture, which amounted to Jewish apocalypticism. This doctrine
was then promoted by several Bible conferences on eschatology. Premillennialism was based on the promise in the Old Testament of a kingdom to
come. Jewish apocalypticism expressed it as a golden age of peace to come
on earth. This was based on a Messianic hope of a Messianic king. *The
Apocalypse of Baruch,* Chapters 29, 72, 73, and the *Book of Enoch*, Chapters
11 and 19 reveal the preposterous claims of the Jewish golden age.

According to Rall, the basis then of modern millennialism had its
roots in the eschatology of Judaism and not in Scripture. Premillennial
dispensationalism grew out of a climate of eschatological turmoil as to the
second coming of Christ and the end of the age. At that time, many were
prophesying the end was at hand. The offshoot of this came from Bible
conferences on eschatology. Out of this came the Plymouth Brethren's

stand, developed by John N. Darby, which became known as "premillennial dispensationalism." It was officially developed by 1830.

At the same time, Joseph Smith wrote the *Book of Mormon* in 1830. Next, we have William Miller with his theology in 1831. He started the Seventh Day Advent movement and prophesied that the end of the world would come in 1843. Then along came the Jehovah's Witnesses in 1880 with Millennial Dawnism.

DOCTRINES PRODUCED DURING THE 1800S

Revelation 9 talks about smoke that will billow out of the pit of hell when a host of demons come out and darken the sun. Does the sun speak of Christianity? A look at doctrines produced during the 1800s will reveal the origin of modern false cults and their beliefs.

Seventh Day Adventism was enhanced by Ellen G. White. She was converted to Adventism in 1842 at the age of fifteen. Adventists today hold her as their prophet equal to those of the Bible. She had over two thousand visions, on which they base their beliefs. One of her doctrines was that Christ had a sinful fallen nature.

Jehovah's Witnesses was started by Charles Russell (1852-1916). Russell was the founder of the International Bible Students Association. Russellites have now split off and formed the Jehovah's Witnesses. They deny Christ's deity.

Mormonism was started by Joseph Smith in 1830. Mormons claim Joseph Smith was a prophet equal to Christ. Under the leadership of Brigham Young, in 1847 the Mormons settled in Utah. They are now known as The Church of Jesus Christ of Latter Day Saints. Mormons deny the deity of Christ.

Christian Science was started by Mary Baker Eddy in 1866. Eddy was the author of Christian Science. She went to Europe to study under George W. F. Hegel and came up with the view that sin was not a reality. She stated that the blood of Christ was no more efficacious to cleanse sin when it was shed on the cross then when it was flowing in His veins (but see Hebrews 9:22).

Darwinism was begun by Charles Darwin (1809-1882), an English naturalist. Darwin wrote the *Origin of Species,* published in 1859, which spawned the theory of evolution. In 1835, Darwin went to the

Galapagos Islands and came up with the concept that all species of plants and animals developed from earlier forms of hereditary transmission of slight variations in successive generations. Out of this arose "the survival of the fittest" theory.

Marxism (or *Communism*) was started by Karl Marx (1818-1883). Communism, or religious atheism, arose as Dialectic Materialism. Marx wrote *The Communist Manifesto* in 1848 and *Das Kapital* in 1867. Marx, born of Jewish parents in Rhenish, Prussia, was a German philosopher of history. His coworker was Freidrich Engels. Marx was strongly influenced by George W. F. Hegel. Most early communist movements were in religion, based on a literal interpretation of Scripture (*Encyclopedia Britannica*). At age twenty-five, Marx said, "Religion is the opiate of the people." Marx did not find the answer to his communist movement in religion but in a system of social organization based on common property. In 1824, his father, a lawyer, embraced Christianity, and all the members of his family were baptized Protestant.

Two proponents of Communism were Vladamir Lenin (1870-1924) and Joseph Stalin (1879-1953). Lenin was brought up in the Russian Orthodox Faith, but at the age of sixteen, he ceased to believe in God. Under his leadership, the Bolsheviks (originally a radical branch of the Socialist Democratic Party in Russia) came into power in 1917 and formed the Communist Party. Stalin was later premier and marshal of the Soviet Union.

Hegelian Philosophy was begun by George Hegel (1770-1831). Hegel was a prophet of Absolute Idealism, which affirmed that "only the rational is real." In his view, the irrational, so called sin and evil, has no true reality. Mary Baker Eddy received this teaching.

Psychoanalysis was developed by Sigmund Freud (1856-1939). Freud, who was Jewish, fathered a modern-day psychology of psychoanalysis that left God out of the picture of man's make-up.

The *"God Is Dead"* theory, introduced by Friedrick Nietszche (1844-1900), stated that man could perfect himself through forcible self-assertion.

The *Modern Liturgical Revival* (1850) was a movement that sought to take away individual liberty and experience before God.

Existentialism was developed by Fyodor Dostoevsky (1821-1881). There are many aspects to existentialism. In it, man's ideas, experiences, and formulations become determinative.

Dispensationalism was officially introduced into Christianity in 1830. Authors of this theory dissect God's Word into seven dispensations, and supposedly interpret the Bible literally. They advocate two and three comings of Christ instead of one.

In *Modern Humanism,* the emphasis is on the secular, centered on human interests rather than on natural interest and religion. Self-realization comes through reason. Proponents of Modern Humanism reject the supernatural.

Unitarianism was developed by William Channing (1819-?). Channing said Christ was a being distinct from the one God and thus did not have the same status as God.

Scofield developed the dispensational premillennial system in the *Scofield Reference Bible*, edited in 1909. People took his notes to be the Word of God and ran with them. Blackstone then wrote his book *Jesus is Coming*, which was based on dispensationalism, and had it sent to many ministers and missionaries worldwide. It is reported that he changed his mind later—but the damage already had been done.

DISPENSATIONALISM IS A NEW DOCTRINE

That dispensationalism is a relatively new doctrine is well stated by its own writers as well as others. Charles Ryrie, speaking about informed dispensationalists, says, "They recognize that as a system dispensationalism was largely formulated by Darby" (Ryrie 1965, 66). He adds, "It is granted by dispensationalists that as a system of theology dispensationalism is recent in origin" (Ibid., 67).

In *An Examination of Dispensationalism*, William E. Cox says, "In speaking of the dispensational teaching that the church was not prophesied in the Old Testament, Harry A. Ironside (*Mysteries of God*, p. 50), boasts of the fact that this teaching was non-existent until introduced by John Darby in the nineteenth century" (Cox 1977, 2). Jon Zens, in his book *Dispensationalism,* dates Darby's origin of two separate purposes in history to 1827 (Zens 1978, 16). It is an historical fact that Darby's eschatology began with the utterance of Barbara McDonald. This, Tregelles said at the time, was from a false spirit.

No true biblical doctrine can arise out of such a quagmire. From this, we can see that the origins of doctrines are very important!

Chapter 19

WORSHIP IN THE MILLENNIUM

According to dispensationalists, worship in the millennium will revert back to the law and animal sacrifices. They take this from Ezekiel 40–45, a portion of Scripture that was given to Israel while they were in Babylonian captivity. It would apply to them when they returned back into the land, had re-established worship, and had rebuilt the temple that was destroyed by Nebuchadnezzar in 586 B.C.

Ezra returned with a portion of the captives to rebuild the temple and restore pure worship under the law of Moses. Nehemiah returned and rebuilt the walls and the city. Haggai and Zechariah, contemporaries to Ezra and Nehemiah, both spoke to the problems that ensued during the rebuilding of the temple. In comparison to the temple of Solomon, this temple was as *nothing* to those who saw it (Hag. 2:3). God gives a vision of the temple the Messiah would build in Zechariah 6:12-13. Haggai 2:7 says a day will come when God would shake all nations and "the Desire of All Nations [the Messiah]" would come. He would fill the temple with glory (Hag. 2:7). This is how John sees Jesus (John 1:14). Then, in Haggai 2:9 it says, "'The glory of this latter temple shall be greater than the former,' says the Lord of hosts, 'And in this place I will give peace.'" This is a true picture of Jesus and His new temple (John 2:18-21; Eph. 2:19-22).

Because the literal fulfillment of Ezekiel was not seen by dispensationalists, they transferred Ezekiel 40–48 to the millennium (a good hiding place for many things). However, there is no thousand-year millennium taught in the book of Ezekiel or any other place in the entire Old Testament. James Hastings has stated, "The doctrine of the millennium is not found in the Old Testament." A millennium was never heard of until the book of Revelation was written, which was at least forty to sixty years after the death of Christ. Christ Himself never taught a millennium. Neither did any of His disciples. It was a scheme to fill in the gap of dispensational eschatology. It became the only way they could see a "golden age for Judaism."

It was Jewish apocryphal writings that spoke of a "golden age for Judaism." In those writings, the Jews were to have Jerusalem restored to them, the temple rebuilt, and a form of worship that would accommodate Judaism. Is it not amazing that it was Judaizers who opposed Paul all the way through his ministry while he was establishing the foundation of the Church under the New Covenant? Because of his revelation from God that did not entail the keeping of the Mosaic law and a national kingdom for Israel, Paul was imprisoned and ultimately put to death on that very account.

In order to worship in the millennium, the temple must be rebuilt and Old Testament worship restored. Dispensationalists must put Christ in there some place, so they have Him come down from heaven in His glorified state, sitting on the throne of David in the city of Jerusalem, ruling over people in their mortal bodies. Jesus is supposed to sit there for a thousand years and watch animals be slain as a sacrifice to replace His sacrifice that was once and for all and forever! How amazing! There will also be a restored priesthood that follows the Mosaic pattern.

There are many who have stated that there is no way a Jew today can come up with a genealogy that puts him in the line of being an Old Testament priest from the line of Levi. Furthermore, what are they going to do with the priesthood of every believer that was established by the New Covenant (1 Pet. 2:5-9)? Did Christ not cancel Old Testament priesthood forever? Is Christ not the only true high priest after the order of Melchizedek, who preceded and was higher than the Aaronic priesthood? Christ is the only Mediator (1 Tim. 2:5). Nevertheless, this is what worship in the millennium would be like. Jesus never taught a restored Judaism or a restored national Israel. There is no explicit Scripture that states this. It is a human invention that man has constructed. If dispensationalists are to sustain this theory, they must do so entirely apart from Scripture.

WHAT IS NEW TESTAMENT WORSHIP?

What does the Bible say about worship after the New Covenant was established? What kind of worship does the New Testament present? As to the temple itself, in Matthew 21, Jesus entered the temple (v. 13) and said, "My house shall be called a house of prayer." At this point, Jesus owns the temple as *His house.* He then cleanses the temple. It had been defiled! Then, from Matthew 21–24:3, He teaches in the temple before leaving it. In His teaching, Jesus was drawing the Jews to a conclusive decision as to *who* He really was (Matt. 22:42-45). They rejected Him as being the Son of God, the Messiah, the Son of David, David's Lord, and God's Shekinah glory. On leaving the temple, Jesus disowned it by saying, "*Your house* is left to you desolate" (Matt. 23:38, emphasis mine). He no longer claimed the temple as His house.

From that point on, the temple was no longer God's house. It was left with no further spiritual value. Christ pronounced it desolate and powerless. The real presence of God, the Shekinah, was Jesus Himself (John 1:14). In the careful reading of Ezekiel 9–11, it will be seen that because of Judah's sins, the Shekinah glory of God was hovering over the temple, trying to find entrance. Finding no place of entry, God's Shekinah glory lifted up from the city and went to the mountain east of Jerusalem (Ezek. 11:23).

This is the very picture we get of Jesus in the temple for the last time (Matt. 21-24). Jesus says, "O Jerusalem, Jerusalem…how I would have gathered you as a hen gathers her chicks under her wings, but you were not willing" (Matt. 23:37). Jesus then departs from the temple and goes to the Mount of Olives on the east of Jerusalem (Matt. 24:3, enacting Ezek. 11:23). The spiritual power of the temple was Jesus, the Shekinah glory (John 1:14), which Israel now rejected. The city and the temple would be destroyed, with not one stone left upon another. This was fulfilled in A.D. 70. God allowed the Romans to destroy both the temple—the center of worship—and the city.

After the city of Jerusalem and the temple were destroyed, the Jews had no center of worship or place to offer sacrifices. Their calling under God was over. Their ultimate mission had been accomplished by bringing the Messiah into the world, but because of their blindness and misinterpretation of their own scriptures, they did not know who Jesus was (Acts 13:27). They later killed the Lord of glory (1 Cor. 2:8).

WHAT IS THE TEMPLE IN THE NEW TESTAMENT?

God had forewarned that Christ would be rejected: "He came to His own, and His own did not receive Him" (John 1:11). In John 1:14, John states that Jesus is the new tabernacle: "And the Word became flesh and dwelt [*eskenosen*, "tabernacled"] among us." Jesus had taken the place of the tabernacle and would now establish the "new Temple" (John 2:13-21). In cleansing the temple at the Passover of the Jews, Jesus had declared in John 2:19, "Destroy this temple and I will build it in three days." Verse 21 declares, "He was speaking of the temple of His body."

The New Testament temple is Jesus Christ Himself. The true temple and place of worship under the Old Testament was where God had placed His name and where the Shekinah glory, "God's presence," came and filled both the tabernacle and the temple. Jesus now takes the place of and fulfills the function of both the tabernacle and the temple of the Old Covenant.

On the Day of Pentecost (Acts 2:1-4), the followers of Christ were in the upper room praying when the Holy Spirit fell on them and filled the *new temples* with the Holy Spirit. Out of the old temple came the new temples filled with the Holy Spirit! In the Old Testament, God filled both the tabernacle and the temple with the Shekinah glory before their use. Notice in Acts 2:42 that the apostle's doctrine was taught, not that of the law or the Old Covenant.

THE PLACE AND ORDER OF WORSHIP CHANGED UNDER THE NEW COVENANT

After Calvary, the temple was no longer the center of worship. Acts 17:24 states, "God who made the world and everything in it, since He is Lord of heaven and earth, *does not dwell in temples made with hands*" (emphasis mine). Paul quotes this as part of Stephen's address in Acts 7:48-59. For making such a statement, Stephen paid the price of being stoned to death. This was a part of the accusation that was finally brought against Paul (Acts 25:8). All of Christ's apostles paid the price for living up to the teachings of Jesus.

THE PHYSICAL BODY OF THE BELIEVER IS THE TEMPLE

What was in the revelation that was given to Paul on the subject of the temple? "Do you not know that you are the temple of God and that the Spirit of God dwells in you?" (1 Cor. 3:16; 6:19-20; 2 Cor. 6:16, where Paul quotes from Lev. 26:11-12). Paul said this about the tabernacle where God would dwell among them and place His name. Paul now applied this to the body of the believer becoming the tabernacle of God, because God had now come to live in His new temples through the Holy Spirit. Peter calls his physical body a tabernacle when speaking about his death, "I must put off my tent [*skenomatos,* "tabernacle"]" (2 Pet.1:14).

CORPORATELY, THE NEW TESTAMENT TEMPLE, THE BODY OF CHRIST, IS THE CHURCH

In Ephesians 2:11-22, Paul declares that the Gentiles who were converted to Christ have now come into that which Israel was in the Old Testament. The middle wall of partition has been broken down by the flesh of Christ being crucified on the cross (Eph. 2:14-15). By so doing, God made one *new man* out of two: the saved Jew and Gentile. He called them God's building, a holy temple, God's dwelling place through the Spirit. Therefore, the Church as the body of Christ is corporately God's temple. The Old Testament place of worship was where God was present and placed His name, *Jehovah Shammah,* meaning, "the Lord is there [present]." Under the New Covenant, Jesus took this place as the Son of Man, *present* among the lamp stands (Rev. 1:12-13) even in times of discipline (Matt. 18:20).

WHAT SACRIFICES ARE TO BE OFFERED IN GOD'S NEW TEMPLE?

Hebrews 13:15-16 states that the sacrifice to be offered in God's new temple is the sacrifice of praise to God; that is, the fruit of our lips giving thanks to His name "to do good and to share, for with such sacrifices God is well pleased." First Peter 2:5, 9, states that we are "a spiritual house, a holy priesthood to offer up spiritual sacrifices acceptable to God through Jesus Christ. And to proclaim the praises of Him who called you out of darkness into His marvelous light."

Hebrews 10:20 states, "We worship by a new and living way." In Philippians 2:17, Paul speaks of his ministry as "being poured out as a drink offering on the sacrifice and service of your faith." These are Old Testament Jewish terms of sacrifice that Paul relates to his service to the Gentiles in the New Testament Church. In Psalm 51:17, David speaks in these same terms under the Old Covenant: "The sacrifices of God are a broken spirit, a broken and contrite heart—these, O God, You will not despise."

What a transfer from a physical building, made by man, to something that God Himself is doing in and through man! God ordered the center of Old Testament worship, the temple, and Jerusalem to be destroyed so that He could further transform His people, the body of Christ, into a *new Jerusalem*—the Jerusalem that is above, the mother of us all (Gal. 4:21-31). Paul in this passage in Galatians calls the Church, God's people, the *new Jerusalem*. The book of Hebrews sustains and affirms this interpretation. The Jewish converts who have come to Christ have not come now to Mount Sinai that burned with fire and blackness, but "have come to the Mount Zion, the city of the living God, the heavenly Jerusalem, to an innumerable company of angels, to the general assembly and church of the firstborn...to Jesus the Mediator of the New Covenant" (Heb. 12:18-24). To what new heights God elevated His people!

Gleason L. Archer wrote, "Because the temple was destroyed it must be rebuilt for worship in the millennium and that the temple that was here when Christ was here did not fit the pattern of the temple of Solomon, 'Therefore we conclude that a third temple is to be built on Mount Moriah, to serve as a center of worship during the millennium'" (*Decision Magazine*, January 1979). This statement counters everything Jesus, Paul, and Peter taught about the temple and New Testament worship. There is no place in the Bible that explicitly states that the physical temple will be rebuilt or that worship will again be held there!

Archer goes on to say, "That Temple will serve as the headquarters of worship and praise for all the citizens of the glorious, messianic Kingdom, over which Jesus Christ will reign for a thousand years after he comes again to claim the earth for God." Psalm 24:1 says that the earth has always been the Lord's. When did He lose it? This is what dispensational millennialists believe, and it is a part of their theology for a Jewish millennium. But does this fit into the pattern of New Testament teaching on the subject of the temple and its worship? It certainly does not!

JESUS INSTITUTED A NEW METHOD OF WORSHIP

What are people really doing when they desire to worship in Jerusalem? In John 4, Jesus spoke to a Samaritan woman. She expressed her side of what and where to worship as opposed to the Jewish system. Jesus countered by stating, "The hour is coming when you will neither on this mountain nor in Jerusalem, worship the Father…But the hour is coming and *now is*, when the true worshipers will worship the Father in Spirit and truth; for the Father is seeking such to worship Him (John 4:21-23, emphasis mine).

Did Jesus not state that there would no longer be need for worshiping in Jerusalem and that there would be no special place in which God's people would have to go to worship God? Why then would He return to have worship centered in Jerusalem as millennialists say? Who is it that would dare to counter what Jesus said? Would not that be heresy? But then, this is what dispensationalists have written and on which their theory is built.

In John 7:37-39, Jesus stood in the temple at the Feast of Tabernacles and declared He was the One who was represented in the symbolic pouring out of water by the priests. He then called them to come to Him and drink. This is the fulfilling of the Feast of Tabernacles, the calling of the unsaved world to come to Christ and drink of the living waters (as seen in John 4 to the woman at the well). This important factor is reiterated in Revelation 22:17 as a call to everyone: Come to those living waters before time runs out.

What does the Book of Hebrews say concerning worship after the cross when Christ's body was rent and His blood was shed? Are we to continue to worship according to a Jewish covenant that has been abrogated by Jesus Himself (Heb. 10:9)? Since the Old Covenant has been abrogated by an act of Jesus, why are millennialists trying to bring back the Old Covenant? Does this not touch on the purpose of the shed blood of Christ and reverse why He shed His blood? Is this not against Scripture and the atonement, for which Christ shed His blood?

Hebrews 10:19-22 declares that because Christ shed His blood, we have a new way of worship! "Therefore, brethren, having boldness to enter the Holiest by the blood of Jesus, by a new and living way which He consecrated for us, through the veil, that is, His flesh, and having a High Priest over the house of God, let us draw near with a true heart in full assurance of faith, having our hearts sprinkled from an evil conscience and our bodies washed with pure water." In this passage, we are told that we have a *new* and *living* way of worship. Furthermore, as New Testament priests, we have the right to enter directly into the Holy of Holies because of the blood of Christ. Verse 20 states that the veil in the temple represented the rent flesh of Jesus Christ, which now would allow entry into the very Shekinah of God. Not even Old Testament priests had the favor of entering the holy of holies. They would have died in the process. But now the New Testament believer can enter the Holy of Holies based on the blood of Christ, not on the blood of a sacrificial animal.

The old has been fulfilled in the new. Behind the veil was the Ark of the Covenant, the throne room of God, who dwelt between the cherubim (Ex. 25:22; Num. 7:89; 1 Chron.13:6). The New Testament believer is now given access to that very throne in prayer (Heb. 4:16). Millennium worship turns the book of Hebrews upside down and drains the person and work of Jesus Christ completely out of it.

The New Covenant of Jesus Christ has changed forever the method and form of worshiping God. The Bible declares that God does not dwell in a man-made temple (Acts 17:24-25). In summation here are some great thoughts by an author whose identity I have lost:

> The Institutions of Judaism have passed away! The Shadow has been replaced by the Substance! Inarticulate symbols have given way to the Divine Word made flesh! We need no earthly tabernacle or earthly temple to assure us of God's interest in our conflicts, joys, and troubles. God, Himself, has become one of us, the Word has been made flesh and was tempted and tried in all points as we are. We need no golden candlestick to fill with rich tranquil light, the darkness of the holy place and to remind us that the Eternal God is always listening to the sighs and cries of the contrite. Why? Because He ever liveth to make intercession for us and we know that He fainteth not neither is weary, nor will this High Priest ever die, or be replaced by another. We need no tables with its loaves and wine to remind us that our earthly possessions should be consecrated to God and that our life belongs to Him. For we have a table to eat of whereof they who served the tabernacle have no right to eat. And now we know that we are not our own for we are bought with a price and whether we now live or die, we do it unto the Lord. We need no golden altar of incense to assure us that our worship and petitions are acceptable to God. For God saw the travail of Christ's soul and was

satisfied. And we are accepted by God in His Beloved, and now He tells us that whatsoever we ask the Father in His name He will give it to us. For now we have received power to become the sons of God and He has given us the Spirit of adoption that assures us we are His. We need no Cherubim to tell us of God's majesty and to testify of His creative power, wisdom, and goodness. For we have seen Him ourselves and the splendor of the world has become dim in the brightness of His presence as we have seen it in the face of Jesus Christ. We need no miraculous pot of manna preserved for us as a memorial of His bounty and divine providence. For we have that true bread from heaven, even Jesus Himself, and with Him, God now freely gives us all things. We need no ark of the covenant to remind us of His presence, His everlasting relationship and mercy for us. We have His divine presence with us at all times, for He has said, Lo I am with you always, even to the end of the world, and I will never leave you nor forsake you.

Wonderful are Christ's divine perfections that cover the tables of the broken law, that required a perfection we could not fulfill. He has now perfected forever, them that are sanctified. We need no priest to sanctify the people now. Both he that sanctifieth and they that are sanctified are one! I am in Christ, and Christ is in God, so how much closer to God can anyone ever get than that! Christ in His stainless purity has become my mercy seat, by His unfaltering obedience to God. We no longer come to Sinai with its thunderings and lightnings of God wherein Moses said I do exceedingly fear and quake. But we are no more reminded by the broken law, of the anger of God. For his body was broken for me and though He was angry with me, now in Christ, His anger is taken away. We need no longer look for God in types, ceremonies, temples, and furnishings. For Christ is the Highest revelation of God; whoever has seen me, Jesus said, has seen the Father. The Shadows, The Symbols have disappeared. We now have Jesus, the fullness of Him, that filleth all in all. He is my completeness! For I am complete in Him without any ark, any tabernacle, any temple. I am in Him for in Him I live, and move, and have my being.

Chapter 20

SACRIFICES IN THE MILLENNIUM

A shock runs through my soul when I think of animal blood sacrifices replacing the blood of Christ and becoming a memorial for atonement of sin that is to last for a thousand years. Animal blood could never forgive sin in the first place; only cover it. How is it then that Christ's blood will be put into the background, when it took His blood to complete the redemption of sins under the first covenant (Rom. 3:24-25; Heb. 9:15)? Since the law and its animal sacrifices made nothing perfect (Heb. 7:19) and Old Covenant saints could not be made perfect without us (Heb. 11:40), how could there even be a thought of returning to imperfection? It would be a return to Judaism!

What does this do to the *blood of God* (Acts 20:28), our Savior and Shepherd, the true Lamb of God? It is sacrilege to think millennialists would replace our Savior's blood so soon. Some time back there was an Associated Press article entitled, "Red Heifer: Sign of Messiah or Just a Cow?" Melody was the name of a "red heifer" born in Palestine, the first to be born there in two millenniums, and was acclaimed by some to be the harbinger of the Messiah. "Gershon Solomon, head of a group dedicated to rebuilding the ancient Jewish Temple said, 'The red heifer is one of the most important signs that we are living in a special time.' Of more recent date many Evangelicals have been spiritually moved when looking for the ashes of the last 'red heifer.'" Is it not true that this promotes the

266

theology of Judaism over and against the Bible? Does a "red heifer" carry more weight than the blood that speaks better things than that of Abel (Heb. 12:24)?

Dispensationalism draws its worship, as such, from Ezekiel 43:18-27. This, however, was written of Israel while they were in Babylonian captivity and was applied to them on returning from that captivity after their release by Cyrus. Scofield says on Ezekiel 43:18-27, "Doubtless these offerings will be a memorial looking back to the cross, as the offerings under the Old Covenant were anticipatory looking forward to the cross" (Scofield 1945, 890).

How can Scofield and his followers believe such a thing when their theology is that Christ came to set up the Davidic kingdom, not to go to the cross? "When Christ appeared to the Jewish people, the next thing, in the order of revelation as it then stood, should have been the setting up of the Davidic kingdom" (Ibid., 998). This surely would have bypassed the cross. Where in Scripture is it stated that *the next thing in order of revelation* was that Christ was to set up the Davidic kingdom? It is interesting what passes off for Scripture that is not Scripture!

In a January 1979 article in *Decision Magazine*, Gleason L. Archer, Jr. wrote:

> We may therefore be confident that the sacrifices mentioned in Ezekiel 43 have nothing to do with atonement for sin. But rather, their function *will be parallel* to that of *the Lord's Supper*…But it should be noted that the Eucharist of bread and wine celebrated by the New Testament Church is intended only for this present dispensation…. But during the age of the millennial Kingdom, when our Lord Jesus Christ will come again to set up the rule of God over all the earth, what type of communion ordinance will *replace our present Lord's Supper* with its bread and wine? Apparently it will be in the form of blood sacrifices again…They were used in this Old Testament prophecy because they furnished the Hebrew believer with the closest available analogy to *the future millennial offerings.* (emphasis mine)

What is Gleason Archer, Jr., telling us? First, he is saying that the sacrifices in the millennium *will be parallel to that of the Lord's Supper.* In the dictionary, "parallel" means "to show something equal to." How sad that the Lord's blood would be equal to animal blood. Second, Archer is saying that the present Eucharist of bread and wine was *"intended only for this present dispensation."* Where is this stated in Scripture?

In fact, this is the exact opposite of what Jesus said in Matthew 26:29 when speaking of the Lord's Supper: "But I say to you, I will not drink of this fruit of the vine from now on until that day when I drink it new with you in My Father's kingdom." Jesus said it would be *the fruit of the vine*, not animal sacrifices, that would be the memorial. Animal sacrifices *will replace our present Lord's Supper?* This is sacrilege!

Archer is also saying that there will be *future millennial offerings*. There is no mention in Ezekiel (or any other Old Testament book) of a millennium, period. It is assumed. Man's theology has been superimposed upon the text.

Harry Ironside, former pastor of Moody Memorial Church, said the sacrifices in the millennium will be figurative. How can a literalist say sacrifices will be figurative? They are not faithful to their own hermeneutic of literalism. A.M. Morris, in his book *The Prophesies Unveiled*, says this:

> How should we view those predictions that use the phraseology common to Israel in foretelling the fortunes of the Israel of God under the gospel? ... As the prophets took their illustrations type-prophecies from the then reigning order of things, we see why they used David, the temple, sacrifices and other types, to foretell the gospel. There is a definite idea in burnt-offering, sin offering, peace-offering, and the like, and such language used, (typically), sets forth the literal antitype or fulfillment. It is manifest that the burnt-offerings, sin offerings, and the like among the Jews were ordained as types to be observed till they were redeemed in their anti-types, but not later. We are now living in a house built for a habitation of God through the Spirit. Any other interpretation brings out opposite and contradictory results and can not be true.

> There is not a typical and anti-typical system of sacrifices to be in effect at the same time. Jesus abolished the typical forever. There is not to be the law in one hand, restored and in the full force in earthly Canaan, by the fleshly seed of Abraham, with circumcision, clean meats, appointed sacrifices, a magnificent temple, richly dressed priest-hood, gorgeous ritual, ancient Levites in full dress performing their ancient duties, and the nations going up in caravans to annual feasts, and the antitypes of all these existing at the same time. It is not Jesus or Moses; but it is

Jesus predicted and typified by Moses and the prophets, or Jesus rejected for a carnal tradition, with Moses and all the prophets upholding the claims of Jesus and rejecting and condemning the blind traditionists. The Jews read the prophets with a veil on their hearts, the veil of Tradition. We should not veil our hearts to the simplicity and beauty of the prophecies concerning Christ and his spiritual kingdom, for the rejected tradition of a temporal kingdom of Christ yet to be set up according to the Jewish hope.

(Morris 1944, 48-49)

Since the millennium is supposed to be the perfect age, how is it that God is going to go back to a system that the book of Hebrews says made nothing perfect (Heb. 7:11-12)? This would be pure Judaism and a devaluation of the blood of our Savior. Because Christ is the end (*telos*) of the law, how can the law ever appear again (Rom. 10:4; 7:4-7)? It has been abrogated. Since the law itself was imperfect, how can that which was imperfect ever become perfect? It cannot. It has been replaced with the perfect. "For by one offering He has perfected forever those who are being sanctified" (Heb. 10:14). "God having provided something better for us, that they should not be made perfect apart from us" (Heb. 11:40).

Hebrews 10:9 declares Christ "takes away the first that He may establish the second." If Christ took away the first covenant, who has the right, power, or authority over Him to re-establish it? God forbid! I feel like Joel when he said, "Blow the trumpet in Zion, and sound an alarm in My holy mountain" (Joel 2:1). Have we waited too long to sound the alarm against such false devaluation of the sacrifice of Christ as well as the purity of God's Word?

Furthermore, Hebrews 7:27, 9:12, 26, 28 and 10:10 state that the blood of the Savior was shed once and for all, never to be replaced by such a memorial as animal sacrifices. By using Ezekiel's sacrifices and referring to them, the millennialists are running counter to Hebrews 10:18, which states that where forgiveness of sin is "there is no longer an offering [*prosphora*, "sacrifice"] for sin." To re-offer blood sacrifices, therefore, has to be diabolical.

How can dispensationalists say that Christ, our present High Priest, forever after the order of Melchizedek, will revert to that of a Jewish high priest that bypasses His own sacrifice and eternal covenant (Heb. 13:20) and thus revert to an outdated and abrogated system? David Brown put it well in his book, *Christ's Second Coming:*

> That the unbelieving Jews should look for a rebuilt *temple*, a re-estab-lished *priesthood*, the restoration of their *bloody sacrifices*, and an Israelit-ish *supremacy*—at once religious and civil—*over all nations of the earth*, when their Messiah comes, is not to be wondered at. With these views of Old Testament prophecy, their fathers rejected Jesus and put him to death, as he neither realized their expectations, nor professed to do so; but on the contrary, directed his whole teaching to the uprooting of the prevalent conceptions of Messiah's character, work, and kingdom, and to the establishing of views directly opposite. Unless they had been prepared to abandon their whole scheme of Old Testament interpretation, they could not consistently have acknowledged Jesus to be the Messiah. But that any *Christians* should be found agreeing with the unbelieving Jews in their views of Old Testament prophecy—that there should be a school of Christian interpreters, who, while recognizing Jesus as the promised Messiah, and attached in all other respects to evangelical truth, should nevertheless contend vehemently of Jewish literalism, and as a necessary consequence, for Jewish altars, sacrifices, and supremacy—is passing strange...But characterized as they were by low views of the Person and Work of Christ, as well as of every thing else in religion, their existence was brief and outside the orthodox Church; nor have such Judaizing opinions ever been able to raise their head, save in a few isolated cases, till the present day. The most remarkable fact of all is, that those who held the premillennial theory in the second and third centuries, seem not to have believed in any literal, territorial restoration of the Jews at all—much less in their millennial supremacy over all nations, and the re-establishment of their religious peculiarities.
>
> (*Christ's Second Coming*, pp. 338-339)

Let us reiterate that which Jesus Himself said would be a memorial in the age to come: "As they were eating, Jesus took bread, blessed and broke it, and gave it to the disciples and said, 'Take eat; this is My body.' Then He took the cup, and gave thanks, and gave it to them, saying, 'Drink from it, all of you. For this is My blood of the New Covenant, which is shed for many for the remission of sins. But I say to you, I will not drink of this fruit of the vine from now on until that day when I drink it new with you in My Father's kingdom'" (Matt. 26:26-29).

Jesus plainly did not refer to animal sacrifices as the memorial, but to the *fruit of the vine*. Why deny or denigrate that which Jesus said? In conclusion, it must be said that the doctrine of sacrifices in the millennium is subjective and that it prescribes a man-made method that God is supposed to use. It is not found in Scripture and is the selling out of Christ and His sacrifice.

Chapter 21

ABERRATIONS OF MILLENNIALISM

Speaking of Jerusalem in the millennium, Pentecost says, "Jerusalem will become the center of the worship of the age." (Pentecost 1978, 509). How can Jerusalem become the center of worship in the millennium when Jesus has already denied that charge and changed that form of worship? In John 4:21, Jesus said, "Woman, believe Me, the hour is coming when you will neither on this mountain, nor in Jerusalem, worship the Father." Was Jesus wrong?

In Revelation 11:8, Jesus told John that the present Jerusalem is called Sodom and Egypt. Has Jesus changed His mind on Jerusalem from the Gospels to the book of Revelation? Would that not be a biblical contradiction and also render divine inspiration of the Scriptures invalid?

How can people living in human flesh inherit the millennium when God has told us in His Word that "flesh and blood" shall not inherit the kingdom of God that comes at the time of the resurrection (1 Cor. 15:50)? At the resurrection, *death* shall be destroyed, "swallowed up in victory" (1 Cor. 15:54). If there is a millennium after the resurrection takes place, how can people die after that?

How could it be possible that Christ in His glorified body, together with all the righteous in their glorified state, rule over mankind for a thousand years, who are still in the body of this flesh? Where in the Bible is such a doctrine taught? Revelation 20 does not speak of reigning on earth; rather, it is to reign with Christ where He was—and that is in heaven. The martyrs are the ones whom Christ is talking about in this passage, and it is they who are called the "first resurrection" (Rev. 20:4-5). And where in the Bible is it implied that Christ will become a political Messiah and reign physically on earth, especially after He said, "My kingdom is not of this world" (John 18:36)?

Christ at His second coming in glory with His angels will judge every person according to his or her works (Matt. 16:27). This precedes the millennium, at which time the wicked are destroyed and "the Lord Jesus is revealed from heaven with His mighty angels in flaming fire taking vengeance on those who do not know God…these shall be punished with everlasting destruction from the presence of the Lord and from the glory of His power" (2 Thess. 1:6-10). How can there be anyone left to go into the millennium for the righteous to rule over?

Dispensationalists teach that when Christ returns after the resurrection, He will set up His millennial kingdom. In this kingdom, they say, people will still marry and have children (Wilkerson and Boa 1983, 518). This is a complete perversion of Jesus' plain teaching, "For in the resurrection they neither marry nor are given in marriage, but are like angels of God in heaven" (Matt. 22:30). The language of Scripture is plain and should not be twisted or tortured to mean the opposite of that which Christ stated. After the resurrection, no person living on earth will be in his or her natural body. The believers will be transformed in a moment in the twinkling of an eye, and the wicked will be sent into eternal damnation (2 Thess. 1:7-10).

Jesus Christ was sent into the world to provide redemption for "His people" (Matt. 1:21). His people were the elect Jew and the elect Gentile (Gen.12:3). Christ said, "I have finished the work you gave me to do" (John 17:4). What purpose is there for a millennium in which the nation of Israel is to be saved when redemption has already been provided for them? Was not the Jew in God's saving act on Calvary? Why did Jesus state what He did in Luke 24:45-47 if there were no covenant of salvation for the Jews now? To say that redemption for all mankind was not complete at Calvary is to deny the redemptive act of God in Christ by the cross. Why is a thousand years needed for Christ to finish His redemptive work, when from the cross He already proclaimed, "It is finished" (John 19:30)? Where in the Bible is it stated that Christ at His second coming will do what He failed to do at His first coming—set up a kingdom in favor of the Jews so they will then accept Him—when Revelation 22:11-12 says just the opposite?

To quote Romans 11:26 in favor of all Israel getting saved at Christ's second coming is to take Scripture out of context and contort it (Rev. 22:11-12). In Romans 11:26, Paul is not reprophesying the prophecy of Isaiah 59:20-21, he is applying it by stating that Christ the Redeemer has already come out of Zion: "And so all Israel will be saved," meaning, in this manner, through the Redeemer that has already come out of Zion. What manner is that? It is that of Romans 11:23-24, which says Israel will be grafted back into that from which they were cut off. That is into the same thing in which the Gentiles—the wild olive branch—have been grafted, outside of which there is no salvation (Acts 4:11-12).

If the Redeemer has not come out of Zion, then according to verse 27, there is no covenant yet for Israel's sins. This would be heresy. If there is a covenant for Israel's sins, it would mean the Redeemer has already come out of Zion. Matthew 21:5 states that on Jesus' triumphal entry into Jerusalem on Palm Sunday, the prophecies of Isaiah 62:11 and Zechariah 9:9 were fulfilled. "Tell the daughter of Zion, 'Behold your King is coming to you.'" Israel is called the daughter of Zion, and Christ is the king. What a direct fulfillment! How could one miss it?

According to the account in John 4, the woman at the well proves that the Jewish faith had been contaminated by Persian and Babylonian mysticism and apocalypticism. Both the books of Ezra and Nehemiah testify of the same. Jesus Himself never spoke of a golden age or a millennium after His second coming. He told His followers He would come back for them and they would be with Him in heaven with His Father (John 14:3; Matt. 26:29).

THE REIGN OF CHRIST

"Rule in the midst of Your enemies!" (Ps. 110:2). Millennialists take this psalm to be fulfilled in the millennium. They teach that there will be a thousand years of peace during the reign of Christ, called the "golden age" or the millennium. Some say when Christ reigns, there will be no enemies. However, the Word of God says in Psalm 110:2 the Messiah is to "rule in the midst of [His] enemies." Dispensationalists say Christ will not reign until He returns the second time after the so-called "great tribulation" when He sets up His kingdom. Therefore, there is no present reign of Christ.

If Christ is not reigning now and in charge of all things, who is? If the dispensational position is not scriptural and Christ *is* reigning now, how is He reigning? It is certain that when Christ left this earth He did not leave it in charge of Satan. Let's consider four points of Christ's victory over Satan:

1. Christ began His ministry in Matthew 4:1-11 by meeting Satan head on. He met and overcame all of Satan's temptations, one of them being the ownership of the kingdoms of this world.
2. In Matthew 12:22-29, Christ bound Satan so he could no longer claim the kingdoms of this world. When Jesus told His disciples of His coming death by being lifted up on the cross, He said, "Now is the judgment of this world; now the ruler of this world will be cast out" (John 12:31-32).

3. In John 16:7-11, Jesus announces that upon His ascension and the coming of the Holy Spirit, "The ruler of this world is judged." Christ has already defeated and judged Satan and his hosts (Col. 2:15; Phil. 2:9-10; Heb. 2:8-9, 14; 1 Pet. 3:22).

4. After Christ's death and resurrection but before the ascension, He said to His disciples, "All authority has been given to Me in heaven and on the earth. Go therefore and make disciples of all nations" (Matt. 28:18-19). Since Calvary, Christianity has invaded and is planted in the kingdoms of the world. Does this not prove that Christ is reigning over the world from His new position in heaven?

This can mean nothing less than Christ is reigning now and is in charge of all things in heaven, earth, and under the earth (Phil. 2:10). Revelation 1:5 declares Christ to be "the ruler over the kings of the earth." What greater status could be given Him?

By the time Paul wrote Ephesians, he could say Christ was at the right hand of God, seated far above all principalities and power, might and dominion, and every name that is named has already put all things under His feet (Eph. 1:20-23). How then can anyone say Christ is not in charge or He is not presently reigning?

In 1 Corinthians 15:25, Paul states, "He must reign till He has put all enemies under His feet." The declaration is Christ is presently reigning and he will do so until He has put all enemies under His feet. The last enemy, being death (v. 26), will be destroyed at the resurrection, the last trumpet (1 Cor. 15:51-52). It is when believers are changed in a moment in the twinkling of an eye.

However, since the present reign of Christ is denied, it must be proven from Scripture that Christ upon His ascension is seated on the throne of David and is reigning from heaven during this present age. Acts 2:29-35 states that Christ was resurrected to sit on the throne of David, which was the fulfillment of Psalm 132:11. Christ's first act on the throne was the outpouring of the promised Holy Spirit (Luke 24:49, Acts 2:1-4, 33).

The reign of Christ is usually taught on the basis of His reigning literally and physically on earth in the literal city of Jerusalem on the literal throne of David, in literal Palestine, for a literal thousand years after His second coming. Stanley Horton says, "Jesus will come and set up a literal kingdom, just as real as the empires of the past but without their imperfections" (Horton, *Bible Prophecy,* *"Student Manual,"* *#10).* Some people take this as their pattern and then isolate Scripture as proof texts of their theory. Yet the Bible does not speak to this position.

In *The Millennium,* George B. Fletcher questions how anyone can make the glorified Christ to be a political Messiah. "To assume that Christ offered to the Jews a temporal world power kingdom, and then, perceiving their official rejection of it, postponed it to a thousand-year period of time *AFTER* His Second Advent, is as contrary to Scripture as anything could be" (Fletcher undated, 8). The text dispensationalists use is in Revelation 20:4-6:

> And I saw thrones, and they sat on them, and judgment was committed to them, then I saw the souls of those who had been beheaded for their witness to Jesus and for the word of God, who had not worshiped the beast or his image, and had not received his mark on their foreheads or on their hands. And they lived and reigned with Christ for a thousand years. But the rest of the dead did not live again until the thousand years were finished. This is the first resurrection. Blessed and holy is he who has part in the first resurrection. Over such the second death has no power, but they shall be priests of God and of Christ, and shall reign with Him a thousand years.

The question is: Does this passage of Scripture teach what dispensationalists say it does; that is, a literal reign, in literal Jerusalem, and on the literal throne of David? It is nowhere found in the text! Nor does the text indicate the time when this will take place.

A KING OF RIGHTEOUSNESS IS PROMISED

Throughout Old Testament history, the Bible teaches that man has been incapable of even ruling over himself. Jeremiah said, "O Lord, I know the way of man is not in himself; It is not in man who walks to direct his own steps" (Jer. 10:23). Israel always had trouble ruling themselves and were often ruled by foreigners. Haggai must have had this in mind and looked for the rulership of the Messiah when he wrote "the Desire of all Nations shall come" (Haggai 2:7 KJV).

As history advanced, God revealed that one day the Messiah would come, be their king, and rule and reign in righteousness. Isaiah said,

"Behold, a king will reign in righteousness" (Isa. 32:1). Jeremiah 23:5-6 echoed the same truth. To some in Israel this was taken literally, while to others it meant God was their king and was ruling them through the Word of God and the prophets (Neh. 9:30). At the time of Christ, Israel was looking for a king that would overcome Rome and restore their kingship. When Christ did not do this, they rejected Him. This is known as the eschatology of Judaism.

Some of the more salient scriptures on the subject of the Messiah's reign are put forth in the book of Daniel. At Daniel's time, the entire Jewish nation was under Gentile domination. Jeremiah had prophesied that Judah would be under Gentile rule for seventy years in Babylon, and that God would then let them return to their homeland (Dan. 9:1-2; 2 Chron. 36:21; Jer. 25:8-12; 27:6-8; 29:10).

Daniel was favored with wisdom to interpret the dream God had given to Nebuchadnezzar. This dream consisted of four Gentile powers who would rule the entire then-known world, after which time God Himself would set up His kingdom on earth through the Messiah, the stone cut out without hands (Dan. 2:31-45). These four kingdoms were presented in the king's dream as an image of man.

In the sequence of events, Daniel was told that *in the days of these kings,* the God of heaven would set up a kingdom. A stone cut out without hands would smite the image on the feet. The image would be crushed like the chaff of a summer threshing floor that the wind would drive away, and no place would be found for it anymore. Then the stone would become a great mountain and fill the whole earth. Notice the text says the entire image was "crushed together, and became like chaff from the summer threshing floors; the wind carried them away so that no trace of them was found" (Dan. 2:35). This included the toes, and therefore precludes a revival of a so-called Roman Empire as taught by dispensationalists. No further scriptural refutation is necessary. Let Scripture speak for itself.

A vision of the same time period was later given to Daniel when he saw one like the Son of Man coming to the ancient of days and set up His kingdom upon the ruins of the four kingdoms (Dan. 7:9-27). This kingdom was to be of such a nature that it would endure forever (v. 14). This prophecy was fulfilled by Christ in Revelation 1 where He is seen as glorified, and in Revelation 4–5 where Jesus takes the throne in heaven at the right hand of God.

Isaiah had already prophesied of the Messiah's coming into the world, setting up His kingdom, and ruling on the throne of David (Isa. 9:6-7). This prophecy was to commence at Christ's birth and to proceed "from that time forward, even forever." Peter interpreted this as being fulfilled by Christ's death, resurrection, and ascension (Acts 2:29-36). This is a very important point, as some say Christ had already postponed His kingdom. Yet if this were true, why in Acts 1:3 did Christ continue to give instructions to His disciples "of things pertaining to the kingdom of God?" This was forty days after His resurrection.

Ezekiel, who lived in the time of Jeremiah, also prophesied that the Messiah's kingdom would be through the greater son of David (Ezek. 34:23-25; 37:24-28). David himself had been dead for several hundred years by this time. Therefore, it could not apply literally to David. God foretold this to David through Nathan the prophet in 2 Samuel 7:1-19. David's throne "shall be established forever" (v. 16), but this was to be "for a great while to come" (v. 19). Peter interpreted these Old Testament prophecies as being fulfilled by Christ at His first coming (Acts 2:29-36; 3:22-26).

When the Messiah was born into the world, God used the angel Gabriel to tell Mary the babe she would bring into the world would be called "the Son of the Highest; and the Lord God will give Him the throne of His father David. And he will reign over the house of Jacob forever, and of His kingdom there will be no end" (Luke 1:31-33). In this passage, we see Jesus, the King, coming from the house of David to take David's throne and reign forever.

Luke 1:72-73 states that Jesus' coming from the house of David was also the fulfillment of the covenant that God made with Abraham "to perform the mercy promised to our fathers and to remember His holy covenant, the oath which He swore to our father Abraham." There can be no doubt as to the fact that Jesus Christ brought to fulfillment all the Old Covenant redemptive and kingly functions of both the Abrahamic and Davidic covenant, which all the prophets had spoken of "since the world began" (Luke 1:70). To delay these functions until after the Church has been taken to heaven is to rob the Church of her kingdom status and her spiritual birthright.

Wilfred C. Meloon writes, "So, the church is lulled to sleep as though her songs were lullabies and her 'gos-pill' were tranquilizers. Of course, there are many 'spiritual sedatives.' There are many sources of somnambulism which have entered into the church of which have worked on it from without; but I think of no greater cause of the church's weakness today than the subtle facetiousness of one of its own great bulwarks— DISPENSATIONALISM" (Meloon 1971, 11). Philip Mauro concurs to the same in his pamphlet, *I Was Robbed.*

THE REIGN OF CHRIST INCLUDES SALVATION FROM SIN

The dispensationalists do not include present-day salvation as a part of the reign of Christ. The reign of Christ included salvation from sin by the shedding of His blood. In Luke 1:68 and Matthew 1:21, the angel bore witness to the truth that the Messiah came to save His people from their sins. This Christ did by the shedding of His blood. Jesus Himself said He came "to give His life a ransom for many" (Matt. 20:28). Hebrews 9:22 states that "without the shedding of blood there is no forgiveness." Sin had a powerful grip on mankind that only God could break. Redemption was the Messiah's victory over sin and Satan's hold on mankind. Christ's shed blood became His reign over sin and was the fountain for cleansing from sin.

Scofield says, "Zech. 12-14 'is the return of the Lord and the establishment of the kingdom'...the cleansing fountain (Zech. 13:1) then to be effectually 'opened' to Israel" (Scofield 1945, 976). This would mean that from the time of Christ until the millennial kingdom, the cleansing fountain had not been effectually opened for Israel. This is startling, especially when Matthew 1:21 says Jesus came to "save His people [Israel] from their sins."

Isaiah prophesied that the Messiah's reign would be over sin. "How beautiful upon the mountains are the feet of him who brings good news, who proclaims peace, who brings glad tidings of good things, who proclaims salvation, who says to Zion, 'Your God reigns'" (Isa. 52:7). Paul in his salvation chapter in Romans 10:15 cites Isaiah 52:7, which declared "our God reigns" and it finds its fulfillment in the salvation brought to us in Christ. The reign of Christ is seen in the fact that through personal salvation, He has delivered us from the power of Satan and sin, "For sin shall not have dominion over you, for you are not under law but under grace" (Rom. 6:14). Every time the gospel of the kingdom is preached and a soul comes to Christ, it takes the sinner out from under Satan's dominion and places him in the kingdom of the Son (Col. 1:13; Acts 26:18).

Therefore, the salvation of God is grace reigning in the life of the saved person. This is why Jesus told Nicodemus that to be saved meant to enter the kingdom of God, of which He was the king (John 3:3-5). Nathanael was the first one to see this: "Rabbi, You are the Son of God, You are the King of Israel" (John 1:49).

THE GENTILES WERE INCLUDED IN THE MESSIAH'S KINGDOM

In His covenant to Abraham, God gave the promise that "all the families of the earth" would be included (Gen. 12:3). Isaiah prophesied that the Gentiles would be included as a part of the Messiah's redemptive kingdom "in Galilee of the Gentiles. The people who walked in darkness have seen a great light" (Isa. 9:1-2). Luke 1:79 says this was fulfilled by Christ "to give light to those who sit in darkness." These prophecies and their fulfillment assure us the Messiah's kingdom has come, was to last forever, and it will have no end. Other scriptures that verify the fact that Christ as king was to come and set up His kingdom are Psalms 2, 8, 45, 89, and 110 and Isaiah 2:1-4. The New Testament verifies these references as fulfilled by Christ at His first advent (Acts 4:25-26; Heb. 2:4-6; Matt. 22:44).

THE MESSIAH WOULD ESTABLISH DAVID'S KINGDOM AND SIT UPON HIS THRONE

What is the house of David that God would build for him as seen in 2 Samuel 7:1-19? In Luke's text, the house of David is called "the house of Jacob." This certainly broadens the realm to more than just David's time. In the prophecies Jacob gave in Genesis 49:8-10, 22-24, the scepter in Judah and the shepherd stone of Joseph were Messianic and should not be left out of the Messianic picture.

Second Samuel 7:16 states three things God was going to build for David: (1) David's house, (2) David's kingdom, and (3) David's throne. The Messiah, David's seed, would establish these three things forever (2 Sam. 7:12-13). Let us take them in reverse order.

The Throne of David. "The Lord has sworn in truth to David; He will not turn from it: 'I will set upon your throne the fruit of your body'" (Ps. 132:11). Peter says this prophecy was fulfilled by the Lord Jesus Christ upon His resurrection and ascension into heaven, at which time He was seated upon the throne of David. "Therefore, being a prophet, and knowing that God had sworn with an oath to him that of the fruit of his body, according to the flesh, He would raise up the Christ to sit on his throne, he, foreseeing this, spoke concerning the resurrection of the Christ, that His soul was not left in Hades, not did His flesh see corruption" (Acts 2:30-31).

To the chagrin of classical and revised dispensationalists, progressive dispensationalism has now accepted the truth of Christ being on the throne of David (see Chapter 6 of *Progressive Dispensationalism* by Craig A. Blaising and Darrell L. Bock).

The Kingdom of David. When Christ the Messiah began His public ministry according to Mark, He did so by announcing "the Kingdom of God is at hand" (Mark 1:14-15). When Jesus said "the time is fulfilled," He was referring to an ancient prophecy of the Old Testament. Most assuredly it was from Daniel 2:44-45, as the fourth kingdom, Rome, was in power when Christ came. The prophecy stated that in "the days of these kings" the stone kingdom of the Messiah was to be set up. This announcement from Christ had been preceded by John the Baptist, who likewise told his hearers that the kingdom of God had now arrived (Matt. 3:1-12).

Furthermore, Jesus said, "The law and the prophets were until John. Since that time the kingdom of God has been preached, and everyone is pressing into it" (Luke 16:16). This does not leave us in the dark as to when Christ instituted His kingdom. (As to the interpretation of "at hand," see Chapter 3, "The Kingdom of God in this Present Age.") The kingdom of God was inaugurated and set up when Christ was on earth. He was born king (Matt. 2:1-6). He claimed He had a kingdom (John 18:36-37). He rode into Jerusalem as king (Matt. 21:5) and as the Son of David (v. 9). The entrance to this kingdom was to be through experiencing the new birth (John 3:3-7).

The House of David. David's house certainly meant his kingdom rule in Israel as well as the continuity of his seed, being Christ, the Messiah, as well as the raising up of the tabernacle of David. This was fulfilled in that Gentiles are now included in the Church (Acts 15:14-18). The Jews, on the other hand, were looking for a different form of the kingdom—a kingdom that would destroy Roman power and put Israel back in a reigning position. However, they had misinterpreted their own prophecies concerning the Messiah (Acts 13:27-39). They said, "We will not have this man reign over us" (Luke 19:14). They then crucified the king, "the Lord of glory" (1 Cor. 2:6-8).

THE REIGN OF THE KING

Because Scripture stipulates that the king has come and has set up His kingdom, we now enter into the phase of the reign of the king. But how does Jesus Christ reign? If Christ is a king, He must have a kingdom. And whom does He reign over? To be king, He must have subjects. Are we His subjects?

When we speak of Christ's kingdom, we do not mean a literal geographic location on planet Earth such as a political kingdom of man (which some advocate). Jesus said, "My Kingdom is not of this world" (John 18:36).

Note that Revelation 20:1-6, which dispensationalists use as a proof text for a millennium, actually says nothing about Christ coming to earth or of Christ literally and physically reigning on earth. To say this is the case would be adding to the text, which we are strictly warned not to do or to go beyond that which is written (1 Cor. 4:6). We cannot play Ping-Pong with God's Word.

Christ was born king (Matt. 2:2; Mic. 5:2). This is irrefutable. Christ reigned as king. He reigned as king over sickness, disease, nature, and death, (Mark 1:40-45; 2:1-12; 3:1-5). He reigns over angels (Matt. 26:53) and over demons (Mark 5:1-20; Matt. 12:22-29). He reigns over things under the earth (Phil. 2:10).

Christ bound Satan. On His ascension into heaven, He cast Satan out, never again to appear in heaven (Rev. 12:4-10). When this was done, a loud voice in heaven was heard saying, "Now salvation, and strength, and the kingdom of our God, and the power of His Christ have come, for the accuser of our brethren, who accused them before our God day and night, has been cast down" (Rev. 12:10). Dispensationalists say this verse applies to a time yet future. If this is so, then there is *no salvation or kingdom* now. That would be the reverse of an entire body of Scripture.

Christ reigns over nature. He walked on water (Matt. 14:22-33). He turned water into wine (John 2:7-11). He stilled the stormy sea (Mark 4:35-41). He reigned over the fish of the sea (Luke 5:1-11). He ruled over the timing the rooster crows (22:34). Furthermore, He reigns over death. He raised Lazarus from the dead (John 11). After His own death and resurrection, He said He had the keys of both death and hell (Rev. 1:18). Christ was resurrected (Isa. 11:1, 10) to reign over the Gentiles, as affirmed by Paul in Romans 15:12.

Christ reigns over sin (Matt. 9:2-6). Sin shall not have dominion over you (Rom. 6:14). And He is presently reigning (1 Cor. 15:25). In Colossians 1:13, Paul says the Colossian believers, being Gentiles, were in the kingdom of His Son. How then could the kingdom have been postponed if at this date Gentiles were still coming into the kingdom? In other words, there is not any place where Christ does not reign. The Bible teaches that Christ wrought about thirty-four miracles to manifest His glory and reigning power.

CHRIST, THE KING OF THE KINGDOM

Christ died as king. He entered Jerusalem for the last time on Palm Sunday as king (Matt. 21:1-16). That He was the greater Son of David is irrefutable. That He died a king is recorded in Mark 15:26 and John 18:33-37.

Christ rose from the dead as king. The kingdom did not end with Christ's death on the cross. He announced to His disciples after His victory over death and the grave that all authority was given to Him both in heaven and on the earth and that the gospel of the kingdom should be preached until the end of the age (Matt. 24:14; 28:18-20).

It is also interesting that on the very day of His ascension into heaven, Jesus continued to speak about the kingdom to His disciples (Acts 1:3-8). They were to tarry in Jerusalem to be endued with the power of the kingdom. If Jesus had already postponed the kingdom, why did He forget about it here? The postponed kingdom is a fallacy.

Christ presently reigns as king from the throne of David. In Acts 2:29-35, Peter said Christ took the throne of David upon His resurrection and ascension into heaven. To controvert this biblical truth and postpone the kingdom until a so-called millennium is to take from the Church the very essence of Christ's gospel as well as the kingdom of God. Christ did *not* postpone His kingdom. Rather, He took the kingdom of God away from Israel and gave it to the Church (Matt. 21:42-43). The Church is the nation that fulfills Isaiah 66:7-8 (this is affirmed in 1 Peter 2:6). Revelation 7:9-10 states that the Kingdom has invaded the entire world and is made up of every kindred, tribe, and tongue.

CHRIST, THE INAUGURATED KING

Revelation 4–5 depicts the inauguration of Christ as king in heaven, where He went after He left earth. These chapters are the fulfillment of Psalm 24:7-10. Redemption is now complete. Christ sits enthroned and is ruling from heaven on David's throne (Acts 2:29-36). To deny this is to deny that Christ sent the promised Holy Spirit. So, if it is true that Christ is not reigning from heaven, is He just sitting in heaven not using His authority and power? What would Matthew 16:18-19 and Philippians 2:10 then mean?

Christ is the king! He is alive and on the throne today. This is according to His own words in Revelation 3:21. His kingdom is being advanced everywhere the gospel of the kingdom is preached. Christ is alive and is reigning from heaven over His Church, of which He said the gates of hell would never prevail (Matt.16:18). The true Church of Christ is marching on and will continue to do so until He comes. This is His promise. Christ's victory is our victory now, not reserved for some future date or time.

That the Messiah was to be king is prophesied throughout the Old Testament (Gen. 49:8-12; 22:17-18; 24:60). Psalm 2:6 proclaims the same message: "Yet I have set My King on My holy hill of Zion." Acts 4:25-26 declares this prophecy was fulfilled in Christ. Likewise, the following references have been fulfilled by Christ's first coming: Isaiah 60:1-3; Luke 2:32; 24:26; Matthew 4:16; Galatians 3:16; Colossians 2:15; Hebrews 2:7; and 1 Peter 1:11.

OF WHAT DOES THE REIGN OF CHRIST CONSIST?

How is Christ reigning today? There is much confusion on this subject, as the eschatology of Judaism has taken over the hearts and minds of many people. This type of eschatology, now known as dispensationalism, teaches that Christ will not reign until a so-called millennium, at which time He will return and re-establish the Jewish nation. This is a man-made theory and contradicts the entire body of Scripture. As already stated, Christ took the kingdom of God away from Israel and gave it to the Church (Matt. 21:42-43; 1 Pet. 2:2-10). It is never stated that He will take it away from the Church and give it back to national Israel. According to Galatians 6:16, the Church has been constituted as the Israel of God.

Paul states that Christ is reigning now and that His reign is through grace. "For if by the one man's offense [Adam] death reigned through the one, much more those who received abundance of grace and the gift of righteousness will reign in life through the One Jesus Christ" (Rom. 5:17). In this passage, Paul contrasts the *reigning of death through Adam* with the *reigning in life through Christ.*

No one can deny that death reigns. Why should we then deny the reign of grace in Christ after He won the victory over sin that caused death? This victory was secured by the resurrection of Christ from the dead, "So that as sin reigned in death, even so grace might reign through righteousness to eternal life through Jesus Christ our Lord" (Rom. 5:21). To deny this is to deny John 3:16 and 10:28, which promise eternal life to all who believe and are Christ's sheep. This, in essence, would also be denying the power of the gospel that we are sent to proclaim (Rom. 1:16; 1 Cor. 4:20).

To say the reign of the believer is only to be with Christ in heaven is to deny what God has already stated: "Those who receive the abundance of grace and the gift of righteousness will reign in life through One Christ Jesus" (Rom. 5:17). We are to reign in life, not only after death.

All believers have been given the gift of the righteousness of God in Christ (2 Cor. 5:21). Grace has been given to the believer to enable him to reign in righteousness unto eternal life through Christ Jesus (Rom. 5:21). "For sin shall not have dominion [reign, have kingship] over you, you are not under law but under grace" (Rom. 6:14).

In Titus, Paul tells us what kind of grace God gives to the believer: "For the grace of God that brings salvation has appeared to all men, teaching us that denying ungodliness and worldly lusts, we should live soberly, righteously, and godly in this present age" (Titus 2:11-12). Paul further accentuates the reign of Christ in this present age: "There shall be a root of Jesse; And He who shall rise [be resurrected] to reign over the Gentiles, in Him the Gentiles shall hope" (Rom. 15:12). Paul quotes this from Isaiah 11:1,10, which dispensationalists say belongs to the millennium. However,

Paul did not think so. He declared it had been fulfilled by Christ in this age. One of the specific reasons for Christ's resurrection was to *reign* over the Gentiles. Christ's reign therefore is universal in scope. It thus eliminates all geographical and political boundaries.

Why is it so hard to believe what these scriptures state? Why turn them around to mean the exact opposite of what they teach? Does that not make the Bible self-contradictory? George E. Ladd says the following regarding Christ's reign:

> Paul portrays the entire mission of Jesus in terms of his Kingdom or reign, and associates the Kingdom of God with the resurrection and salvation. Christ's reign as Messiah began with the resurrection. It will be concluded only when "He has put all his enemies under his feet" (1 Cor. 15:25). By his reign, he will destroy every rule and every authority and power, the last of which is death. When his messianic reign is completed, he will turn over the Kingdom to God the Father (1 Cor. 15:24). Here the Kingdom is the redemptive, dynamic rule of God exercised in Christ's total messianic mission to bring order to a disordered universe, to accomplish God's total redemptive purpose.
>
> (Ladd 1974, 410)

Christ was promised the throne of David as the fulfillment of David's covenant promises (2 Sam. 7:12-19; Isa. 55:3; Luke 1:31-33; Acts 13:22-39). This is to say nothing of the Messianic Psalms 2, 8, 89, and 110. Zechariah 6:12-13 states that the Messiah was to be both priest and king on the throne and that He would build the temple of God. This temple that Christ built is seen in John 2:18-21, Ephesians 2:19-22, 1 Corinthians 3:16, and 2 Corinthians 6:16. Paul tells us that God no longer dwells in temples made with hands (Acts 17:24). Therefore, God will have nothing to do with any future physical temple structure.

By now, we have seen that the kingdom of Messiah was not to be a political power wielded over nations but one of saving grace by its delivering power over sin. Did Jesus not say, "My kingdom is not of this world" (John 18:36)? Christ's reign is spiritual, and so is His kingdom through which He is now reigning!

THE SCEPTER OF CHRIST'S KINGDOM

Every reigning king has a scepter that tells of the objective of His reign. Jesus Christ was given the scepter that was promised the Messiah in Genesis 49:10: "The scepter shall not depart from Judah, nor a lawgiver from between his feet, until Shiloh comes; and to him shall be the obedience of the people." This scepter is also mentioned in Numbers 24:17 and Psalm 45:6. Hebrews 1:8 states, "But to the Son he says: 'Your throne, O God, is forever and ever; a scepter of righteousness is the scepter of Your kingdom.'"

Isaiah declared, "Behold, a king will reign in righteousness" (Isa. 32:1). Jeremiah states that David's greater son is called "a Branch of righteousness; A King shall reign and prosper, and execute judgment and righteousness in the earth.... His name by which He will be called: The Lord Our Righteousness" (Jer. 23:5-6).

In the New Testament, Christ is our righteousness. "But of Him you are in Christ Jesus, who became for us wisdom from God—and righteousness and sanctification and redemption" (1 Cor. 1:30). "For He made Him who knew no sin to be sin for us, that we might become the righteousness of God in Him" (2 Cor. 5:21). There is no other righteousness that can supersede the righteousness of God.

No other construction can be put on Jeremiah 23:5-6 other than Christ is presently reigning. Christ reigns because He is Lord (Acts 2:36). This He will do until the last enemy, death, is destroyed. Death will be destroyed by the resurrection at Christ's second coming (1 Cor. 15:50-56). This takes place, Paul says, at the last trumpet when all living believers will be changed in a moment in the twinkling of an eye. Christ reigns because He ascended to the throne of David (Acts 2:29-35). In Revelation 1:17-18, Christ conquered both death and hell, and those keys are now in His possession. Death was the devil's greatest weapon against mankind (Heb. 2:14).

At Pentecost, the apostles were convinced by the sound from heaven and the tongues of fire that Christ's universal Lordship was now established and that He truly was on David's throne pouring out the Holy Spirit (Acts 2:1-36). This resulted in three thousand Israelites being brought into the kingdom of God.

Jesus said in Mark 9:1 that some of those to whom He was talking would not see death until they saw the kingdom come with power. Either the kingdom has come with power or the people to whom He was talking are alive today. Which is it? The kingdom came with power at Pentecost (Acts 1:8). The Mount of Transfiguration was a prefigured manifestation of the king in His glorified state of power and rulership.

Jesus, the very day of His ascension into heaven, spoke about the ongoing of the kingdom, its power, and how it would be spread (Acts 1:1-8). Today, the uttermost parts of the earth are being reached with the gospel of His kingdom. Christ reigns because He said all authority was given to Him (Matt. 28:18). If this is not true, then Matthew 16:18, in which Christ promised victory to the Church over and against the gates of hell, has no meaning.

Isaiah saw Christ's victory when he wrote about Christ's death: "Therefore will I divide a portion with the great and He shall divide the spoil with the strong" (Isa. 53:12). This Jesus did when He gave His disciples power over demons (Luke 10:19).

CHRIST REIGNS FROM THE RIGHT HAND OF GOD

David prophesied of Christ's reign in Psalm 110:1-2, "The Lord said to my Lord, 'Sit at My right hand, till I make Your enemies Your footstool. Rule in the midst of Your enemies.'" Isaac Ambrose, born in 1591, wrote about what it means for Jesus to be at God's right hand.

> What is the right hand of God? I answer, 1. Negatively, It is not any corporal right hand of God, if we speak properly, God hath neither right hand, nor left hand; for God is not a body, but a Spirit, or a spiritual substance. 2. Positively, the right hand of God, is the majesty, dominion, power, and glory of God. Ps. 118:15; Ex. 15:6; Ps. 89:13; Isa. 48:13.
>
> (Ambrose 1896, 499)

Psalm 110 is quoted at least twenty-one times in the New Testament. Each time, it is applied to Christ and His present action of reigning power from the right hand of God. Christ did not go back to heaven defeated, or to do nothing until He came back the second time. The following references prove that Christ is actively busy and reigning on behalf of His people:

1. Matthew 22:44: Jesus applies Psalm 110:1 to Himself as proof that He is both David's son, and David's Lord. This verse explicitly

implies that Jesus was to rule from the *right hand* of God, until all of His enemies were made His footstool (see Mark 12:36 and Luke 20:42-43).

2. Matthew 26:64: Jesus said to the high priest, "Nevertheless, I say to you, hereafter you will see the Son of Man sitting at the right hand of Power, and coming on the clouds of heaven."

3. Mark 16:19: "So then, after the Lord had spoken to them, he was received up into heaven, and sat down at the right hand of God." This is Christ's new reigning position.

4. Acts 2:25: On the Day of Pentecost, Peter quotes a prophecy from Psalm 16:8-11 that Jesus, in spite of His death, was alive and sitting at the right hand of God.

5. Acts 2:33: On His ascension, Jesus took the throne of David and is set down at the right hand of God.

6. Acts 2:34-35: Peter ascribes that Jesus, on His resurrection and ascension, was positioned at the right hand of God as His place of enthronement.

7. Acts 5:31: Jesus as prince and savior reigns from the right hand of God, granting repentance and forgiveness to Israel.

8. Acts 7:55-56: The reigning Jesus stands from His seated position at the right hand of God to welcome home His first martyr, Stephen.

9. Romans 8:34: A part of the reign of Jesus is that He intercedes for His people from the right hand of God (see Heb. 7:25).

10. Ephesians 1:19-21: The power that raised Christ to the right hand of God and placed Him far above all principality and power is the same power that He now grants to His Church. The Church has been robbed of this power because it has been taught that Christ will not reign until the millennium. Truly, we have been robbed.

11. Colossians 3:1: To obtain that reigning power, the Church is asked to seek the things that are above where Christ sits at the right hand of God. This certainly proves the present reign of Christ on behalf of His people.

12. Hebrews 1:3: For the believer, sin has forever been taken care of by Christ, who having purged our sins sat at the right hand of God. God has already done everything necessary for the forgiveness of sin. Christ reigns over sin!

13. Hebrews 1:13: Angels are not as high in dignity and rank as Christ. Therefore, they are not elevated to the right hand of God. Jesus alone is the true Son of God. He reigns over angels.
14. Hebrews 8:1: Jesus is our great high priest who reigned over sin by making atonement and is now sitting at the right hand of the Majesty in the heavens. He is both king and priest on the throne in the fulfillment of Zechariah 6:12-13. He is now building God's temple.
15. Hebrews 10:12: Christ now reigns over sin by the one sacrifice of Himself, after which He sat at the right hand of God.
16. Hebrews 12:2: We are to look to Jesus who is at the right hand of God for the reigning power of faith, because He is the author and finisher of our faith.
17. First Peter 3:22: The believer who lives in Christ has no fear of principalities and powers, as they are all now subject to Christ who is at the right hand of God.

Christ is actively reigning on behalf of His people. Hebrews 4:16 tells us that Christ is presently busy and active on the throne, granting mercy and grace to help in our time of need.

The Pharisees knew that if they accepted Christ as their Messiah, they would be subjects of His reign, therefore they said, "We will not have this man to reign over us" (Luke 19:14). If Christ is not presently reigning over His Church, then Matthew 16:18 means nothing, for He must reign till He has put all enemies under His feet. The last enemy that will be destroyed is death (1 Cor. 15:25), which occurs at the resurrection. Truly, Christ is King on the throne and is reigning in regal power now.

As to the reign of Christ in the kingdom of God, dispensationalists say that it takes the physical presence of Christ on earth to constitute that reign. The Bible does not teach such a literal interpretation. Paul went so far as to say that "even though we have known Christ according to the flesh, yet now we know Him thus no longer" (2 Cor. 5:16).

Jehovah was Israel's king, but never in a physical sense. Upon Israel's victory through the Red Sea, their victory song was, "The Lord shall reign forever and ever" (Ex. 15:18). Israel considered their exodus from Egypt as God reigning in their affairs. Regarding this passage in Exodus 15, F. F. Bruce states, "This is the first explicit mention of the Kingdom of God in the Bible, and from it we learn that His Kingdom is not to be understood territorially…exercised over nations as seen in His curbing the Red Sea, and over men; both in His vindication of those who put their trust in Him and in His judgment of their enemies" (Bruce 1978, 5).

God reigned in the kingdom that in the Old Testament was in Israel without being physically present. God is not a physical being. Jehovah's presence was in the Ark of the Covenant, which served as God's reigning throne. From the time He made Israel a nation and a kingdom of priests, His divine presence was manifested in and through the Ark of the Covenant. Through the wilderness, God's manifest presence led the Israelites by a pillar of cloud by day and a pillar of fire by night.

The sons of Aaron found out how real that presence was. When the Philistines captured the Ark, their god, Dagon, found out how powerful the Jehovah God of Israel was. When David set out to retrieve the Ark, Uzzah soon found out that the God of Israel was a God of power. God reigned by His invisible presence amid the nation of Israel.

Romans 5:14 states that death reigned from Adam to Moses. There was no physical presence of Satan in that reign. How then can dispensationalists say it takes the physical presence of Christ to constitute the reign of His kingdom? Such a statement is unscriptural and absurd. Christ established His kingdom while He was on earth. As A.T. Robertson has so aptly expressed it, "The kingdom came with the presence of the King." It is stated in the book of Acts that after Christ had ascended into heaven, the Christians had "another king—Jesus" (Acts 17:7).

John, the Revelator, said he was in the kingdom of Jesus Christ (Rev. 1:9). This kingdom was without the physical presence of Jesus on earth. Revelation 15:3 states that Jesus is "King of saints." Paul, after his revelation of Christian truth (Gal. 1:11-12), continued to preach the kingdom of God until his death (Acts 28:30-31). This may seem redundant, but scriptural truth should not be denied. We may deny truth, but we can never get away from it. Truth is like the hound of heaven and one day will judge us (John 12:48).

THE BIBLE TEACHES THAT THERE CANNOT BE A MILLENNIUM

Dispensationalism teaches that upon Christ's second coming, He will institute the New Covenant (of Jeremiah 31:31-33) with the Jews and set up His millennial kingdom. The Bible does not teach this theory for the following reasons.

First, the Bible teaches that there were only two redemptive covenants. All other covenants are covenants within covenants. The two covenants are called the first covenant and the second covenant (Heb. 10:9). Christ took away the first covenant to establish the second. The first covenant was that of the law, while the second covenant is the one Christ instituted (Matt. 26:26-29; Luke 22:20).

If dispensations were biblical, Hebrews 10:9 would read that Christ took away the fifth dispensation to establish the sixth. But the Bible does not say that. The book of Hebrews teaches that the New Covenant of Jeremiah 31:31-34 is the covenant Christ fulfilled (Heb. 8:6-13; 10:1-21). Hebrews 13:20 verifies the fact that Christ's covenant is called the eternal one. Therefore, there cannot be another covenant made with the Jews after Jesus comes. To ratify another covenant, there would have to be the death of the Testator (Heb. 9:16-17). This would mean Christ would have to die again. Is that a biblical possibility (see Rom. 6:9-10)? That would be heresy!

This tells us God deals with man's sin on the basis of covenants, not on the basis of dispensations. The word *dispensation* is a Latin word that has been transported into the Bible and used in an endeavor to replace the word *covenant*. The Greek word οικονομια, with its cognates, is rightly translated "steward" or "stewardship," not dispensation. In the Bible, it never is used as a period of time but as a duty to be performed.

If the Bible taught dispensations as to elements of time, it would have said so in Matthew 1:17. Rather, this scripture divides periods of time into generations, not dispensations. Does this not also teach that there is no set length of time, even for a generation? God introduced redemption through covenants, not through dispensations. Dispensations are a man-made, pre-supposed plan, in which God's plan fails every time. Never do we find redemption for sin in dispensations. Redemption for sin is found only in covenants:

- Under the covenant of Adam (Hos. 6:7), God provided redemption for fallen man (Gen. 3:21).
- Sacrifice was renewed in the covenant with Abraham (Gen. 15; 17).
- The covenant of law (Ex. 19; 20) was added to the Abrahamic covenant until the Seed, Christ, should come (Gal. 3:19).
- The Davidic covenant was an extension of the Abrahamic covenant under which God promised a "king" through Abraham's line (Gen. 17:16). The Davidic covenant therefore deals with the kingdom and the kingship of Christ, the Messiah from the seed of David. After Israel's backslidings and the breaking of God's covenant, they were sent into Babylonian captivity. While in captivity, they were promised by God a covenant they could not break (Jer. 31:31-34). This became Christ's covenant (Heb. 8:7-13; 10:15-18), and it is an eternal covenant (Heb. 13:20).

If the truth of the New Covenant was that Jesus Christ failed to bring perfection (which He did not—see Hebrews 10:14 and 11:40), then God would have had to set up a seventh dispensation for a thousand years, which also would fail because Satan would rise up to ruin Christ's reign. Where would that put God with failure after failure? Thus, dispensations are absurd and ridiculous. No, there is no fifth, sixth, seventh nor any other dispensation. God simply took away the first covenant to establish the second. There is no other covenant to come.

Christ has never failed. His Church will never fail. We have His promise (Matt. 16:18). Furthermore, Hebrews 10:14 states, "For by one offering he has perfected forever those who are being sanctified." Perfection has already been brought in by the covenant that Christ instituted. Therefore, there remains no need for a millennial age. Christ must remain in heaven (Acts 3:21) until all things are restored that have been spoken by His holy prophets since the world began. When Christ does return, according to 2 Peter 3, all things will have been restored. He will then usher in the new heavens and the new earth, not a millennium.

Scofield says in his comments on Ephesians 1:10 that *the fullness of times* belongs to the millennial age. However, Galatians 4:4 states that *the fullness to time* began when God sent forth His Son into the world. This makes the Church Age *the fullness of time*. Revelation 10:6 states that at the sounding of the seventh trumpet, time (*kronos*, not delay) will be no longer. Time will then end and eternity will begin.

According to the following references, the Bible teaches that there is only one bodily resurrection to come: John 5:28-29; 1 Corinthians 15:12-55; 1 Thessalonians 4:16; Revelation 11:15-19; Isaiah 26:19; Ezekiel 37:12; and Job 14:12,14; 19:25-27. The Bible never uses the word *resurrection* in the plural. Jesus said the time of the resurrection would be "at the last day" (John 6:39-40, 44, 54; 11:24). This would have to include 1 Thessalonians 4:16. Second Peter 3 states that when Jesus comes as a thief in the night, the present earth as we know it will be renovated, and we will then enter into the new heavens and the new earth. There is no room here for a millennium. Revelation 20:1-6 does not teach a bodily resurrection.

If the righteous are resurrected on the last day (John 6:39-40, 44-45, 54; 11:24), there can be no millennium, because there can be no days after the last days. Furthermore, if all the holy prophets since the world began (Acts 3:21) and those since Samuel have spoken of these days (Acts 3:24), what other days are there? Acts 2:17 and Hebrews 1:1-2 confirm that the last days began with the Church Age. What other age does the Bible talk about except the eternal age after this one (2 Pet. 3:10-13)?

The Bible teaches that there is no rapture of the Church apart from the second coming of Christ and the last trumpet (Matt. 24:3, 31; 1 Cor. 15:51-54; Rev. 11:15-19; 1 Thess. 4:13-18). The Bible teaches that the wicked and the righteous will be judged and rewarded at the same time, not seven or more years apart (John 5:28-29; Matt. 13:36-43; Acts 10:42;

2 Tim. 4:1; 1 Pet. 4:5; 2 Thess. 1:6-10; Rev. 11:18; Dan. 12:2). The Bible teaches that there is but one general judgment to come (John 5:27-29; Rev. 20:11-15; 11:15-19; 2 Thess. 1:6-10; 2:1-10; Matt. 13:36-43; 25:31-46; Acts 24:15; 10:42).

The Bible teaches that Christ upon His ascension to the right hand of God was seated on the throne of David and is now reigning from that position (Ps.110; Matt. 22:41-46; Isa. 9:6-7; Luke 1:31-33). The Lamb is on the throne of David (Acts 2:29-36). The throne of Israel on which David and Solomon sat is called the throne of the Lord (1 Chron. 29:23). (For Christ on the throne, see Revelation 3:21; 4:2-3; 5:6. For Christ reigning, see Romans 5:17, 21; 15:12 and 1 Corinthians 15:25.)

Did Christ teach a millennium in Matthew 12:32 when He said there was only one age to come and it would be the Father's kingdom (Matt. 22:29)? Since the handwriting of ordinances of the Old Covenant that were against us has been nailed to the cross, how can they ever be brought up again in a millennium (Col. 2:14)?

Did Paul teach a millennium? In Ephesians 1:21, speaking of Christ's authority, he said it would be "not only in this age but also in that which is to come." In Ephesians 2:19-21, there is no other building that God will yet have to build. Paul says the next age will be God's heavenly kingdom (2 Tim. 4:18) not an earthly millennium.

Does Hebrews 9:26 teach a millennium when it says, "Christ appeared once at the end of the ages"? After the end of the ages eternity will be ushered in.

Did Peter teach a millennium in 2 Peter 3:13?

Did John teach a millennium on earth after Jesus returns (Rev. 20:1-6)? If he did, then he contradicted himself in Revelation 11:15, where he said when Christ does come, He comes to reign eternally and not just for a thousand years. It is impossible that the Bible could so contradict itself. A millennium holds out a false hope to both the Jewish and Arab people. Both are to be evangelized and brought into the Church, which is God's fullness.

You Shall Not Add to the Word of God

To add to a text or to say something is in a text that is not there is adding to God's Word. God warns us not to add to His Word.

Deut. 4:2	You shall not add to the word which I command you, nor take away from it, that you may keep the commandments of the Lord your God which I command you.
Prov. 30:6	Do not add to His words, lest He rebuke you, and you be found a liar.
Ps. 119:89	Forever, O, Lord, Your word is settled in the heaven.
Matt. 5:18	For assuredly, I say to you, till heaven and earth pass away, one jot or one tittle will by no means pass from the law till all is fulfilled.
2 Cor. 4:2	But we have renounced the hidden things of shame, not walking in craftiness nor handling the word of God deceitfully, but by manifestation of the truth commending ourselves to every man's conscience in the sight of God.
1 Cor. 4:6	Now these things, brethren, I have figuratively transferred to myself and Apollos for your sakes, that you may learn in us not to think beyond what is written.

Gal. 3:15

Brethren, I speak in the manner of men: Though it is only a man's covenant, yet if it is confirmed, no one annuls or adds to it.

2 Pet. 3:16

As also in all his epistles, speaking in them of things, in which are some things hard to understand which untaught and unstable people twist to their own destruction, as they do also the rest of the Scriptures.

2 Pet. 3:17

You therefore, beloved, since you know this beforehand, beware lest you also fall from your own steadfastness, being led away with the error of the wicked. [Note: "Error of the wicked" means deception, fraud, delusion, seduction, being unrestrained or licentious.]

Rev. 22:18-19

For I testify to everyone who hears the words of the prophecy of this book: If anyone adds to these things, God will add to him the plagues that are written in this book; and if anyone takes away from the word of the book of this prophecy, God shall take away his part from the Book of Life, from the holy city, and from the things which are written in the book.

DANIEL'S STONE AND PROPHETIC BIBLICAL HISTORY

DANIEL'S STONE IN PROPHETIC BIBLICAL HISTORY

1. Daniel 2:31-35, 44-45: Christ, the stone kingdom, crushes all other kingdoms.
2. Genesis 49:24: Messiah is the Shepherd, the Stone of Israel (Ps. 80:1).
3. Genesis 28:11: Jacob slept on a stone; anointed it as El-Bethel (Gen. 35:1-14).
4. Numbers 20:11: Moses strikes the rock (Isa. 48:21; Ps. 78:20; 1 Cor. 10:4).
5. Exodus 24:12: The decalogue is on two tables of stone.
6. Ezra-Nehemiah: The stone wall of the city a symbol of salvation (Isa. 26:1).
7. Isaiah 32:1-2: A king was to reign as a great rock in a weary land.
8. Isaiah 8:14: The stone was to be a stone of stumbling (Rom. 9:32-33).
9. Isaiah 28:16: The stone was to be a foundation stone laid in Zion (1 Pet. 2:6).
10. Psalm 118:22: The stone was to be rejected by the builders (Matt. 21:42).
11. Isaiah 5:1-7: The stone was in Israel, God's vineyard (Matt. 21:33-46).

12. Zechariah 4:7-9: The stone was to be the capstone of the temple (Eph. 2:20-21).
13. Zechariah 3:9: The branch is the stone with seven eyes (Rev. 5:6).

CHRIST'S KINGDOM HAS BECOME THE STONE KINGDOM

1. Matthew 21:33-46; 1 Peter 2:7: Jesus is the rejected stone of Israel.
2. Romans 9:32-33; 1 Peter 2:8: Christ is the stone Israel stumbled over. Therefore Daniel's stone has already fallen!
3. First Peter 2:4: Christ is the living stone.
4. First Peter 2:6: Christ is the chief cornerstone of Isaiah 28:16.
5. Matthew 11:28-29: Christ is our rock in a weary land (Isa. 32:1-2).
6. Acts 4:11-12: Christ is the rejected stone and the only way of salvation.
7. First Corinthians 3:11: Christ is the foundation stone of the Church.
8. First Corinthians 10:4: Christ is the rock that Israel drank from in the wilderness.
9. First Peter 2:5: Christians are the living stones in God's new temple.
10. Revelation 5:6: Christ is the seven-eyed stone of Zechariah 3:9.
11. First Peter 2:8: Christ is the chief corner stone and stone of stumbling.

Jesus Is King of His Kingdom, as Prophesied by the Prophets

1. Genesis 17:15-16: Abraham's offspring through Sarah was to produce kings.
2. Micah 5:2: The king was to be born in Bethlehem (Matt. 2:2).
3. Isaiah 9:6-7: The king was to take the throne of David (Luke 1:32-33).
4. John 1:31: John the Baptist introduces Christ the Messiah to Israel.
5. John 1:49: The Messiah was Israel's king.
6. Matthew 3:1-12: John the Baptist preaches the kingdom of God to Israel.
7. Mark 1:14-15: Jesus preaches the time is fulfilled and that the kingdom of God is here. What time is fulfilled (Dan. 2:44-45; 7:13, 14, 18, 27)?
8. John 3:3-5: Admittance into the kingdom is via the new birth.
9. Matthew 10:7; Luke 10:9: Jesus sends His disciples to preach the kingdom.
10. Matthew 16:19: Jesus gives Peter the keys of the kingdom.
11. Matthew 11:12-13; Luke 16:16: The law and the prophets replaced by Christ's kingdom.
12. Matthew 8:11-12; Luke 13:29: Old Testament and New Testament saints possess the same kingdom (Col. 1:13; 1 Thess. 2:12; Rev. 1:5-9).

13. Luke 1:18-22: Signs of the Messianic king are fulfilled by Jesus.

14. Luke 4:14: Jesus in Galilee preaches the kingdom as composed of all nations.

15. John 1:14: Jesus is the New Testament tabernacle.

16. John 2:18-19: Jesus is the New Testament temple (Matt. 12:6; Zech. 6:12-15).

17. Mark 11:7-11: Jesus dramatizes the Passover of Himself (1 Cor. 5:7).

18. Hebrews 9:26: Jesus' sacrifice was the end of the ages.

19. Acts 2:1-36: The last days arrived in Christ and He was resurrected to sit upon the throne of David (Joel 2:28-29; Rom. 15:8-13; Heb. 1:1-13).

20. Matthew 26:26-29: Jesus establishes His New Covenant and fulfills the prophecy of Genesis 12; 15; 17; Exodus 19:6; Isaiah 55:3; Jeremiah 31:31-34; Hebrews 8:6-13; 10:16-18; 13:20.

21. First Peter 2:2-12: All the prophets are fulfilled in Christ (Acts 3:19-26; Luke 24:24-27).

22. Romans 10:4: Jesus terminates the law (John 1:17; Rom. 6:14; 7:1-7; Gal. 3:19).

23. Hebrews 12:28: Christ's kingdom cannot be shaken.

24. John 18:36: If the kingdom did not come with Christ, why did He say it did?

25. Acts 28:25-31: Paul until his death preaches the kingdom of God.

THE PROPHESIED MESSIAH IS FULFILLED IN JESUS

The prophesied king of the Old Testament is Jesus, the King in the New Testament.

1. Genesis 14:18: Melchizedek, king of righteousness—Jesus is King of Righteousness (Isa. 32:1; Jer. 23:5-6).
2. Second Corinthians 5:21: Jesus Christ reigns as King of Righteousness (Rom. 5:17, 21; 14:17; 1 Cor. 1:30; 15:25-26; Heb. 1:8-9).
3. John 3:3-8, Colossians 1:13, Revelation 1:9: The king's converts enter His kingdom.
4. Genesis 14:18: Melchizedek, king of peace—Jesus is King of Peace (Isa. 9:6-7; John 14:27; 16:33; Eph. 2:14-15; Col. 1:20).
5. Genesis 14:18: Melchizedek served bread and wine. Bread and wine bespeak the Lord's Supper (Matt. 26:26-29).
6. Genesis 14:18: Melchizedek, priest of the Most High God—Jesus, Priest of God (Ps. 110:4; Heb. 5:5-6; 7:1-20).
7. Genesis 17:6: A king would come from Abraham's seed (Pss. 2:6; 89; John 18:36-37). Isaiah saw the king, Jehovah of hosts (Isa. 6:5); John says Isaiah saw Jesus (John 12:41).
8. Genesis 49:10: Jacob prophesied the king's scepter was to come from Judah: "The scepter shall not depart from Judah, nor a lawgiver from between his feet, until Shiloh come; and to Him shall be the obedience of the people."

9. Hebrews 1:8: But to the Son he says, "Your throne, O God, is forever and ever; a scepter of righteousness is the scepter of Your kingdom." Only kings have scepters.

10. Genesis 49:24: The king is to be a shepherd and a stone. "From there is the Shepherd, the Stone of Israel" (Pss. 23; 80:1; John 10:11).

11. Numbers 24:17,19: Balaam prophesied of a scepter from Israel. "A Star shall come out of Jacob; a Scepter shall arise out of Israel... Out of Jacob One shall have dominion."

12. Numbers 23:21: The shout of a king is among them.

13. Isaiah 7:14: The king announced is to be born of a virgin. Therefore, the Lord Himself would give a sign: "Behold, the virgin shall conceive and bear a Son, and shall call His name Immanuel" (Matt. 1:23). This was fulfilled in Jesus.

14. Isaiah 9:6-7: The king prophesied to be born as a child. "For unto us a Child is born, unto us a Son is given; And the government will be upon His shoulder, and His name will be called Wonderful, Counselor, Mighty God, Everlasting Father, Prince of Peace. Of the increase of His government and peace there will be no end, upon the throne of David and over His kingdom, to order it and establish it with judgment and justice from that time forward, even forever."

15. Zechariah 6:12-13; The king shall build the temple of the Lord (Zech. 6:12-13; John 2:18-21; 1 Cor. 3:16; 6:19; 2 Cor. 6:16; Eph. 2:11-22).

16. Zechariah 9:9: The king was to ride into Jerusalem on a donkey. This was fulfilled by Jesus (Matt. 21:1-11).

17. Isaiah 11:1-10; 52:7: The branch is a king that reigns (Rom. 15:12; 5:17, 21; 1 Cor. 15:25-26).

18. Micah 5:1-5: The king's birthplace and kingship announced. "But you Bethlehem Ephrathah, though you are little among the thousands of Judah, yet out of you shall come forth to Me the One to be Ruler in Israel, whose goings forth are from of old, from everlasting [olam is the Hebrew for "everlasting," which means "eternal."]...And He shall stand and feed His flock."

19. Matthew 2:1-6: The king is born in Bethlehem. "Where is He that has been born King of the Jews?" (v. 2).

20. Isaiah 40:3: The king has a forerunner. "In those days came John the Baptist preaching in the wilderness…Repent, for the kingdom of heaven is at hand" (Matt. 3:1-2). "The ax is laid to the root of the trees" (v. 10). This is spiritual as opposed to literal!

21. John 1:29-34: The king is revealed to Israel by John the Baptist. "Behold the Lamb of God who takes away the sin of the world… that He should be revealed to Israel, therefore I came baptizing with water…this is He who baptizes with the Holy Spirit" (vv. 29, 31, 33).

22. John 1:49: Jesus is seen as the king of Israel. Nathanael says, "Rabbi, You are the Son of God! You are the King of Israel!"

23. Mark 1:14-15: Jesus, the king, sets up His kingdom. His mission is to preach the kingdom of God (Matt. 4:23). He tells people to repent and believe the gospel. Man enters the kingdom through repentance.

24. Matthew 3:13-17: The king is baptized in water. The Spirit descends like a dove. Jesus identifies Himself with lost mankind! The Father's voice is heard announcing His Son, in whom He is pleased.

25. John 3:3-5: The king announces the way into the kingdom. "Unless one is born again [from above] he cannot see the kingdom of God."

26. Matthew 4:1-11: The king invades Satan's territory and overcomes him. "Man shall not live by bread alone but by every word that proceeds from the mouth of God. You shall not tempt the Lord your God. You shall worship the Lord your God and Him only you shall serve."

27. Matthew 12:22-29: The king binds the strongman. Jesus the king casts out demons and heals the sick (v.22). Casting out of demons is a manifestation of the kingdom of God (v. 28). Jesus binds the strongman and plunders his goods (v. 29; cf. Isa. 53:12).

28. John 12:31-33: The king casts out the ruler of this world (Rev. 12:7-9; Col. 2:15; Phil. 2:9-10).

29. John 16:11: The king judges the evil one "of judgment, because the ruler of this world [Satan] is judged" (v. 11).

30. John 18:33-37: King Jesus is not a political rival of Caesar. "My kingdom is not of this world."

31. Ephesians 1:19-23: The king has placed His enemies under His feet (Phil. 2:9-10; Heb. 2:8-9).

32. Luke 17:20-21: The king's kingdom comes not by observation. It is inside the believer.

33. Mark 11:9-10: The king's kingdom fulfills the Davidic kingdom. "Hosanna! Blessed is He who comes in the name of the Lord! Blessed is the kingdom of our father David that comes in the name of the Lord! Hosanna in the highest!"

34. Matthew 16:18-19: The king gives the keys of the kingdom to Peter. "Upon this rock I will build my church and the gates of hell shall not prevail against it. And I will give you the keys of the kingdom of heaven and whatever you bind on earth will be bound in heaven, and whatever you loose on earth will be loosed in heaven."

35. Matthew 21:43: The king takes the kingdom away from Israel and gives it to the Church (1 Pet. 2:5-9).

    • The Church is God's spiritual house.
    • The Church is a holy priesthood.
    • The Church is Zion, the place of the chief cornerstone.
    • The Church is a royal or kingly priesthood.
    • The Church is a holy nation.
    • The Church is God's own special people (see Ex. 19:6).

36. Matthew 26:26-29, Luke 22:20: The king inaugurates the New Covenant, the fulfillment of Jeremiah 31:31-34 (Heb. 8:8-13; 10:15-18; 13:20).

37. John 19:19-22, Mark 15:32: The king dies as king of the Jews. Pilate wrote, "JESUS OF NAZARETH, THE KING OF THE JEWS" on the sign above His cross. In John 19:22, Pilate said, "What I have written, I have written."

38. Matthew 28, Mark 16, Luke 24, John 20, Acts 1:1-3: The king is resurrected and returns alive from the dead! He is king over death (Rev. 1:18).

39. Acts 2:29-36: The king is resurrected and ascends into heaven to sit on David's throne. Therefore, this cannot be a millennial event.

This event fulfilled Luke 1:31-33, 2 Samuel 7:1-19, Psalm 89 and 132:11, and Isaiah 9:6-7.

40. Matthew 24:14, 28:18-20, Mark 16:15-20, Acts 1:8: The king commissions His disciples to preach the gospel of the kingdom until the end of the world (Acts 28:25-31).

41. Matthew 13:38: Good seed are the children of the kingdom.

42. Matthew 16:28, Mark 9:1, Luke 9:27: The king promises the power of the kingdom to His disciples.

43. Acts 1:3-8; 2:1-4: The kingdom was not postponed.

44. Luke 22:29: The king bestows the kingdom on His apostles.

45. Acts 2:1-4: The king fulfills His promise and pours out the promised Holy Spirit (Joel 2:28-29; Luke 24:49-53; John 7:37-39).

46. Acts 4:11-12: The king is the rejected stone that brings salvation.

SCRIPTURE REFERENCES TO THE SECOND COMING

Never once in any of the verses following is it implied that Jesus will come twice. The words *revelation, epiphany* and *parousia* happen at the same time. These three words cannot be separated to imply two or three separate comings of Christ.

1. Matt. 16:27 — The Son of Man comes in the glory of His Father.

2. Matt. 25:1-13 — The ten virgins. Bridegroom coming for the bride.

3. Luke 12:35-37 — Be ready and watching.

4. 1 Cor. 3:13 — Everyone's work will be revealed by fire.

5. 1 Cor. 1:7-8 — Christians are to eagerly await the revelation of Christ.

6. 1 Cor. 11:26 — Communion to believers shows Christ's death until He comes.

7. Col. 3:4-5 — When Christ appears [epiphany] we shall appear with Him.

8. Phil. 3:20 — Wait for the Savior.

9. Phil. 1:6 — He who begun a good work will complete it.

10. Phil. 1:9-10 — Be sincere and without offense until the day of Jesus Christ.

11.	1 Cor. 3:13	The day shall declare every man's work.
12.	1 Thess. 1:9-10	Christians are to wait for His Son from heaven.
13.	1 Thess. 4:13-18	Christ comes with, as well as for His saints.
14.	1 Thess. 5:23	We are to be preserved blameless at the coming parousia.
15.	2 Thess. 1:4-7	Jesus will be revealed from heaven.
16.	2 Tim. 4:8	The crown of righteousness to those who love His appearing.
17.	Tit. 2:11-13	Looking for the blessed hope, Christ's glorious appearing.
18.	Heb. 9:27-28	Appointed once to die then the judgment.
19.	James 5:7-8	Be patient until parousia of the Lord.
20.	1 Pet. 1:13	Believer is to be sober until the revelation of Jesus Christ.
21.	2 Pet. 3:4	The parousia (v. 4), is the same event as vv. 10, 12, and 13.
22.	1 John 3:2-3	Believers are to be like Him at His epiphany (Col. 3:4).
23.	1 John 2:28	We are to abide in Him until He appears.
24.	Jude 14-15	Judgment will be upon the ungodly when Jesus comes.
25.	Rev. 1:7	Every eye shall see Him.
26.	Rev. 2:25	Hold fast until I come.
27.	John 5:28-29	The righteous and wicked are resurrected together.
28.	Matt. 13:36-43	Both tares and wheat are harvested together at the end of the age.
29.	Rev. 11:15-19	Everyone is judged and rewarded at the same time.

ABOUT THE AUTHOR

Rev. John C. Egerdahl is a searcher. He has spent his life searching for the truth—not "a" truth, but "the" truth. He has found that truth in Jesus Christ. From the time he was five years old, John realized that not only was there a God, but also that God wanted him. With the first five dollars he earned, he bought a Bible and carried it with him, even into the South Pacific, where he served during World War II. When John was fourteen, God made it plain to him that he was a sinner and in need of salvation. This started within him the search for how to be saved.

Five years later, while at home on leave from the Navy, his aunt invited him to church. After the sermon, the preacher asked, "Is there anyone here who would like to become a Christian?" Those words gripped his heart. The pastor showed him from the Bible how Christ died for his sins and that if he would confess his sins, God would forgive him. When John did, the assurance of salvation and forgiveness became his. This started John's search to really know God.

One of the compelling reasons for this book comes from John's many encounters and interactions with false cults (such as Jehovah's Witnesses and Mormons). He wondered how they, using the same Bible, could come to the opposite conclusions to which he came. His next thought was that if they could know what they believed (even though false) as well as they did, shouldn't he know the Bible better and in such a manner as to convince them of their error? This started the search for the really deep truths in God's Word.

310

There is a biblical principle of rightly dividing the Word of Truth. However, even among Christians, there are some unbiblical flavors. How could John untangle what he'd found and come up with an unbiased and biblical view of divine truth? His quest for truth had been fueled.

God set us free to be true to Him, true to ourselves, and true to others. Truth believed and lived out will set man's soul free and keep it free. Why is this so crucial? It's because a part of our corrupt nature has crept into religion. All too often, we approach the Bible according to our preconceived ideas. Scripture is taken out of context and becomes proof texts of what we want it to mean, and then it becomes a pretext to protect our bias. When that happens, it does not allow God's Word to be free to be interpreted in the light of its own immediate or total biblical context. A big difference between God's truth and our truth!

It is John's hope and prayer that what is said in these chapters may inspire each reader to dig into God's most holy and precious book for the "truth that sets you free," and be blessed.

BIBLIOGRAPHY

Ambrose, Isaac. *Looking unto Jesus*. Harrisonburg, VA: Sprinkle Publications, 1896.

Andrews, Samuel J. *Christianity and Anti-Christianity*. Chicago: The Bible Institute Colportage Association, 1898.

Angus, John. *The Bible Hand-Book: An Introduction to the Study of Sacred Scripture*. London: The Religious Tract Society, 1857.

Archer, Gleason L, Jr., Paul D. Feinberg, Douglas J. Moo and Richard R. Reiter. *The Rapture*. Grand Rapids, MI: Academie Books, 1984.

Armerding, Carl E. and W. Ward Gasque. *Handbook of Biblical Prophecy*. Grand Rapids, MI: Baker Book House, 1978.

Barclay, William. *Letters to the Corinthians*. Philadelphia, PA: Westminster Press, 1975.

Barnes, Albert. *Epistle to the Romans*. New York: Harper and Brothers, Publishers, 1871.

Berkhof, Louis. *The History of Christian Doctrines*. Carlisle, PA: The Banner of Truth Trust, 1978.

Bickerseth. *The Promised Glory of the Church of Christ*. London: Seeley Burnside & Seeley, 1845.

Blaising, Craig A. and Darrell L. Bock. *Progressive Dispensationalism*. Grand Rapids, MI: Baker Books, 1993.

Boa, Kenneth and Bruce Wilkinson. *Talk Thru The New Testament*. Nashville, TN: Thomas Nelson Publishers, 1983.

Booth, Edwin Prince. *New Testament Studies.* Nashville, TN: Abingdon Press, 1942.

Brown, David. *Christ's Second Coming: Will It Be Premillennial?* London: Hamilton and Co., 1882.

Bruce, F. F. *Answers to Questions.* Grand Rapids, MI: Zondervan Publishing House, 1973.

———. *God's Kingdom and Church.* Grand Rapids, MI: Wm. B. Eerdmans, 1978.

———. *New Testament Development of Old Testament Themes.* Grand Rapids. MI: Wm. B. Eerdmans, 1970.

———. *The Book Of The Acts.* Grand Rapids, MI: Wm. B. Eerdmans, 1998.

Bullinger, E. W. *The Foundations of Dispensational Truth.* London: Eyre and Spottiswood Publishers Ltd., 1930.

Buswell, Dr. J. Oliver. *Unfulfilled Prophecies.* Grand Rapids, MI: Zondervan Publishing House, 1937.

Chafer, Lewis Sperry. *Systematic Theology IV.* Grand Rapids, MI: Kregel Publications, 1993.

Chesnut, Lawence J. *Will There Be a Millennium?* Oklahoma City, OK: Self Published,1973.

Clarke, Adam. *Old Testament*, vol.1. New York: Eaton and Mains, undated.

Conybeare and Howson. *Life and Epistles of St. Paul.* London: Longmans, Green, and Co. 1863.

Cox, William E. *An Examination of Dispensationalism.* Philadelphia, PA: Presbyterian and Reformed Publishing Company, 1977.

———. *Biblical Studies in Final Things.* Philadelphia, PA: Presbyterian and Reformed Publishing Company, undated.

Crenshaw, Curtis I. and Grover E. Gunn, III. *Dispensationalism Today, Yesterday, and Tomorrow.* Memphis, TN: Footstool Publication, 1985.

Cumming, Rev. John. *Apocalyptic Sketches.* London: Arthur Hall, Virtue and Company, 1858.

Cumming, Rev. John. *The Church Before the Flood.* Boston, MA: John P. Jewett and Company, 1854.

Dake, Finis Jennings. *Annotated Reference Bible.* Lawrenceville, GA. Dake Bible Sales, Inc. undated.

Davidson, A. B. *The Epistle to the Hebrews.* Grand Rapids, MI: Zondervan Publishing House, 1950.

Edersheim, Alfred. *Biblical History.* New York: James Pott and Company, undated.

Ellis, E. Earl. *Paul's Use of the Old Testament.* Grand Rapids, MI: Baker Book House, 1981.

English, E. Schuyler. *Re-thinking the Rapture.* Travelers Rest, NC: Southern Bible Book House, 1954.

Erdman, Charles R. *The Return of Christ.* New York: George H. Doran and Company, 1922.

Eusebius. *The Ecclesiastical History of Eusebius Pamphilus.* Grand Rapids, MI: Baker Book House, 1989.

Farrar, F.W. *Expositor's Bible.* New York: A.C. Armstrong & Son, 1908.

Fletcher, George B. *Predictive Prophecy.* Sterling, VA: Reiner Publications, 1971.

———. *The Millennium.* Sterling, VA: Reiner Publications, undated.

———. *Prophecy Newsletter–"And So All Israel Shall Be Saved."* Dayton, TN: Gospel Witness Associates, Inc., 2001.

Fort, John. *God's Salvation, Epistle to the Romans.* New York: Loizeaux Brothers, Bible Truth Depot, Undated.

Gaebelien, Arno C. *The Prophecy of Daniel.* New York: Our Hope, 1911.

Gordon, S. D. *Quiet Talks about Jesus.* New York: Eaton and Mains, 1906.

Grant, Frederick C. *The Gospel of the Kingdom.* New York: The MacMillan Company, 1940.

Gregory and Ruter. *Church History.* New York: B. Waugh & T. Mason, 1934.

Halph, Dr. Charles. *The Christian Jew Hour* telecast, March 26, 1993.

Hagenbach, K. R. *A Text Book of the History of Doctrine.* New York: Sheldon & Co, 1861.

Hastings, James. *Dictionary of the Bible.* Edinburgh: Charles Scribner's and Sons, 1908.

Hocking, Dr. David L. *Guidelines on Romans.* La Mirada, CA: Biola University, 1983.

Hodge, Charles. *First Epistle To The Corinthians.* Grand Rapids, MI: Wm. B. Eerdmans, 1953.

Holdcroft, L. Thomas. *Eschatology.* Abbotsford, Canada: CeeTeC Publishing, 2001.

Hottel, W. S. *The Earthly Kingdom and Kingship of the Lord Jesus Christ.* Cleveland, OH: Union Gospel Press, undated.

Kertzer, Morris N. *What Is a Jew?* London: Collier Macmillan Publishers, 1978.

Ladd, George Eldon. *A Theology of the New Testament.* Grand Rapids, MI: Wm. B. Eerdmans, 1974.

——. *The Blessed Hope.* Grand Rapids, MI: Wm. B. Eerdmans, 1956.

Lahaye, Tim and Jerry B. Jenkins. *Left Behind.* Wheaton, IL: Tyndale Publishers, 1995.

Landis, Ira D. *The Faith of Our Fathers on Eschatology.* Lititz, PA: published by the author, 1946.

Lane, G. and Tippett, C.B. *Sermons and Sketches of Sermons.* New York: G. Lane & C. B. Tippett, 1848.

Larkin, Clarence. *Dispensational Truth.* Philadelphia, PA: Rev. Clarence Larkin, Est. 1920.

Lenski. *Interpretation of Hebrews.* Columbus OH: Wartburg Press, 1946.

Lindsey, Hal. *The Terminal Generation.* Old Tappan, NJ: Fleming H. Revell Company, 1976.

——. *There's a New World Coming.* New York: Bantam Books/Vision House Publishers, 1974.

MacArthur, John F., Jr. *The Gospel According to Jesus.* Grand Rapids, MI: Academie Books, 1988.

Mathison, Keith A. *Dispensationalism Rightly Dividing the People of God?* Phillipsburg, NJ: The Presbyterian and Reformed Publishing Company, 1995.

Mauro, Philip. *The Gospel of the Kingdom.* Swengel, PA: Reiner Publications, 1978.

——. *The Hope of Israel.* Swengel, PA: Reiner Publications, undated.

McGarvey, J.W. *New Commentary on Acts of the Apostles.* Cincinnati, OH: The Standard Publishing Company, 1892.

McGavern, C. G. *Rapture or Resurrection?* Grand Rapids, MI: Wm. B. Eerdmans, 1943.

Meloon, Wilfred C. *We've Been Robbed.* Plainfield, NJ: Logos International, 1971.

Morris, A.M. *The Prophecies Unveiled*. Winfield, KS: Courier Press, 1914.

New Heavens and A New Earth. Watch Tower Bible & Track Society, 1953.

Newell, William R. *Hebrews: Verse by Verse*. Chicago, IL. Moody Press, 1947.

Ockenga, Harold J. *The Church in God, Expository Values in Thessalonians*. Westwood, NJ: Fleming and Revell Company, 1956.

Palmer, Earl F. *Salvation by Surprise*. Waco, TX: Word Books Publisher, 1978.

Pember, G. H. *The Great Prophecies Concerning the Gentiles, the Jews, and the Church of God*. Miami Spring, FL: Conley and Schoettle Publishing Co., Inc., 1984.

Pentecost, J. Dwight. *Prophecy for Today*. Grand Rapids, MI: Zondervan Publishing House, 1964.

——. *Things to Come*. Grand Rapids, MI: Zondervan Publishing House, 1978.

Pettingill, Dr. William. *Nearing The End*, Chicago: Van Kampen Press, 1948.

Pink, A. W. *The Divine Covenants*. Grand Rapids, MI: Baker Book House, 1973.

Rall, Harris Franklin. *Modern Premillennialism and the Christian Hope*. New York: The Abington Press, 1920.

Reese, Alexander. *The Approaching Advent of Christ*. London: Marshall, Morgan and Scott Ltd., 1934.

Riggle, H. M. *Christ's Kingdom and Reign*. Anderson, IN: Gospel Trumpet Company, 1918.

——. *The Kingdom of God and the One Thousand Years Reign*. Moundsville, WV: Gospel Trumpet Publishing Co., 1899.

Robinson, A. T. *Word Pictures in the New Testament*. Nashville, TN: Broadman Press, 1930.

Rutgers, W.H. *Premillennialism in America*. Goes, Netherlands: Oosterbaan & Le Cointre, 1930.

Ryrie, Charles C. *Dispensationalism*. Chicago: Moody Press, 1995.

——. *Dispensationalism Today*. Chicago: Moody Press, 1965.

——. *The Basis of the Premillennial Faith*. Neptune, NJ: Loizeaux Brothers, 1978.

———. *The Final Countdown*. Wheaton, IL: Scripture Press Publications, Inc., 1989.

Schaff, Philip. *History of the Christian Church*. Grand Rapids, MI: Wm. B. Eerdmans, 1910.

Scofield, Rev. C. I. *The Scofield Reference Bible*. New York: Oxford University Press, 1945.

———.*Scofield Bible Correspondence Course*. Chicago: Moody Bible Institute.

Small, Dwight Hervey. *Remarriage and God's Renewing Grace*. Grand Rapids, MI: Baker Book House, 1989.

Suerig, Dr. R. F. *A Study of the Testimony*. Denver, CO: R. F. Suerig, undated.

Talbot, Louis T. *God's Plan of the Ages*. Grand Rapids, MI: Wm. B. Eerdmans, 1946.

———. *The Great Prophecies of Daniel*, radio messages. Beverly Hills, CA, 1934.

Taylor, Dr. Charles. *Get All Excited! Jesus Is Coming Soon*. Redondo Beach, CA: Today In Bible Prophecy, Inc., 1974.

Terry, Milton. *Biblical Hermeneutics*. Grand Rapids, MI: Zondervan Publishing House, undated.

Vos, Geerhardus. *The Pauline Eschatology*. Grand Rapids, MI: Baker Book House, 1982.

Walvoord, John F. *The Blessed Hope and the Tribulation*. Grand Rapids, MI: Academie Books, 1976.

———. *The Church in Prophecy*. Grand Rapids, MI: Zondervan Publishing House, 1982.

———. *The Rapture Question*. Grand Rapids, MI: Zondervan Publishing House, 1978.

Weatherhead, Leslie D. *The Will of God* (booklet), New York: Abingdon Press, 1944.

Webb, T. Myron. *Startling Prophetic Events*. Lincoln, NE: Back To The Bible, 1958.

Wickliff, John. *Reformers—Wickliff to Bilney*. London: William Clowes and Sons, undated.

Wilkerson, Bruce and Kenneth Boa. *Talk Thru the New Testament*. Nashville, TN: Thomas Nelson Publishers, 1983.

Williamson, G. A. *Eusebius, The History of the Church from Christ to Constantine.* New York: Dorset Press, 1984.

Woods, Leonard, *Lectures on the Inspiration of the Scriptures.* Andover: Mark Newman, 1829.

Zens, Jon. *Dispensationalism: A Reformed Inquiry into its Leading Figures and Features.* Nashville, TN: The Presbyterian and Reformed Publishing Company, 1978.

Pleasant Word

To order additional copies of this title call:
1-877-421-READ (7323)
or please visit our Web site at
www.pleasantwordbooks.com

If you enjoyed this quality custom-published book,

drop by our Web site for more books and information.

www.winepressgroup.com
"Your partner in custom publishing."

Breinigsville, PA USA
23 June 2010
240443BV00002B/3/P